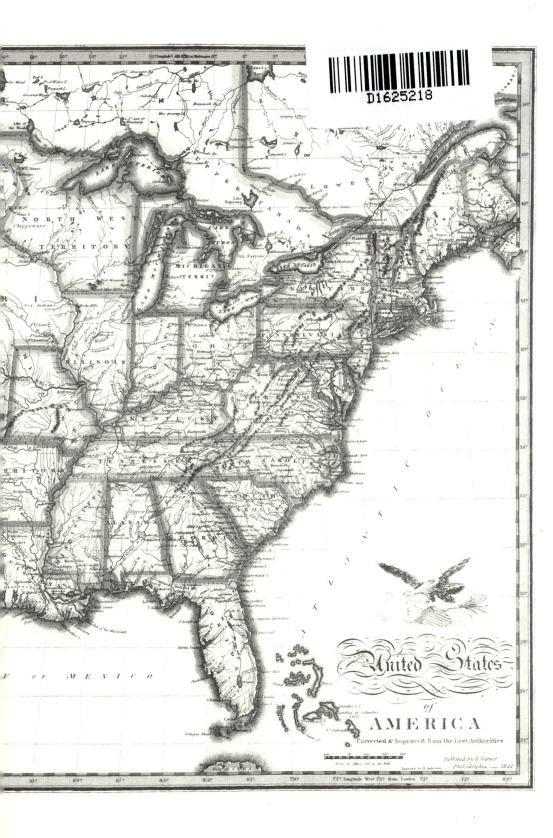

United States of AMERICA

Corrected & Improved from the best Authorities

Scale of Miles 130° to an Inch

Engraved by G. Anderson

Published by B. Warner
Philadelphia ——— 1820

THE
PLACE
WITHIN

EDITED BY

JODI DAYNARD

THE
$\mathscr{P}$LACE
$\mathscr{W}$ITHIN

PORTRAITS

OF THE AMERICAN

LANDSCAPE BY TWENTY

CONTEMPORARY WRITERS

W. W. NORTON & COMPANY NEW YORK / LONDON

Since this page cannot legibly accommodate all the copyright notices, page 269 constitutes an extension
of the copyright page.

Endpaper map courtesy of Historic Urban Plans, Inc.

The text of this book is composed in Garamond Number 3
with the display set in Centaur
Composition by PennSet, Inc.
Manufacturing by the Haddon Craftsmen, Inc.
Book design by Jam Design

Library of Congress Cataloging-in-Publication Data

The place within : portraits of the American landscape by twenty
    contemporary writers / edited by Jodi Daynard.
        p.   cm.
    ISBN 0-393-03999-4
    1. Landscape—United States—Literary collections.   2. Place
(Philosophy)—Literary collections.   3. American literature—20th
century.   I. Daynard, Jodi.
PS509.L3S46   1996
814'.5408032—dc20   96-13708
                                                             CIP

W. W. Norton & Company, Inc., 500 Fifth Avenue, New York, N.Y. 10110 http://web.wwnorton.com
W. W. Norton & Company Ltd., 10 Coptic Street, London WC1A 1PU

1 2 3 4 5 6 7 8 9 0

Contents

INTRODUCTION

AMERICA IS A PLACE THAT HAS ALWAYS INSPIRED ITS INHABITANTS to portray it. For more than two hundred years, our artists—from Edward Hicks to Edward Hopper—have sought to capture not just its face but its polymorphous spirit, as embodied in the land itself.

What draws us to our native terrain? Is it that we are a new nation and haven't had time to grow bored with our own geography? Or that most of us are, in a geographic sense, orphans, cut off from our original homelands—whether Russian shtetl or Welsh mining town or South African village—seeking to define new identities? Whatever the reasons, as a group we have attached ourselves with a passion to our adopted home.

American writers have always been passionate about places, too. As readers nursed from childhood on the novels of William Faulkner or the short stories of Flannery O'Connor, we know that, in our fiction, place is never just the location where events occur, but the vital context without which these events have no meaning. Indeed, such places as Yoknapatawpha County are protagonists themselves, so mammoth and mythic as to dwarf all others.

Perhaps more quietly but just as forcefully, American prose writers have been charting their own terrain as well, carving out a uniquely American genre complete with its own traditions and anti-traditions. It may not be such an exaggeration to say that American philosophy was born at Walden Pond.

Since Thoreau's *Walden*, hundreds of American writers have taken up writing about place as a means to reflect on not just nature but human nature, our desires as individuals and as a society, our moral core. Over the years, the form has proven itself to be remarkably accommodating, allowing writers to combine, in seemingly infinite variations, history and philosophy, politics and autobiography. And yet, in reading essays about landscape from across the generations, one becomes aware of a common thread: that the borders of "individual" and "land," "self" and "other," are far more fluid than we might .otherwise imagine.

In *Journal of a Solitude*, Mary Sarton writes, "Whatever peace I know rests in the natural world, in feeling myself a part of it, even in a small way." Sarton's words echo those of Thoreau, who more than a century earlier wrote in *Walden*, "By a conscious effort of the mind, we can stand aloof from actions and their consequences . . . I may be either the driftwood in the stream, or Indra in the sky looking down on it."

Traces of Thoreau's transcendentalism abound in twentieth-century literature, and there is no lack of that uniquely American spirit in *The Place Within*. But in assembling this book, I sought a far broader definition of "landscape" than Thoreau or his followers would allow. After all, our turf is much more than the natural, rural one. It is also Phillip Lopate's grid-locked "Manhattan" and the "restricted" country clubs of "Suburbia, USA." It is Richard Rodriguez's gay San Francisco and Gerald Early's uneasily "integrated" St. Louis.

There are no picture postcards here; no travelogues. Even for those who write in the naturalist tradition, one finds surprisingly few transcendental ecstasies. Our landscape has grown too complex for that; and those who attempt even modest transcendence—as Scott Russell Sanders wryly suggests in "Mountain Music"—find their words tinged with the mournful toll of elegy.

The process of commissioning essays from writers I most admired was one not so much of discovering why we're drawn to landscapes as the depths and parameters of this desire. The portraits included here are complicated, sometimes ambivalent, sometimes downright outraged. They depict city and suburb, Chicago water and Alaskan fire. What they share is not so much their motivation for seeing but their *means* of doing so, through the artist's inner eye.

For some, writing about landscape is a way to celebrate it. In "A Map for Hummingbirds," Ellen Meloy ponders the subtle migration patterns not just of birds but of her own life. In "Dreaming of Trees," Kathleen Norris meditates upon the way in which solitary objects can change our experience of space itself. In "Clovelly," Suzanne Berne speaks about a place lost and then found by the power of memory. And Gretel Ehrlich's "The Solace of Open Spaces" discovers what may be our first cure for human grief.

Other portraits are far darker in spirit, issuing laments if not outright warnings. Joy Williams's "Florida" reminds us that, however passionately we writers may write about landscape, the razing cranes of "progress" roll forth just the same. In his haunting "Journey to Trinity," Bradford Morrow unearths an eerie parallel between America's frontier cowboys brandishing guns and America's frontier scientists brandishing bombs. Finally, while NASA astronaut Jeffrey Hoffman's piece, "A Place Above America," rejoices in our country, it also gives us an image of its cosmic fragility.

Just as we can be perilously indifferent, both materially and spiritually, toward the places that sustain us, some of these essays remind us how indifferent our land can be toward us. Donald Hall's "Winter" and Robert Finch's "A Day of Roads" take an affectionate view of nature's power. But "Fire in the Valley," by native Alaskan Natalie Kusz; "Chicago Waters," by Susan Powers; and "The Grandeur of the Grand Canyon," by Diane Ackerman, remind us of our terrain's power, the delicate truce we must strike with it to survive.

While nearly all the essays in *American Landscapes* convey, in some measure, the effect of landscape upon the writer, two do so quite directly. Alan Lightman's "Hallelujah" is both a beautiful description of a vacation spot and a revelation of how modern writers manage to do what they do. When he speaks of his summer life on a remote island in Maine following "the rhythm of the tides," he is also rejoicing in a less tangible freedom: the one his mind has to take on its own creative rhythms, its own tides. And in "Swamp as Metaphor," Harry Crews recounts how the Okefenokee has provided him not just with a source of inspiration but with an antidote to despair.

However varied, these essays all share a common bond. It's nothing that can be reduced to a single word or even a sentence. But perhaps William Kittredge gets closest with this concluding paragraph from his book *Hole in the Sky*: "If we want to be happy at all, I think, we have to acknowledge that the circumstances which encourage us in our love of this existence are essential. We are part of what is sacred. That is our main defense against craziness, our solace, the source of our best politics, and our only chance at paradise."

In the end, I'm astonished by and grateful for the diversity of the essays collected here, and the generosity of spirit with which these authors wrote them. Taken together, they form a refreshingly unauthorized vision of America as seen and felt by some of our most talented writers working at the end of the twentieth century. My hope was that *The Place Within* would illuminate the complex, enduring, and ever-changing relationships we have with our terrain, the deep well of feeling and creativity it inspires. In the measure that I've succeeded, these essays are not just new and different, they get us where we live.

—J.D.

ACKNOWLEDGMENTS

I would like to thank all those who lent their support to this project. To Suzanne Berne, Maxine Rodburg, Verlyn Klinkenborg, Brad Morrow, Alan Lightman, and Christopher Sawyer-Laucanno, who brainstormed with me early on about the seemingly limitless possibilities for authors. To Richard Ford, who couldn't contribute, but whose discussions with me about landscapes (and a few other things) helped my notions to evolve. To my family, who provided emotional and financial sustenance while I was working on this. Thanks also to my agent, Faith Hamlin, whose name is perfect for her. And to Jill Bialosky, my editor at Norton, who waited patiently while these beautiful essays meandered in.

THE
PLACE
WITHIN

ELLEN MELOY

Ellen Meloy's writing, deeply embedded in place, is a combination of lyricism, spiritual meditation, and arch humor. Meloy was hesitant about writing an essay on Montana, apologetic about the fact that while many writers live there year-round, she shuttles back and forth between Montana and Utah. But there is nothing apologetic about "A Map for Hummingbirds," in which Meloy's sense of seasonal migration takes center stage. It is a stunning piece, seemingly effortless in its prose, charting not just Montana's bird migration but the instinctive urges in the author's own migratory patterns.

A Map for

Hummingbirds

Montana's wild geese migrate in family units. They navigate by memory and topography—the shape of a mountain, a curve of river—and by an internal compass that responds to the earth's magnetic field. The point bird in the distinctive V-shaped formation is usually a gander, although the geese change position frequently. Updrafts of air behind each wing in the V reduce drag for all but the leader, which must drop back to rest. Think of the V as a single creature: aerodynamically fluid and energy efficient, adjusting its flight pattern by loud honks.

Borne by sturdy bodies and powerful wings, the geese stay aloft for hours. The peoples of old did not underestimate the endurance of migratory birds with large body mass. They also observed, correctly, that hummingbirds migrate but presumed that such tenderly small creatures—birds that must eat constantly to fuel a rapid-fire heartbeat—could not fly long distances on their own without dropping dead. Thus, according to folk belief, big Canada geese would carry tiny, fragile, hitchhiking hummingbirds on their backs when they migrated.

A cold front can trigger migration in the fall, although the precise moment of departure is never predictable. Not all goose families are of like mind about staying or leaving or when. One minute they might be nibbling succulent plant bits in a serene valley, the next minute they rise into the clean blue air above the Montana-Idaho border. Below lies a rumpled cordillera of rocks and ice and a pickup winding along the Interstate highway. Inside the truck are two humans, also migrants, also at odds about staying or leaving or when. Cranked on for the first time in months, the truck heater smells like melting Chihuahuas. The man drives. The woman, who never wears socks south of Pocatello, takes off her battered desert sandals, pulls on a pair of woolies and shoes, then stares down at her feet as if they were freshly embalmed mummies. Paths cross. The distance between sky and road, wing and tire, diminishes sound but not a vague sense of air flowing in opposite directions. The southbound geese comb our northbound hair.

Birds respond to changes in their environment by migrating. In temperate North America the best strategy is to move south for the winter to warmer terrain, where better menus flourish, and to return north in the spring, where the mild season and longer daylight hours favor mating, nesting, feeding, and growing up. Nature, of course, never quite sticks to the grid. Some birds head south when they should head north. My ornithology book defines reverse migration as bird movement that proceeds in a direction opposite the one expected for the season. If a storm or heavy winds sweep them off course, for instance, the birds fly back to the beginning or to a point where instinct reorients them to their preferred lane of passage.

Reverse migration is the metaphor of my life in Montana. My husband's seasonal work as a backcountry ranger and a home we built in southern Utah keep us in the desert during the hottest months, from early spring until late fall. Our slightly delirious Utah life, spent largely outdoors, unfolds in the sensuous red-gold light of a heat-scorched, tense, skinless earth fissured with deep canyons and upthrust in sandstone monoliths. Each winter I haul my lizard pelt and desert soul back to our Montana home, blue-starved. For months I have not seen so much light at this end of the spectrum: thick conifer forests the color of malachite, steel gray peaks creased with cobalt shadows, lofty cornices underlined with blue-violet cusps of snow. Montana is a sojourn in northern light.

The truck moves through an indigo dark. The geese push onward to open water and a rest. At this point in our migration all other vehicles have fallen off Idaho, whose edge meets an abyss into outer space—or so it seems. Our vehicle slips solo up the massive plateau that hovers above the rest of the continent like Coleridge's Xanadu ("That sunny dome! those caves of ice!"), a distant, glittering place undercut by something dark and alluring. The night beyond our high beams obliterates all horizons, all distinction between land and sky. The lights of scattered ranches become stars. Nothing but the ground beneath me tells me that gravity exists. Away from towns scattered like islands in Montana's vast space, few travelers are immune to the floating sensation caused by this blanket of darkness.

Geographers often describe Montana's size with the how-many-states-can-fit-into-it measure. Nearly three Connecticuts. A couple of Vermonts. One slightly distended West Virginia. Stretch the analogy farther: overlay Massachusetts onto southwestern Montana, where I live. The Crazy Mountains impale Boston, tossing half a million people downslope into a rude heap. Cape Cod's curled finger tickles a paltry number of sage-freckled acres west of Twodot, and the Connecticut River disappears into the Missouri like a lost noodle. The Berkshire Hills form a dust cover to the Scapegoat Wilderness. Cowboys from Deer Lodge sell Housatonic gentry a few sizable cattle outfits. The city of Butte pierces the overlay, startling everyone in New Bedford with a giant open-pit copper mine. Yellowstone National Park, however, now sits conveniently in their backyard.

Montana easily fits Gertrude Stein's remark, "more space where nobody is than where anybody is." The journalist Joseph Kinsey Howard called Montana "the space between people," implying that a vehicle and a few tanks of gas are needed merely to bring you close enough to see if the other person's eyes are blue or brown. So much space fosters keen introspection, philosophic abstraction, fierce independence, and narrative inventiveness—desirable traits for writers, cowboys, and that up-and-coming New West prodigy, the golf pro. Under the Big Sky, human and landscape exist in the right proportion to one another; comfort is found in one's own insignificance. As a young, insignificant woman I believed that Montana's humbling and informing scale would provide the proper vessel for my terminal restlessness, my notion that home could be found in movement itself. I felt that rootlessness might find root in a place of this size.

Some birds, notably young gulls, herons, and egrets, do not always migrate in predictable seasonal directions. Juvenile wandering can be linear—the young birds head north as the rest of the colony heads south—or explosive: they move in all directions and at considerable distances from their hatching area. When immature birds cannot compete successfully for food with older birds, they must wander until they find an adequate supply for themselves.

Years ago I came to Montana as a juvenile wanderer, a native westerner exchanging one rural home for another. Behind me I dragged previous lives—student, lifeguard, hermit—and ahead lay a buffet of new ones. I made a living in technical illustration, churning out laboriously stippled pen-and-inks of bones and feathers, detailed diagrams of geological strata and the cell divisions of anxious amoebas. The medium enriched my knowledge of science and gave me thumb calluses, thick reading glasses, and the revelation that my art, so meticulous in nature, was also extremely uptight. For relief I painted barns.

In the Rockies' brief growing season I jump-started my garden inside a junked farm truck, its cab and windshield facing south, its windows adjusted for ventilation. This greenhouse yielded seedlings for tons of unlikely tomatillos and one cantaloupe with the size and flavor of a used tennis ball. Montana's winter weather crossed Seattle with the Yukon: one storm covered the land in humid, brooding skies, the next in brittle, frigid air that burned the skin like poisoned needles. Contrary to predictions, winter didn't kill me. I boldly crawled under the house to thaw my pipes with a blow dryer. When a more severe cold snap froze every molecule of liquid in my house except a tumbler of whiskey, I drank the whiskey. I survived winter's cold but not its length; each year I fled to the desert to cheat it.

In Montana I married a man who called his sleeping bag "Doris" and lived three blocks from where he was born. At the time of his birth, in the early fifties, the neighborhood boasted a hospital, a convent, modest family homes, and one active and at least five former brothels. On one of our first dates he took me to a bird refuge in a remote intermontane valley, where he shot a duck and served me its tiny butchered breasts for dinner. Before I could decide how I felt about dead duck, he told me its name: bufflehead. We were eating bufflehead breasts. In Montana I learned to fly-fish, row a river raft, belly-dance, and herd sheep. I frost-nipped my feet on cross-country ski trips in moonlight and rearranged my knee cartilage on treks across mountains with a heavy pack. The land seemed so vast, each season so deep, adventure became irresistible, even if moments of exquisite beauty had to be earned by extreme pain. These years matched youth to place, reckless energy to a land that does not yield easy living to anyone.

Perhaps the southbound geese that flew above our northbound heads picture their winter grounds as an enormous open-air restaurant; their primary occupation is to eat. On my feeding grounds on the upper Missouri River I exchange the lusty, brainless, overheated, intimately physical life of the desert for winter's distinct mood of reflection, summer's harlotry of color for what Melville called a "fixed trance of whiteness." I trade the wild for shelter.

My street abuts a million acres of timbered high country along the Continental Divide, possibly the last street until the next town nearly ninety miles away. Here, edge of town means a distinct, palpable border. On the tamed side of the wilderness, below our house, lies the old red-light quarter, and wedged into a narrow gulch, a dense cluster of commercial buildings with ornate facades of sandstone and granite. Montana's innards—gold, silver, copper, lead—paid the bill and fed the town's aspirations to worldliness. A delirious mix of architectural elements borrowed from the Italian Romanesque, French Renaissance, midwestern Gothic, and mining-camp Baroque doesn't quite hide a frontier soul. Similar opulence is found on the downtown's other flank, merely a gulch away from the whorehouses, in a neighborhood of stately mansions built at the turn of the century by mining magnates who followed a cardinal rule: The dirtier your mine, the farther you live from it. They lived here, close to their banks.

What could be more western than an endemic confusion of virtues? As towns like mine outgrew their frontier motleyness, civic pride called for churches, schools, and other refinements. Visitors from the East wanted mud and bugling elk and virile men who mumbled about posses and punched each other's lights out. As the nation paved its highways in the thirties, Montana, short on funds and long on need, stretched its blacktop budget by building its highways as narrow as possible. Not that it mattered; traffic was negligible and everyone drove all over both lanes anyway. These days *los hombres de global economy* dress like Wyatt Earp on weekends but demand a four-lane to the ski lift. Everyone wants Montana to be not a state but a state of mind.

The downtown district recently sprouted a thick crop of espresso bars. From my house I can walk this gauntlet and arrive overcaffeinated at my favorite bookstore. The cafés, and weekly calls from realtors hoping to wrest our house from us, portend Montana's demise as a faraway, hostile, possibly coffeeless place. The great interior West is filling. Hoarding the limelight are white supremacists, golf pros, a ranch-hungry Hollywood elite, and nearly everyone else from California who saw the fly-fishing movie. The state's soul, however, perches somewhere between pieces of its own myth as a paradise of raw nature and a backwater of rural primitives in love with sheep.

In winter Montanans become a hearth people, content to shut the door against the howling wilderness. The season exacerbates an insularity in the Montana character, an ease with keeping to oneself without diminishing one's community. A few cope by shooting their refrigerators. Others embrace the pleasure, if not the necessity, of friends and neighbors, one of whom might someday pluck them from a snowdrift. Ranches a tenth the size of Belgium keep a lot of people far apart. Early homesteaders often built their houses on adjacent corners of their sections and lived close to one another. Before long they moved to the other side of their holding, ostensibly because their chickens got mixed up together. Something about this extraordinary land accommodates a desire for privacy without loneliness, seclusion without solitude.

The winter solstice marks the midpoint of our stay in the far north. This calendar suspends me in the purity of a singular season; winter's most evocative qualities freeze-frame in a landscape that wears them to perfection. Days unfold in preternaturally bright sunlight or under a pewter sky weighted against snowy hills with its impending storm. Nights are sudden and complete, with a faint glacial scent. The moon is lilac as it rises, silver at its zenith. I never see the seasons change in Montana, I never see the green, only its scheduled death. For me Montana is always cold, the original and ultimate state of the universe.

January brings the coldest days, bone-chilling polar air that leaves no slack. Every surface freezes so hard it would rip your lips off if you kissed it. Car exhausts spew dry-ice fumes. The air crackles with helium, ozone, neon, argon—air that can be 108 degrees colder than me—yet somehow I remain liquid. Not counting my bathtub, the aquariums in the local pet store have the only open water for miles. Winter's worst grip sends me there for the solace of gurgling water and a fecund, tidal humidity. The same Arctic front sends the derelicts to the library. Some sit cozily next to the heat vent in their baggy parkas and unlaced pack boots. Another sleeps at a table, snoring face down on *La Technique: Cooking with Jacques Pépin*.

Despite the pervasive lethargy of hibernation, things get done. Ravenously hungry after the cold spell, cedar waxwings—tawny birds with black bands across their eyes—strip my crabapple tree of its frozen fruit, then fly off like masked bandits. My husband cleans the basement. Someone resuscitates all those Bostonians heaped at the foot of the Crazies. According to the news, the Romanians are selling their excess bears. I order two. The legislature, which meets here every two years for ninety days, undoes the laws that the previous session repassed in response to laws depassed by the session before that, making everyone so dizzy, we wish they would meet every ninety years for two days. I send out postcards with photos of typical Rocky Mountain ungulates and letters that note a ski trip to the valley of the bufflehead breasts, the lengths of icicles, the blizzards and the chinooks, the shock of exploding color from arriving seed catalogues, an epidemic of imploding marriages among friends—all the riches and wrecks that mark life as *Homo sapiens* on a wobbly, spinning planet that tilts its northern hemisphere away from the sun. Then the season turns and the light slowly climbs the orb.

Before migrating a bird must eat a great deal, storing energy in the form of subcutaneous fat. The bird must also become predisposed to migrate by a metabolic state called migratory restlessness. In spring this condition is controlled by the pituitary gland, which in turn is stimulated by periodicity, or changes in day length. Fat, restless, and physiologically prepared, the bird now needs only the external stimulus of a drop in barometric pressure, the moist, southerly air of a warm front, before it loads those little hummingbirds on its back and takes wing: northbound.

For me the migratory impulse manifests itself in too many trips to the pet store aquariums. The geography wars, the tension between allegiances to two places, escalate. One day I will press my face against a window that frames Montana's crystalline winter purity and I, too, will long for hummingbirds. Fat, restless, and physiologically prepared, aching for the desert, I will turn winter's bend with the geese and take wing: southbound.

H A R R Y   C R E W S

Harry Crews is an American original. His novels, the most recent being *The Mulching of America*, are often raunchy, usually insane, and always hilarious stories, unmistakably rooted in the backwater South Georgia where Crews grew up. And yet, in addition to a prodigious sense of character, Crews also possesses a philosopher's intellect and a poet's sense of detail. "Swamp as Metaphor," reminiscent of the tender prose in *Childhood: The Biography of a Place*, is a disarmingly candid, moving essay about the Okefenokee Swamp and its tributary, the long, long Suwannee River. "Swamp as Metaphor" tells two stories. The first is about Uncle Cooter, the man who showed Crews the river as a child. And the second is about the mystery revealed to Crews as an adult about the strange, saving confluence of swamp and narrative, the novelist's art.

SWAMP

AS

METAPHOR

ON MANY DAYS AS A BOY I FOUND MYSELF STARTING TO WORK IN the first murky light of morning in the nearly impenetrable fastness of the Okefenokee Swamp (first light in the Okefenokee Swamp was always murky); on many days as a man I have found myself trying to work in the murky light of morning in the very nearly impenetrable fastness of fiction (first light in the very nearly impenetrable fastness of fiction is always murky). I suspect many readers will find the sentence I have written more than passing strange. What in the world might a swamp have to do with writing fiction? And isn't the sentence badly overwritten anyway? Couldn't one of the parenthetical phrases—or both—be deleted in a simple revision?

Perhaps, if not for the fact that I want to join quickly and strongly the Okefenokee Swamp and one of the cleanest, most tranquilly beautiful rivers in the country for which the 666-square-mile Okefenokee forms the headwaters: the Suwannee. Moreover, I want to set down, knowing at the outset that it is impossible, how this incredibly wild and strange swamp, combined with the madly twisting and turning Suwannee, has made it possible for me to keep writing at times when nothing else can. I want to try to show how these waters and all that grow in them or on their banks, and fly above them, have been an influence on and a constant support of the writing I've been able to do over the last thirty years.

The doubly difficult thing to make sense of here is that I know the influence of the Suwannee and the support of the Okefenokee have always been there when I've needed them, yet I've never once set a novel or even a scene on the river or in the swamp. I know that over the years I've called the names of the Suwannee and the Okefenokee many times in stories and essays, but nothing of a narrative line or anything of fictional consequence has ever taken place in the swamp or on the river in anything I've written.

But when my work has turned sour, or I'm hopelessly baffled by what I'm looking at on the page in front of me, my head, heart, and imagination, without any conscious effort on my part, drift back to the deep swamp or else ride the wind like a gliding bird just over the surface of the Suwannee as it makes its two hundred and some odd-mile westward journey across the peninsula of Florida to the Gulf of Mexico.

A subject that slowly begins to fail right before the eyes of a writer who is trying to set it down on paper as truly as he is able often causes pain so immediate and severe it's embarrassing to talk about. (I speak only for myself and no other writer, even if it might sound otherwise.) But worse than the pain is the paralyzing doubt that comes right along with the pain. And this doubt not only make me irritable, it also puts me into a murderous rage.

Then comes the flowing image of the river, a river of sweet water that carries no commercial traffic, has only a few small villages along its banks, which are lined with cypress hanging long with gray moss, gnarled old trees that have never had an ax in them. With the image of the river, a coolness and calmness starts to trace through the jungle of my burning nerves.

Maybe I have been struggling for days to discover where the novel I am trying to write is going and I am on the verge of giving up, abandoning a book that I have been thinking about and wanting to write for years. No matter how hard I try, I can find no focus in what I am doing.

Then comes the image of the river, or maybe I put my old labrador retriever in the front seat of my pickup truck with me and we drive over to the bluffs at Old Town above the Suwannee's placid waters, waters turned black from the tannin in the bark of trees. At the first

glance, something—I couldn't tell you what—shifts in my head, or maybe the subtle shift is in my blood.

I neither know nor do I care about the nature of the shift. It may only be some harmlessly sophomoric fancy of mine. All I care about is what it does for me. Despite the fact that I feel as though I am dying with doubt, the broad black waters of the Suwannee carry no doubt. The river bends and twists, but its direction is west. Massively, steadily, implacably, it flows west true as a plumb bob.

It is going where it has always gone, going to the same place it went before the first white man ever laid eyes upon it, the Gulf of Mexico, the sweet water seeking the salt in a cycle that is as natural as the rising and the setting of the sun. The same sleek ospreys are dropping out of the sun and hitting the water from where they unerringly rise with a fish caught in their talons. Red shoulder hawks and redtail hawks wheel and soar over the thick cypress forests. As many as four deer, walking in tandem, might appear on the other side of the river to drink. There is a scale here, a natural balance, that nothing can ever destroy. Everything is of a piece. I immediately feel less confounded, fragmented, less alone and lost.

Once the storytelling part of me is on the river, that ridiculously vain demon that lives in me forces me to joyously take hold again of the mad dream that shamelessly insists that I have a better-than-even chance of reinventing the experience of the world and making it all new again. During that moment when I am hovering over the water, I know that all things are possible. When I get back to my desk, I not only start to write again but to write with pleasure and the solid conviction that what I am doing is not without merit.

What I've been writing thus far did not occur to me in a flash today, or last week, or last month, or ever. I have no idea when I started thinking about all this. But I think I know its source. When my work goes wrong, when I'm stuck and confused and full of rage, I am also *afraid*.

I didn't mention the fear before because I guess I was ashamed to admit it. I am ashamed of the fear because at first glance it seems so stupid. What is there to fear? Why the panic and pain? Just this: I am overwhelmed with the feeling that I have reached the end of my rope. I've gone to the well one time too many and this time the well is dry. What does a writer do if there's nothing left in him to write? The core of my working life has been making novels and stories. The thought of the core disappearing is unbearable.

Since I have no notion whatsoever where novels come from, what am I to do? When I was young it terrified, this business of what is the source of a novel, and how do you go about finding that source. I learned to live with it but I never made peace with it.

Like a great many other writers, I ran into the much talked about, fearsome monster of the dreaded second novel, where so many fiction-writing careers have ended, died without a sound. My first novel was finished, sold, not slaughtered with terrible reviews, and I was ready to get on with the business of being a writer. Then a strange thing happened. In the very first few pages of the second book I found myself something of a dullard, a dullard whose language was foggy and unsure, and whose powers of invention, if I ever had any, had quietly died or else packed up and left town without even saying good-bye.

I had heard entirely too much about these second-novel terrors, and I had also heard that very nearly everybody had some trouble getting a second novel finished, and I was determined ahead of time that such a thing would not happen to me. I would avoid it by not driving myself crazy with anxiety. As it turned out I wasn't just overly anxious, I wanted to shoot myself.

Many people wonder about how fiction writers do what they do. While wondering about such things is a fairly innocent and harmless pastime, it can, and I am convinced often does, terrify writers—particularly if one day they find themselves without a story or novel to write and no way to find one—terrify them enough to make them dive to the bottom of a whiskey bottle and refuse to come up, or drive them into a depression so dark that even God seems unwilling or unable to let in the light.

Struggling to find that second novel, I knew about the despair waiting to drown the writer who had run out of words. I desperately did not want that for myself. Looking back, I know it could have happened to me, and it could have happened *then*. But it happened twenty years later, when I discovered one day that I could find no narrative—none of any kind that was not sophomoric and silly—to write down. I thought it would pass, this dry spell. But the wait was stronger than I was and I spent nine years at the bottom of the bottle myself, and an even longer time stumbling into unnameable things in a darkness so deep I despaired of ever coming into the light again.

I think this horror could have been avoided, but I was older by then and full of myself. I had not forgotten the river and the swamp, but my ignorance told me I was beyond the crutches of an apprentice, for so I had come to regard the Okefenokee and the Suwannee. Refusal to go for help where I had always gone in the past, and an overly high regard for the little I had thus far been able to achieve, almost combined to kill me.

Fortunately, when I hit the wall trying to get started on the second novel, my sensibilities were still enough intact to recognize ignorance when I was drowning in it. I suppose it was inevitable that since I had nobody else to turn to, I remembered the man who had helped me take my first faltering steps into what would be my life's work: Uncle Cooter.

It was Uncle Cooter who had first taken me into the swamp when I was eight years old. He was neither my uncle nor was Cooter his real name. I called him uncle because I had never heard anybody call him anything else. On his right leg he wore a cypress peg that he had carved himself (he owned precious little that he did not make himself) and he had the curious habit of bending down from time to time and scratching it. In that part of the world, you did not ask a man so personal a question as why he scratched his wooden leg since he couldn't feel it. A question like that could get you badly hurt or perhaps killed.

He lived on the edge of the swamp and made his living out of it. He poled a flat-bottomed craft that looked like a canoe but was not, poled it slowly over the black water of the swamp where he kept a trapline and a trotline and seined for crawfish, which he sold for fish bait at a penny a piece. I would never see a boat like his again until I was in the middle of Cajun country in Layfayette, Louisiana. There they were called pirogues. A man with a pegleg couldn't plow a mule but he could turn to the swamp, and if he was as resourceful and inexhaustible as Uncle Cooter, he made a living, a good living. Most men would have been thrown out of the boat and spent a good part of the day trying to get back in, but he moved and poled and stepped over the traps and seines nimble as a cat.

Uncle Cooter came down the steps as nimble as a boy. Despite the pegleg, there was no hitch in his gait as he came across the yard. I was smiling but nothing showed in his seamed, weathered face. No expression was his habitual expression. He didn't say a word until he embraced me, his bewhiskered face rough against mine.

Then against my ear, softly, tender as a woman's: "Son."

"Uncle Cooter," I said.

He held my shoulders and stepped back to look at me. "Thought you'd forgot where I lived."

I felt skunk-nasty for not visiting him in such a long time. I could only shrug, palms up, and look back into his faded blue eyes.

"I know," he said. "Lying out with dry cattle."

Dry cattle is the South Georgia dialect for young women who have not yet had a baby. "I haven't had the time nor the money for dry cattle."

He said: "Don't take neither and you know it."

He nodded his head at the dark wall of the swamp that stretched away on either side of the cabin as far as you could see. You don't smell the Okefenokee, you wear it, palpably thick, a heavy mixture of century-old mulch and day-old grass, the living and the dead nicely layered with swamp. A great many people think it stinks. Not I. I love the way it smells because I love the thing itself, and I love it the way I do because it came to me more through the perceptions of Uncle Cooter than it did through my own. As a boy, sitting in the back of the canoe, I listened to his strong, smooth voice, his voice keeping the same steady rhythm as the pole and the canoe gliding over the dark water, as he told me of the painted naked Indians that once made this their home, of strange birds that flew great distances to make this their home during the winter. He held the egg of an alligator in his hand and let me watch the tiny hatchling gator break out of his shell and into the great world. He taught me even if I got only a fleeting glance to recognize otters, raccoons, wildcats, to tell the difference between sparrow hawks, red shoulder hawks, redtail hawks, to respect the lethargic alligator and how fast he is—swift as a racehorse over the first twenty yards—and a headful of other things.

But he taught me, without knowing he was teaching me, ways of being that would be with me all the days of my writing life: patience, perseverance, and how order is brought out of chaos.

One day about a week before my ninth birthday, we were out pulling fish off his trotline when after a long silence, he said: "Ever been to Fargo?"

"No, sir, I ain't." I thought for a minute. "I don't even know where one is."

He didn't laugh or even get a chuckle from my ignorance. He only turned and looked at me with his stoic face, deeply lined and toothless even then. "It's a place, a little town. I'll ask your ma about taking you over there on your birthday. You ought to see it." He stopped with the fish he was taking off a hook and seemed to think about something for a moment. "It's where the Okefenokee changes itself into something else."

I leapt to my feet, rocking the canoe pretty good. "Hot damn, that must be something to see."

"It's not so much something to see as it is something to think about."

"I'll like that," I said.

He heard the lie in my voice. "Maybe you will and maybe you won't. First we have to ask your ma."

Uncle Cooter and I ran the trapline, and to celebrate my visit, he cooked us a couple of thick bear steaks he had curing in his smokehouse. A bear steak is as pretty a piece of meat as a man is ever likely to see and it was Uncle Cooter's favorite food. I hated the stuff, but I ate it every time Uncle Cooter took it into his head to cook one. To do otherwise would have been intolerably bad manners. There's two things about bear steak I don't like. The longer you chew it the bigger it gets. And it tastes like a wet dog smells.

My mother not only gave me permission to go, but she was happy as she could be that her baby—I was four years younger than my brother—was going to have *something* for his birthday. Cake with candles or a single present wrapped in colored paper were pretty much unknown to the children of tenant farmers.

The trip to Fargo and back took a single day. We left before daylight and got back after dark, but while it was only one day, it was a day that has remained with me now for better than thirty years. As Uncle Cooter had promised, there was little enough to see. Actually, in little-boy terms, there was *nothing* to see.

On the edge of Fargo, Uncle Cooter had pulled his truck off to the side of a dirt road. He climbed a fence and I followed. We went across a field and into some marshy woods.

Uncle Cooter looked at me and said: "We got to take our time at this so don't go getting in a hurry. She changes every year, sometimes two or three times in the same year, so I'll have to look for her."

Look for *her*, I thought. That made no sense at all to me. But I wasn't about to tell Uncle Cooter that. I followed wherever he went and he went through gall berry patches, palmetto thickets, briars and brambles, sometimes through mud and sometimes through pine flats that were dry as a bone. And uncharacteristically, he was a little frantic, like a rabbit hound that has found a hot trail.

Finally he stopped. Appeared to sniff the air, look east, west, north, south, up at the sun and then down at his feet. For some time he looked at his feet and did not speak.

"What is it?" I asked when I could wait no longer.

"I've found her," he said.

I looked hard because I did not want him to think I was a dummy. But finally I had to ask: "What? What is it you found?"

"The Okefenokee."

Out of the ground at his feet was a little shelf of flint rock off which drops of water fell.

He bent down and caught several drops of water in his hand. He lifted it up to my face. "That right there is the Okefenokee."

"Uncle Cooter, you mean *some* of the Okefenokee. It ain't even a tablespoon there in your hand."

"Ahh, son, you're a good boy with a good head on your shoulders, but you've got to listen hard to this. But listening hard you still may not get it. Not today, anyway. Or next month or maybe next year. But if you think on it long enough it'll change the world you walk in, and everything you think you know, you won't know. And everything you don't know, you will come to know."

My first thought was that he had lost his mind, either that or he was playing with me. I opened my mouth to speak but he raised his hand and I was quiet.

He caught another little handful of water and lifted it between us. "That right there in my hand is the Okefenokee." He glanced over his shoulder. "And the hundred and some-odd miles behind us—all that muck and mud and twisted things growing there and the ten thousand furred things that eat each other and are then ate by something else—is the Okefenokee, too. The drops in my hand couldn't be there without the deep swamp behind us. The biggest thing in the world has to start with the littlest thing in the world and the biggest thing in the world has to one day be part of the littlest thing in the world. Everything is a piece of everything. It cain't be no other way."

I felt on the verge of tears and I didn't know why. I certainly wasn't afraid of Uncle Cooter. I thought the feel of tears had come because Uncle Cooter sounded a lot like my grandpa when he got started talking about the Bible, which I didn't understand either.

"Why did you do this, Uncle Cooter, bring me here?"

He actually smiled, a full, generous smile that made me realize how much I loved him. "Because it's your birthday and because when I was about your age my grandpa brought me here. It was the best thing my grandpa ever gave me and I thought it was the best thing I could give you. I never forgot it, and forgive the pride of an old man, but I don't think you'll ever forget it either."

I didn't forget it either, although at the time I did not know what it was I would not forget. It is also the reason why the swamp and the river have been at the heart of my writing even though neither has ever been the subject of anything I've written.

"It was a great birthday present, Uncle Cooter, and I'm glad you brought me."

"Oh, we're not through yet, son. Come on."

I followed him up to his truck and he drove to the paved road and turned west and we drove in silence for about forty miles, Uncle Cooter draining his tobacco into a spit cup and I trying to imagine what I'd been shown and why. We turned off onto a dirt road and followed it between walls of oak, black gum, and cypress trees.

"Hop out and take a look at this, son."

But I had already seen it before I got the door open, a river totally unlike any I'd ever seen before except in geography books at school. In Bacon and Ware County where I'd grown up, there was not a stream or creek you couldn't drive a mule and wagon across, much less an honest-to-God river like this one, or if there was, I hadn't seen it. I couldn't even imagine how wide it was.

"Know what that is?"

"I know it's a river, but I never seen anything like it."

"Yes, you have. Its size just had you fooled."

I could only stare at him.

"Remember that water that was dripping off that rock into my hand?"

"Yes, sir."

He pointed to the river and said, "That's Okefenokee water. Only now it's called the Suwannee River. Sometime, a long time ago, before they was even any Indians in here, the Okefenokee decided to change itself into something else." He paused and looked up the river. "And it's still doing it."

That was a revelation to me—one of the biggest of my life—that an unimaginably huge tangle of muck and mud and literally thousands of different kinds of life (both plant and animal that had taken eons to twist themselves together) could remake itself into something that had integrity, coherence, direction, and strength by so simple an act as falling off a flat piece of flint rock one drop at a time.

I heard that when I was nine years old, and it would be two decades later when I discovered that what I had heard that day as a child was a nearly perfect description of how a narrative is formed. Nothing can be written the way it happened—*nothing*—because things happen simultaneously, and the limitations of pen and pencil dictate that only one thing can be written at a time, one word at a time. Therefore, time will always be distorted in any narrative, and since time *has* to be distorted anyway, all writers of consequence try to distort it to their own best advantage.

An old man, a little boy, and water falling from a flat rock are worth a dozen books on the "craft of fiction" or "the creative personality." A swamp and a river are enough to bring at least one writer back from the raging edge of despair to a place where calm, sane work can at least be attempted.

ALAN LIGHTMAN

*I*f only time could be as elastic as Alan Lightman imagines it in his beautiful first novel, *Einstein's Dreams*, life would be far easier for we harried moderns. In "Hallelujah," Lightman recounts his own experience of elastic time as he experiences it on a remote island of Maine. Here, as in his two novels, Lightman displays a dazzlingly spare yet lyrical and evocative prose style. The theme of time is pervasive, as is that of the conflict between the waking, rational mind and the sleeping mind of dreams and desires. On this island, far from fax machines and telephones, Lightman finds his life taking on not just "the rhythm of the tides," but the rhythm of his own creative heartbeat. "Hallelujah" is a subtle, delicate piece about the saving grace of solitude.

HALLELUJAH

I SPEND SUMMERS ON A SMALL ISLAND IN MAINE. IT'S A SKINNY finger of land, several hundred feet wide and half a mile long, pointing northeast and southwest like the other islands in Casco Bay. Apparently, all the landmasses in the region were carved long and thin by the great retreating ice floes some twenty thousand years ago. However, land shapes can be deceiving at sea. When I go out in my boat and look at the island end-on, it doesn't appear as the tip of a finger but as a round dollop, with spruce trees sticking up from its crown like green bristly hair. A high ridge runs down the spine of the island, a hundred feet above sea level, and my house lies on the north end of the ridge. From there, the ocean is a stone's throw in all directions but south. To the south, there are four other cottages, cloaked from each other by a dense growth of trees. On cold winter nights, as I sit in my city house near Boston, brooding about the next day's assignments, I imagine I'm on the island, wearing shorts and sandals, smelling the sweet ocean air, listening to sea gulls and ospreys.

The island basks in its isolation. There are no roads or bridges, no ferries, no telephone service, no fax machines, no electronic mail. The rest of the world is a light-year away. However, like Thoreau in Concord, I've traveled far and wide on the island. I know each cedar and poplar, each cluster of spruce, each clump of wild rose, *Rosa rugosa*, each patch of blueberry bushes and raspberry brambles and lush moss.

I know every indentation of the shoreline, which my nine-year-old daughter and I have often circumnavigated in our water shoes. On the south end of the island, a flat grassy area nestles unexpectedly amid heavy spruce trees. It's rumored that an eccentric man who owned the island a century ago made a garden in that spot for his lady friend from Portland. On the west, down the hill from my house, an underwater cave gurgles at midtide. About midlength on the east side of the island, an osprey nest perches atop a high tree. Several summers ago, I watched as a mother osprey taught her two children how to fly. One at a time, each of the babies was shoved out of the nest, rose into the air, and began flying, then endlessly circled the nest while emitting the most pitiful squawks, unable to perform the stalls and backdrafts needed to slow down for a landing. The mother, during the ordeal, flew helpfully nearby and let out with a constant stream of high-pitched instructions. Father osprey watched nonchalantly from a tree.

Our dock lies on the east side of the island, approached by a series of stone steps down from the house to a short, level path covered with sienna spruce needles, then again down a long flight of wood steps to the ramp and the float on the water. When I get up early in the morning, I love to make a mug of black coffee and, while everyone is sleeping, walk down to the dock and watch the sun rise over the trees on the far shore. At that time of day, and in that spot, I can for once let my mind think about what *it* wants to think about. Solitude is so rare nowadays. One morning, I was there on the dock just as a light fog began moving in. The rising sun became a gauzy fire. Suddenly, the air started to glow. Fog scattered the sunlight, bounced it around and back and forth until each cupful of air shone with its own source of light. In all directions, the air beamed and shimmered and glowed, and the gulls stopped their squawking and the ospreys became silent. The ocean was still as a held breath. For some time I stood there spellbound by the silence and the glowing air. Then the fog burned away and the glow disappeared.

It is on this summer island, away from the rush of the world, that I do most of my writing. To me, the island is far more than its physical beauty; it is my inner life, the center of my creativity, part of my bloodstream. I write in a small room in the corner of the house, with our family's two Maine coon cats curled up happily on a rug at my feet, their favorite spot when I am writing. Windows surround my desk on three sides. To the south I can gaze out on a needle-covered path that winds across the spine of the island; to the east I look through spruce trees down the hill to the ocean. But after some moments at my desk, the spectacular views become meaningless, for I have transported myself to a place without body or time. How curious that I have sought out this physical paradise in order to write, only to abandon it as soon as I begin writing. At these times I am so far away that I do not notice even the day's changing light, the dazzling strips of sun across my desk in the morning and the even soft glow after noon.

In the early morning, however, before the writing day has begun, I am much attentive to the light. In the early morning my wife and I are treated to a light show on our bedroom ceiling. Sunlight, reflected off the ocean below, shines through the east windows and shudders with each passing wave in the bay, each ripple on that vast blue-green mirror. I like to think that a single bluefish swimming close to the shore can create enough of a wave to flutter the sun on our ceiling, leaving a trace of its slender body forever in my memory. By eight o'clock or so, the angles of incidence and reflection are no longer right, and the light show comes to an end. Then, we must wait until eight in the evening, when the sun setting over the mainland throws its long spiky light sideways through the west windows and onto the opposite wall, creating homemade movies out of any objects in its path. This performance lasts about ten minutes.

Unconsciously, our lives on the island follow the rhythm of the tides, two high tides and two low every day. In our neck of the ocean, the difference between high and low tides can get up to twelve feet. At high tide, the land area of the island shrinks by a sixth. The ocean seems practically at our doorstep. Familiar rocks and ledges near the island disappear, submerged. The ramp leading down to our float becomes practically horizontal. Midtide, when the tidal current is swiftest, we can hear the water trickle by the rocks on the shore. A V-shaped water wake trails downstream of each lobster buoy in the bay, as if each buoy were a little boat rushing forward against the current. At low tide, we get our island back. The ramp to the float again makes a steep drop. Down on the shore, gold sea kelp drapes over the rocks like braided hair and hisses with popping air bubbles.

Some rocks on the shore are uncovered only at low tide, timidly peering above the surface for their brief hour of air, each with its own headdress of sea kelp, attached periwinkles, and visiting gulls. At super-low tides, when the sun and moon are lined up with the earth and both pull together, our boat becomes grounded and we happily stranded, all aquatic excursions put on hold until more water is at hand.

Other times, we become stranded by dense fog. There is little more lovely than a heavy fog moving in, taking its time. In the beginning, the air slightly thickens, becomes milky, diaphanous. The mainland, a half mile away, grows fuzzy and blurred. Distant houses lose their edges, piers on the water become gradations of air mass, trees turn to smudges. Colors fade first, leaving blue tones and grays. Then these too melt away, into white. The wooden fishing boat moored near the marina across from the island turns gauzy and white, its gunnels grow cotton, its engine turns to a strange mound of snow, it fades and is gone. Lobster buoys dissolve one by one, the most distant first, then nearer and nearer, in decreasing circles. When the mainland and ocean are gone, the island itself disappears, beginning with the spruce trees to the south, then the dock, usually visible from the house, the bottom of the hill to the east and the west. Finally, as we sit looking out, our small house becomes the last material substance on earth, everything else dissolved into chalky oblivion. Our house floats in nothingness. Yet we continue to look out the window, staring into that nothingness, as if we could still see the invisible world. Sometimes at that moment, I imagine that I am sitting in my city house on a cold winter night, watching the obliterating snow fall outside while I ponder invisible appointments and invisible urgent electronic messages. I imagine that way for a while, angry at myself for recalling the world I want to escape, uncertain which place I inhabit. Then my daughter, who has no such uncertainties, shouts for the Monopoly board, and we lay up some popcorn for the duration of the fog.

We try to keep our summer visitors to a minimum, aside from occasional dinners with other residents of the island, but two guests always welcome at the end of a long writing day are Greta Waterman and her husband George. The Watermans hail from South Freeport. They motor over in George's ancient green lobster boat, making a giant wake that announces their visit several minutes before they arrive. "I don't know where the summer's gone to," says Greta, smiling. "But here we are." Greta is a small, fragile, silver-haired woman who grows beautiful heather in her garden and sells it to locals. George is the opposite in appearance—huge and hulking like a bear, barrel-chested, enormously strong. He once studied to be a classical musician, before he was captured by the outdoors of Maine, and will often compare ocean sunsets to Handel's *Messiah* or the sound of wind through the trees to a Beethoven symphony. George works on the water. He builds piers, ramps, and floats, and a variety of other marine constructions, lazily traveling from one job to another in his boat. The more logistically difficult and challenging a project, the more he enjoys it. All of his work has a wonderful blend of unquestionable practicality and aesthetics of design. The ramps of his floats are solidly anchored at both ends, yet arc gracefully into the air. His piers are often octagonal.

George doesn't go anywhere without his cellular phone, even when having a leisurely dinner with me on the island. He claims to need it for incoming business calls, but I've never seen him receive any. I believe the phone is a dutiful connection to some other life, which he must constantly rub against whether he wants to or not, just as I find myself unable to stop visualizing the other, time-ridden world or measuring the duration of sunsets. We joke about it but cannot change our behavior, cannot fully capture our freedom.

In addition to the phone, which he carries in a heavy metal box, George always wears a dozen or more tools strapped around his waist on a leather harness. As he walks, taking his big, bearlike steps, the tools clank and rattle. For some odd reason, however, whenever George comes over to build something at my house, he never has the one tool he needs. He'll roll his eyes for a moment, with the recognition that he's forgotten some specialized wrench or drill, then break out with a mischievous grin that says he's figured out how to make do with whatever equipment he has on hand. George prides himself in his resourcefulness, and sometimes I think that he intentionally leaves behind a key tool or part just to prove to himself he can live without it. He once came over to build a door to the lattice skirting under my house. As it turned out, he'd forgotten the door handle and latch. Within ten minutes, he constructed a perfectly fine handle and latch out of wood and a bent nail, which I still use to this day. After much admiration of his handiwork, we went down the hill with a bottle of wine and watched the sun turn red and puffy, him humming one of Handel's serenatas.

A great variety of boats pass by the island, but the ones I like best are the small skiffs loaded with kelp. The kelp can be sold to restaurants and fishing wholesalers, to keep lobsters and other fish moist. The kelp fishermen coast slowly up to the shore at low tide, then shovel the kelp into their boats like farmers shoveling hay. They don't stop until the kelp is piled high in two huge mounds fore and aft and their boats seem in imminent danger of sinking. At dusk, the silhouettes of their kelp-laden boats, slowly heading home, look like double-humped camels on the desert.

Living close to wildlife is a fine island pleasure. For several summers running, a family of phoebes returned to a nest under our house. Actually, I'm not certain they were the same birds every summer, but it was always phoebes who took up residence in that nest, happily shouting, "Fee Bee, Fee Bee." They would fly in and out through the small holes in the wood lattice at great speed, never slowing down but never colliding with the cross struts, somehow gauging their aerial position with the precision of F-15s. I grew attached to the birds but eventually dismantled the nest when a more knowledgeable friend told me that nests used over and over are dangerous to the birds because of bacterial buildup. The ospreys don't seem to have the same problem and use the same nest every summer with no mishaps. Besides a variety of birds, red squirrels abound on the island, and they have a ferocious self-confidence and irreverence. Last summer I was having a picnic with my family, out in the woods, when a single red squirrel made off with an entire bag of chocolate chip cookies, probably twice its own weight. Absconding with just one cookie wasn't worth its time. Then, when the fellow was safely away and its loot stored, it climbed a tree and mocked us with a loud chatter in our direction.

Deer come to the island in winter, but leave early spring. Each November, just at the beginning of the hunting season, several of them miraculously swim over from the mainland, a quarter mile through deep, frigid water, to escape the guns of the hunters. When I come to open up the house in late spring, I often see deer tracks and droppings, chewed-up blueberry bushes. I wish the deer would stay longer. I once came to the island in January, hoping to spot them. It was right after a snowfall and the island was covered in a beautiful, thick white, and dead quiet. The only footprints I saw, however, were my own. I have never felt so alone in my life, and the feeling wasn't bad. As I walked down the spine of the island in my winter boots, the snow crunching underfoot, a wind whipped through the ice-laden tree branches sounding like huge support cables giving way, as if the great dome of the sky were about to crash down. I looked up and was relieved to see a deep, steady blue.

Other animals I see in great numbers live in the ocean, down by the dock. In June, the water temperature is just right for jellyfish, and a platoon of those translucent creatures can be spotted in the water just off the float, slowly contracting and dilating their soft liquid sacs. The jellyfish are harmless, but my daughter won't swim in the water until they are gone. Other times, she will leap in, regardless of the temperature, and dare me to swim with her out to some buoy halfway to the mainland. At midtide, we often see crabs fidgeting around on the rocks down below. My daughter, who is growing up with the outdoors in her blood, fishes for crabs with a bit of meat attached to the end of a string. She shrieks with pleasure when she catches one, then quickly throws it back in when I suggest we cook it for dinner. Some summer days, millions of minnows swim just below the surface. Every second, there is a bright flash as one of the millions of fish has wriggled at just the right angle to reflect sunlight from its silvery body.

A few years back, when I arrived at our house at the start of the season, I was startled to find a yellow horseshoe-shaped life vest, fastened upright around a tree stump near the shore. Evidently, during the winter the vest had been tossed up by the ocean at high tide and deposited there. The word "Hallelujah" was written on it in black letters. I figured that life vest was some sign from providence, and I left it untouched on the stump, where it still rests.

DIANE ACKERMAN

iane Ackerman looks at we humans with the curious eye of a benevolent extraterrestrial. Here, as in her books *A Natural History of the Senses* and *The Moon by Whalelight: Other Adventures Among Bats, Penguins, Crocodilians and Whales*, she displays an uncanny ability to stand back from the natural world with a refreshing sense of the unfamiliar. Seamlessly weaving science, history, and personal narrative, "The Grandeur of the Grand Canyon" achieves the *ostranennie*, or "making-strange," that Anton Chekhov believed to be a necessary component of any moving prose. Such "making-strange," however, is not just the essay's method but its subject: unlike the other essays in *The Place Within*, "The Grandeur of the Grand Canyon" is about the failure of the observer to "humanize" a place as utterly inhuman as the Grand Canyon.

The Grandeur

of the

Grand Canyon

Nothing prepares you for the visual thrill of sailing over the rim, from a state of flatland predictability suddenly into one of limitless depth, change, and color. All at once we are down into its jungles of rock, plunging toward sheer crevices, skimming limestone jags by only a few yards, then swooping down even farther to trace the winding path of the Colorado River, rocketing up toward a large butte, wing left, wing right, as we twist along the unraveling alleyways of rock, part of a spectacle both dainty and massive. Who could measure it, when we are the only certain size moving through the mazes? Off one wing tip, a knob of limetsone curves into arrowhead edges and disappears at the base of a half-shattered tree whose open roots catch the sunlight in a cage of iridescence.

When we land, we begin to explore the Grand Canyon on foot from lookouts and trails along the rim. Hypnotized by the intricate vastness, I hike from one triangulation station to another, finding two of the ninety bronze survey disks that were installed decades ago by the Boston Museum of Science/National Geographic expedition. Sitting alone on a plinth jutting far over the emptiness, I listen to the monumental silence and find my mind roaming over the notion of wonder.

The canyon is, in part, a touchstone to other wonders, revealing the uncanny work of erosion, a great builder of landscapes; five geologic eras piled one on top of the other like Berber rugs; the evolution of life viewable in a fossil record; and the fumings of the Colorado

River (whose color changes during the year from deep green to bright red, or even to milky blue). Gigantic as the canyon is—217 miles long—it is the world in miniature: seven environments (from Sonoran to Arctic Circle); desert barrenness to spring lushness. It is certainly the grandest American cliché, explored by many but an enigma nonetheless. No response to it seems robust enough.

In a world governed by proportion—in which the eye frames a moment, digests it, frames another—scale is lost; visual scale, mental scale, emotional scale. If your lips purse in a silent *wow* at the sight of Niagara Falls, what is suitable here where your heart explores some of its oldest dwellings? The mind makes its own lavish prisons; rarely does one confront in nature a prison unimaginable. How can you explain an emptiness so vast and intricate, an emptiness rare on this planet? Not the sprawling, flat, oddly clean emptiness of a desert or Arctic region but an emptiness with depth. There are no yardsticks, unless one is lucky enough to catch sight of a dark speck moving along the canyon floor which is a mule and rider. But that is part of the puzzle of this labyrinth, a maze both of direction and of proportion, a maze in three dimensions.

It's easy to forget how ugly nature often seemed to people before Romanticism reexplored the unevenness of natural beauty. Early nineteenth-century writers found the canyon grotesque—not just dangerous and obstructive and rife with bloodthirsty Indians but actually a vision of evil. C. B. Spencer described it as "Horror! Tragedy! Silence! Death! Chaos! . . . a delirium of Nature," while another writer called it "the grave of the world." After two world wars and assorted smaller ones, with all the atrocities attendant to them, it's no longer possible to find works of nature horrible, tragic, deadly, chaotic; humankind has personalized those traits forever. Now the canyon is just the opposite: a sanctuary, an emblem of serenity, a view of innocence.

The Cardenas expedition of 1540 discovered the canyon for the Caucausian world but felt no need to name it. For three hundred years it was too overwhelming to report except in whole phrases and sentences. And then in the 1850s and 1860s "Big Canon" and "Grand Canon of the Colorado" came into use, as if it were *one* of anything. For it is not one but thousands of canyons, thousands of gorges and buttes, interflowing, mute, radiant, changing, all with a single river among them, as if joined by a common thought.

In the canyon's long soliloquy of rock, parrots of light move about the grottoes and real swifts loop and dart, white chevrons on each flank. The silence is broken only by the sound of air whistling through the gorges, and the occasional whirring of a helicopter. Now and then one hears the sound of a furnace whumping on: a bird is taking flight. There is no way to catalogue the endless dialects and languages and body types of the tourists encountered at the rim. With binoculars as various as they are, visitors search the canyon for trails, mules, signs of other people. The need to humanize the marvel is obsessive, obvious, and universal. With glass lenses extending real eyes, canyon visitors become part of the evolution on show. If we cannot go backwards in time, we can at least creep into it, above desert floors and red-rock mesas and ponderosa pine, then suddenly slip over the rim of dreams and down through the layers of geological time.

What is *grandeur* that it should form rapidly in the mind when one first sees the Grand Canyon? Why do we attach that concept to this spectacle? Is it merely the puniness of human beings compared with the gigantic structures of rock? The moon, the biggest rock most of us know, has been domesticated in literature and song, but the canyon has resisted great literature. Like the universe and the workings of nature, there is no way to summarize it. The ultimate model of a labyrinth, it is gargantuan and cryptic, full of blind alleys and culs-de-sac. We are compulsive architects; to see engineering as complete, colossal, and inimitable as this—still far beyond our abilities —is humbling indeed. As John Muir said in 1896, upon first viewing the canyon: "Man seeks the finest marbles for sculptures; Nature takes cinders, ashes, sediments, and makes all divine in fineness and beauty—turrets, towers, pyramids, battlemented castles, rising in glowing beauty from the depths of this canyon of canyons noiselessly hewn from the smooth mass of the featureless plateau."

Most of all, the canyon is so vastly uninvolved with us, with mercy or pity. Even the criminal mind is more explicable than this—a quiddity we cannot enter, a consciousness that does not include us. We pass through much of our world as voyeurs and yet we are driven, from sheer loneliness, I suppose, to attribute consciousness to all sorts of non-conscious things—dolls, cars, computers. We still call one another totemic names by way of endearment: we would like to keep the world as animate as it was for our ancestors. But that is difficult when facing a vision as rigidly dead as the Grand Canyon. It is beautiful and instructive and calming, but it cannot be anything other than it is: the absolute, intractable "other" that human beings face from birth to death.

Perhaps that's why tourists mainly respond to it with a long pause of recognition, the momentary twisting of a brow as they try to construe it, and then a long, slow silence as they sit and behold it, until their bus must go, or the fading light leaves the thinnest catwalk between the blue sky and the bluer outlines of rock.

Consciousness is the great poem of matter, whose opposite extreme is a Grand Canyon. In between, matter has odd fits and whims: lymph, feathers, Astro Turf, brass. Cactus strikes me as a very odd predicament for matter to get into. But perhaps it is no stranger than the comb of an iris, or the way flowers present their sex organs to the world, or the milky sap that often oozes from inedible plants. There is something about the poignant senselessness of all that rock that reminds us, as nothing else could so dramatically, what a bit of luck *we* are, what a natural wonder.

At the south rim, brass sighting tubes make arbitrary sense out of the vista. Lay the lensless tube into a slot marked "Battleship" and there will be a facsimile in rock. The other sites are mainly temples: Vishnu Temple, Wotan's Throne, Zoroaster Temple, Brahma Temple, Buddha Temple, Tower of Ra, Cheops Pyramid, Osiris Temple, Shiva Temple, Isis Temple, and so on. One of the most dramatic, tall, and precarious buttes is referred to as "Snooopy" because, they say, it resembles the cartoon dog lying on his doghouse. All this demotion of the spectacle troubles me. Why define a site by another site that is smaller and in some cases trivial? Why vulgarize it with pop culture icons? The word *"vulgar"* didn't originally mean to debase or cheapen but to make suitable for the common people (from the Latin *vulgus*). Do visitors to the canyon really need to have it tamed before they can appreciate it? Nothing can compare with the Grand Canyon, and that is part of its true marvel and appeal.

It was John Wesley Powell who, in 1860, gave the salient buttes their temple names. Now that the gods who instructed us are remote, we are quite obsessed with temples. We have moved our gods farther and farther away, off the planet, into the solar system, beyond the Milky Way, beyond the Big Bang. But once upon a time, when time was seasonal, the gods were neighbors who lived just across the valley on a proscribed mountain. Their deeds and desires were tangible; they were intimates.

Today on the Hopi mesas close to the Grand Canyon, in rituals older than memory, people still dress as kachinas—garish, expressionist re-creations of the essences of their world. There is a kachina of meteors, and maize, and water vapor. In the winter months the kachinas dwell on the twelve thousand-foot slopes of Humphreys Peak, and in the growing season they come down to move among humans. The Hopi have traditionally traveled into the canyon to perform some of their rituals, and there is a spot on the bank of the Little Colorado where, they believe, humans may first have entered the world.

Indeed, the whole area around the Grand Canyon is full of lore and natural wonders. The volcanic field just north of Flagstaff is the largest in the United States, and flying over it you can see where the black paws of lava stopped cold. The aerial turbulence at midday evokes the early turbulence from which the canyon was partially formed, and long before that the chaos of the Big Bang. At the Lowell Observatory, in Flagstaff, Pluto was first sighted. In half a dozen other observatories, astronomers cast their gaze upward while, close by, a million tourists cast theirs down into the canyon.

There would be no canyon as we perceive it—subtle, mazy, unrepeating—without the intricate habits of light. For the canyon traps light, reveals itself in light, rehearses all the ways a thing can be lit: the picadors of light jabbing the horned spray of the Colorado River; light like caramel syrup pouring over the dusky buttes; the light almost fluorescent in the hot green leaves of seedlings. In places the canyon is so steep that sunlight only enters it, briefly, at noon; the rest is darkness.

It is hard to assimilate such a mix of intensities; it is too close to the experience of being alive. Instead, we order it with names that are cozy, trendy, or ancient. It is like the conscious mind, smitten with thought, whose crevices spread open silently before us. Available, viewable, definable, reducible to strata of limestone and fossil, they are still mysterious crevices, still unknowable, still overwhelming, still ample and unearthly, still the earth at its earthiest.

The Douglas firs crop out, under, around, between, through every place one looks; they survive the rock. Many of their twisted, light-ning-licked limbs are still in leaf. The cottonwoods, growing over a hundred feet tall, can use more than fifty gallons of water each day. There are a thousand kinds of flower and species of squirrel and bird indigenous to the canyon (some nearly extinct). And endless otters, skunks, beavers, ring-tailed cats, deer, porcupines, shrews, chip-munks, rats, and wild burros. In the low, common desert of the inner canyon depths, only the prickly-pear cactus survives well the high temperatures and rare precipitation. It is not erosion on a large scale that has formed the canyon but small daily acts of erosion by tiny plants and streams, reminding us what the merest trickle over lime-stone can achieve. From rim to floor, the canyon reveals the last two billion years of geological history and thus typifies the processes of evolution and decay in which we all take part.

But mainly there is the steep persuasion of something devastatingly fixed, something durable in a world too quick to behold, a world of fast, slippery perceptions, where it can sometimes seem that there is nothing to cling to. By contrast the canyon is solid and forever; going nowhere, it will wait for you to formulate your thoughts. The part of us that yearns for the supernaturalism we sprang from yearns for this august view of nature.

At nightfall, when we reboard the plane for our flight back to Phoenix, there is no canyon anywhere, just starry blackness above and moorish blackness below. Like a hallucination, the canyon has van-ished, completely hidden now by the absence of light. Hidden, as it was from human eyes for millennia, it makes you wonder what other secrets lie in the shade of our perception. Bobbing through the usual turbulence over the desert, we pick our way home from one cluster of town lights to another, aware from this height of the patterns of human habitation. Seven skirts of light around a mountain reveal how people settled in waves. Some roads curve to avoid, others to arrive. Except for the lights running parallel along the ridges, people seem desperate to clump and bunch, swarming all over each other in towns while most of the land lies empty. The thick, dark rush of the desert below, in which there is not one human light for miles, drugs me. Looking up drowsily after a spell, I'm startled to see the horizon glittering like Oz: Phoenix and its suburbs. That, or one long, sprawl-ing marquee.

S U Z A N N E   B E R N E

uzanne Berne's rich, descriptive prose is
suffused with a sense of place. In her stories
and other essays, this place is typically the
landscape of New England, where she has lived
most of her adult life. And yet, much as Berne
thinks of herself as a New Englander,
"Clovelly" reveals an author's southern roots.
The essay finds Berne writing for the first time
about that sprawling, aristocratic, anachronistic
Virginia estate on which she was born. It is a
wry, tender, sensual portrait of an unusual
childhood and the author's "casual embrace of
the extraordinary." More so, it is a piece about
the "stubborn alchemy of looking back," the
creative power of memory. One may leave a
place, "Clovelly" seems to suggest, but one
never loses it.

CLOVELLY

IN 1961, THE YEAR I WAS BORN, MY FATHER BOUGHT A TWO HUN-
dred and fifty–acre horse farm in Fauquier County, Virginia, a place
called Clovelly. One of my first memories is of sitting in a field there
in a nest of cut grass, pretending to have been just hatched. We lived
in Virginia for ten years, surrounded by pastures and low green hills,
with a pond and a creek, and a barn and a stable, in a house that had
been built before the Revolution. Not far from the house was a family
graveyard with slate headstones so old that the names chiseled into
them had worn away in the rain. It wasn't hard to believe that Clovelly was one of those places that had always been there and would
always be there.

But eventually we left it to move to the city, and became city
people, and after a while I stopped noticing how temporary everything
else seemed. Ten more years went by, and another ten, and a few
years more. Then last summer I went back to Fauquier County for a
funeral and drove by Clovelly again, and saw the pastures shimmer
under a hot August sun.

It was a humid morning, over a hundred degrees. On the way I'd
passed fields and old stone walls banked by honeysuckle and mountain
laurel, all shimmering also, a soft world of blurred boundaries that
reminded me of what I saw whenever I took off my glasses. The road
had been resurfaced and a housing development was going up on what
used to be a farm called North Wales. But the other farms I'd passed

looked pretty much the same, with names like Elway Hall and St. Leonard's painted on quietly imposing little signs that hung over wrought-iron gates. Horses grazed in the distance on bright green grass, as they always had. On the opposite side of the road, a girl wearing jodphurs and a T-shirt trotted along on a big bay horse with yellow ribbons braided into its mane. It seemed that I had seen her before, although when I passed by she was no one I recognized. Overhead coasted a pair of turkey vultures, so high in the sky they looked like sparrows.

I've come to consider myself a New Englander, but driving through the slow, dazed Virginia countryside that morning, with its ripe smell of hay and manure, and the buzz of cicadas, and the Blue Ridge Mountains truly blue in the distance, I found myself wondering what it would be like to live there still. This feeling grew stronger as I drove along until my heart was beating as fast as if I were on my way to meet an old lover.

You can't see much of the house itself from the road, so I turned in at the gates and drove down the long driveway as far as the stable, where the drive forked and the boxwood began. The people who now lived at Clovelly owned three fat Doberman pinschers, which ran up to my car and barked at the doors, so I stopped and gazed through the windshield at the old house beyond, its white pillars half-hidden behind cedar trees that had grown higher than the roof.

Not much had changed. The new owners had painted the green trim brown and those tall cedars looked ragged, a little mysterious in the way they blocked the view; otherwise it was the house I remembered. The stone-flagged courtyard was still there, and my mother's rose bushes. The car began to get very hot. But I sat a bit longer, wishing I could walk around the house and see if the duck pond was still there surrounded by weeping cherries, or if the spring house was still there surrounded by watercress, or if the graveyard was still there where my sisters and I had buried little dead animals among the headstones, or if the creek was still there running to the Rappahannock, or if there was still a hill in the cow pasture where persimmon trees grew.

Of all the places I've known, I suppose the house at Clovelly still seems the loveliest and most graceful. It was already over two hundred and fifty years old when we moved in, with four chimneys and a fieldstone verandah that rose above terraced lawns and flowering trees—the kind of beautiful old house you find in that part of Virginia and nowhere else. But when I lived there, I didn't see it as beautiful. I thought it was haunted.

I believed a Yankee soldier's chopped-off head had been stuffed up one of the chimneys and that a rabid ghost dog lived in the furnace room. I believed the Devil slept all day in the front hall closet and came out at night to type on my father's Royal typewriter wearing a black homburg hat.

Our housekeeper, an immense country woman named Mrs. Weaver, also thought the house was haunted. "You all got haints," she once told my mother, widening her pink-rimmed eyes. "Buncha haints. They run up and down them back stairs and leave crumbs on the floor." Mrs. Weaver was fond of ghost stories and liked to tell them right before bedtime when our parents were away. "This is a true story," she would begin. "It happened just down the road a piece." Whatever followed was guaranteed to give us bad dreams. Mrs. Weaver never had nightmares herself and once asleep was very hard to wake up. She slept through the time lightning struck a tree right outside her window. Even if you did succeed in waking her by shrieking and pounding on her bedroom door, she would appear in the doorway with her head bristling with metal clips, and no matter how terrible your nightmare, order you back to bed. The only person in my family Mrs. Weaver admired was the baby, who at two years old quietly insisted that she had been spanked by a ghost named Kemper, which was the name of the people buried in the little graveyard.

Yet even with its ghosts, the house didn't seem exceptional to me then, although it had been part of the Underground Railroad and was pocketed with secret compartments, walled-up passageways, and false-backed closets. But this is the lost secret of childhood, this casual embrace of the extraordinary. In those days, I saw Clovelly simply as my home, where I lived, mine the way my parents were mine. It was unthinkable that I would live anywhere else, just as it was unthinkable that my parents would ever stop being married.

Not far from the house was the stable, which also looked the same, a long-roofed clapboard building I remembered as being full of horse stalls and hay bales and shafts of dusty light. A few barn cats always slunk around the open double doors or lay in blades of sun beside the tractor. Sometimes the cats had kittens in the hayloft, most of which died in pathetic and grisly ways and were conducted to the graveyard, but always a few had hung on to be chased by our dogs. Thin-legged young men in plaid shirts and Sears bluejeans used to lounge around the stable door with the cats, squinting and smoking as they waited to take horses out to exercise in the pastures. We didn't have horses ourselves. The stalls were rented out to people who owned racehorses but had nowhere to keep them.

The grooms rarely spoke to me. They came and went in the warm brown gloom of the stable like country gods, their thin forearms splendidly sinewed, their boots dirty, their light-colored eyes squinting toward something which perhaps had to do with the coming evening, and perhaps not. They were impatient, brooding, not much older than eighteen. Whenever they finished smoking a cigarette— always a Lucky Strike—they flicked the butt onto the ground and stepped on it with a twist of their boot heel. I was in love with all of them, even though several had no front teeth, and they had names like Ephraim and Elmer and Jimmy Cornfield. Sometimes I glimpsed them in town when my mother took me to buy shoes at Lerner's or to my Saturday ballet lessons. They looked just as moody and restless there, leaning against a lamp post or sitting hunched on a bench by the drugstore, except maybe they had dusted off their boots. They would nod to my mother as we passed by, call her "Ma'am" in a smoky tone that made me shudder, and go back to staring.

The stable had been forbidden to me as a child, and so of course I went there every chance I got. I liked to sink my hands into the wheelbarrow of oats that always stood below the hayloft, sliding the oats through my fingers, pretending to be Midas while the chaff rose, itched my fingers, and made me sneeze. Sometimes I threw oats to a Brazilian stallion named Amerigo that had won a quarter of a million dollars in track money and now, accompanied by a billy goat, had been put out to stud.

Amerigo was crazy. He spent most of each day kicking his stall, occasionally splintering a board; the goat was the only live thing that could calm him down. A crazy racehorse seemed very romantic to me then and I used to stand for twenty minutes at a time listening to that dull, hectic kicking, hoping Amerigo would swing up his head and show his yellow teeth and roll his eyes. He must have been homesick, I figured, and trying to kick his way back to Brazil. When no one was looking, I leaned against his door and whispered promises to him while the barn cats twisted around my legs and dust rose in little puffs at my feet. Once one of the grooms caught me with my hand on the stall latch. After that someone put a padlock there.

But the real reason I visited the stable was that I liked to slip into the tack room and peer into its dark bathroom with the torn ochre-colored shade where the grooms kept their black combs and bottles of Vitalis. The toilet seat was always up and always a few flies circled the sink. I would stand in the doorway, shivering a little, hoping and fearing, but hoping more intensely, that one of the grooms would come in and catch me there. What I would do if this happened I had no idea, and since it never did, I never found out. The tack room itself held an old deal desk and a broken-down leather sofa under a spotty print of four dogs playing poker. The farm's caretaker, a crab-faced man named Mr. Leach who had an epileptic daughter, often drank whiskey in there late at night, muttering as he scratched at the desktop with his thumbnail. Afterwards he went home to his stone cottage and slapped his wife.

Then one January night when the whole farm was lost in snow, a groom wrapped himself in a horse blanket and fell asleep drunk on the tack-room sofa with a lit cigarette in his hand. The cigarette caught fire to the blanket, then the sofa, and before the groom woke up he had burned himself to death. All the horses were saved, and except for the tack room, so was the stable. No one else seemed to be hurt. But the next morning one of the other grooms walked up the driveway, knocked at the kitchen door, and asked if he could borrow my father's bicycle. My father said of course. The groom ped-aled away past the cold glitter of the fields, his little cap pulled low, and we never saw him or the bicycle again.

For years I tried to keep straight the name of the groom who died and the one who disappeared with our bicycle, and whether I had actually seen the fire from my bedroom window or only heard about it later. Strange how something like that could grow hazy while other things stayed so clear. I had no trouble, for instance, remembering every foot of the farmyard behind the stable, with its collapsing barns and corn cribs and the chicken coop. But then, dead and vanished young men were one thing, and chicken coops another; at least that's how you'd think it would be.

The chicken coop at Clovelly was a tall, lopsided shed, dim and musty as a cave, where banty hens laid speckled eggs in tiers of straw gemmed with white droppings. If you tried to steal an egg from under a setting hen, she rose up squawking and beat her wings; she might even peck your hand. But still it had been a privilege to collect eggs, since we weren't usually allowed in the farmyard at all and had to sneak there on our own. The eggs rocked gently if you held them in your palm. Every so often when we broke one open for breakfast we found the cloudy red beginnings of a chick inside, and then my sisters and I would cry and ask to bury it and refuse to eat poached eggs for a week or two.

In those days Amerigo's goat liked to hide behind the chicken coop, then gallop out to butt you with his knobby head. It was better if you brought a dog with you on visits to the farmyard because then he might chase the dog. Once, right after Amerigo died, the goat jumped up and set his front hooves on my older sister's shoulders and glared at her with cracked yellow eyes. "He's trying to hypnotize me," she shrieked. We thought the goat had supernatural powers because of his beard. When I got up the courage, I used to run alone from the stable to the chicken coop—pausing once to let the goat have a chance at me—and then, heart walloping, I would run out again, run and run until my eyes leaked tears and my chest felt bruised.

Sometimes I ran all the way down to the cow pasture to the salt licks, big blocks of salt put out for my father's herd of Black Angus cattle, most of which died from hoof-and-mouth disease a year after he bought them. I liked to kneel down on the cropped grass and, when I'd stopped panting, lick those blocks myself, which tasted not just of salt but of earth, while around me grasshoppers chirred, and the dogs hunted ground hogs, and cloud shadows rushed across the hills, disappearing into the creek.

At one end of the cow pasture, down in a hollow full of thistles, sat the pigpen. Next to the graveyard and the tack room, the pigpen had been my favorite place to visit because of its stench of mud and rotting corn cobs and pig dung. The smell was so terrible that I sniffed it like a drug. If you climbed onto the fence, the pigs hurried over and rammed their hairy sides against the slats, grunting and tossing their delicate pale snouts. I had been told that pigs would trample you to death with their hooves if you fell into the pen; but I remember thinking their little eyes looked resigned instead of murderous, and confused, as if they could not figure out how they came to be what they were. Whenever I could, I fed the pigs sugar cubes filched from the silver bowl on my mother's buffet. Their names were Happy and Lucky, and one spring we ate them.

The stable and the farmyard still seem the most wild and thrilling of places: where bent nails in the dirt waited to give you tetanus and the dark, glossy smell of horses mixed with the stink of pigs, a place where you might find anything, bloody chicken feathers, a dead rat in the corn crib, love, grief, one of Mr. Leach's empty whiskey bottles. If we'd never left Clovelly I'm sure it wouldn't have stayed that way.

But we did leave Clovelly, and five or six years later my parents divorced. It's odd how remembering one time in your life can bring you to another, which you didn't intend to remember at all. And yet there's nothing casual about memory, just as there's nothing casual about a racehorse: they both have their tracks they circle, forever in the same direction. It's in the blood, to run that way. But I guess I've learned that revisiting what you've lost can make you crazy after a while, and so you need something as persistent and bossy as a billy goat to keep butting you along.

Above the house, the cedar trees rocked. It was getting late; I had a funeral to go to. But I sat in the car a few minutes longer, looking at the house and the pastures alongside. I had been certain Clovelly would have changed so much, and there it was, not much different at all. The grooms had been replaced by other grooms, and barn cats by other barn cats, and pigs by other pigs. The haunts were the same. And yet it was as different as a place can be and still be the same place. My sisters and I had gone on with our lives, had grown up, got married ourselves, and some of us got divorced ourselves, and all of us had wandered around to get wherever we were. Now we lived in cities and suburbs, and none of us had a farmyard, or a horse, or even a chicken coop. As I drove back through Clovelly's gates that morning, I wondered if I would ever see it again.

But this is the stubborn alchemy of looking back, that you can have the things you don't have, live in a place you've lost. The present is flat; the future unfocused. With its clear right angles of fields and clouds and stable roofs, the past offers the most inhabitable dimension, furnished with graveyards and duck ponds, corn cribs and persimmon trees, peopled with epileptic daughters and far-sighted boys in Sears bluejeans, and always, behind everything, the echo of a creek running in and out of the shadows.

RICHARD RODRIGUEZ

ichard Rodriguez has much to say about himself as a gay man and the son of Mexican-American immigrants, but it may not be precisely what any member of these groups wants to hear. For years his essays have gone against the grain of those who would pigeonhole him, as in the essay "Aria," in which he argues against bilingual education. "Late Victorians" is an elaborate pastiche in which San Francisco comes alive in all its contradictions. Beneath his wry, colorful portrait of this "painted lady," however, is a serious meditation on life and death in the age of AIDS, and what it means to be living, geographically or otherwise, at the end of the road.

LATE
VICTORIANS

ST. AUGUSTINE WRITES FROM HIS COPE OF DUST THAT WE ARE REST-
less hearts, for earth is not our true home. Human unhappiness is
evidence of our immortality. Intuition tells us we are meant for some
other city.

Elizabeth Taylor, quoted in a magazine article of twenty years ago,
spoke of cerulean Richard Burton days on her yacht, days that were
nevertheless undermined by the elemental private reflection: This
must end.

On a Sunday in summer, ten years ago, I was walking home from
the Latin mass at St. Patrick's, the old Irish parish downtown, when
I saw thousands of people on Market Street. It was the Gay Freedom
Day parade—not the first, but the first I ever saw. Private lives were
becoming public. There were marching bands. There were floats. Banners blocked single lives thematically into a processional mass, not
unlike the consortiums of the blessed in Renaissance paintings, each
saint cherishing the apparatus of his martyrdom: GAY DENTISTS.
BLACK AND WHITE LOVERS. GAYS FROM BAKERSFIELD. LATINA LES-
BIANS. From the foot of Market Street they marched, east to west,
following the mythic American path toward optimism.

I followed the parade to Civic Center Plaza, where flags of routine na-
tions yielded sovereignty to a multitude. Pastel billows flowed over all.

Five years later, another parade. Politicians waved from white convertibles. "Dykes on Bikes" revved up, thumbs-upped. But now banners bore the acronyms of death. AIDS. ARC. Drums were muffled as passing, plum-spotted young men slid by on motorized cable cars.

Though I am alive now, I do not believe an old man's pessimism is necessarily truer than a young man's optimism simply because it comes after. There are things a young man knows that are true and are not yet in the old man's power to recollect. Spring has its sappy wisdom. Lonely teenagers still arrive in San Francisco aboard Greyhound buses. The city can still seem, by comparison with where they came from, paradise.

Four years ago on a Sunday in winter—a brilliant spring afternoon —I was jogging near Fort Point while overhead a young woman was, with difficulty, climbing over the railing of the Golden Gate Bridge. Holding down her skirt with one hand, with the other she waved to a startled spectator (the newspaper next day quoted a workman who was painting the bridge) before she stepped onto the sky.

To land like a spilled purse at my feet.

Serendipity has an eschatological tang here. Always has. Few American cities have had the experience, as we have had, of watching the civic body burn even as we stood, out of body, on a hillside, in a movie theater. Jeanette MacDonald's loony scatting of "San Francisco" has become our go-to-hell anthem. San Francisco has taken some heightened pleasure from the circus of final things. To Atlantis, to Pompeii, to the Pillar of Salt, we add the Golden Gate Bridge, not golden at all, but rust red. San Francisco toys with the tragic conclusion.

For most of its brief life, San Francisco has entertained an idea of itself as heaven on earth, whether as Gold Town or City Beautiful or the Haight-Ashbury.

San Francisco can support both comic and tragic conclusions because the city is geographically *in extremis*, a metaphor for the farthest-flung possibility, a metaphor for the end of the line. Land's end.

To speak of San Francisco as land's end is to read the map from one direction only—as Europeans would read it or as the East Coast has always read. In my lifetime San Francisco has become an Asian city. To speak, therefore, of San Francisco as land's-end is to betray parochialism. My parents came here from Mexico. They saw San Francisco as the North. The West was not west for them. They did not share the Eastern traveler's sense of running before the past—the darkening time zone, the lowering curtain.

I cannot claim for myself the memory of a skyline such as the one César saw. César came to San Francisco in middle age; César came here as to some final place. He was born in South America; he had grown up in Paris; he had been everywhere, done everything; he assumed the world. Yet César was not condescending toward San Francisco, not at all. Here César saw revolution, and he embraced it.

Whereas I live here because I was born here. I grew up ninety miles away, in Sacramento. San Francisco was the nearest, the easiest, the inevitable city, since I needed a city. And yet I live here surrounded by people for whom San Francisco is the end of quest.

I have never looked for utopia on a map. Of course I believe in human advancement. I believe in medicine, in astrophysics, in washing machines. But my compass takes its cardinal point from tragedy. If I respond to the metaphor of spring, I nevertheless learned, years ago, from my Mexican father, from my Irish nuns, to count on winter. The point of Eden for me, for us, is not approach but expulsion.

After I met César in 1984, our friendly debate concerning the halcyon properties of San Francisco ranged from restaurant to restaurant. I spoke of limits. César boasted of freedoms.

It was César's conceit to add to the gates of Jerusalem, to add to the soccer fields of Tijuana, one other dreamscape hoped for the world over. It was the view from a hill, through a mesh of tram wires, of an urban neighborhood in a valley. The vision took its name from the protruding wedge of a theater marquee. Here César raised his glass without discretion: To the Castro.

There were times, dear César, when you tried to switch sides, if only to scorn American optimism, which, I remind you, had already become your own. At the high school where César taught, teachers and parents had organized a campaign to keep kids from driving themselves to the junior prom, in an attempt to forestall liquor and death. Such a scheme momentarily reawakened César's Latin skepticism.

Didn't the Americans know? (His tone exaggerated incredulity.) Teenagers will crash into lampposts on their way home from proms, and there is nothing to be done about it. You cannot forbid tragedy.

By California standards I live in an old house. But not haunted. There are too many tall windows, there is too much salty light, especially in winter, though the windows rattle, rattle in summer when the fog flies overhead, and the house creaks and prowls at night. I feel myself immune to any confidence it seeks to tell.

To grow up homosexual is to live with secrets and within secrets. In no other place are those secrets more closely guarded than within the family home. The grammar of the gay city borrows metaphors from the nineteenth-century house. "Coming out of the closet" is predicated upon family laundry, dirty linen, skeletons.

I live in a tall Victorian house that has been converted to four apartments; four single men.

Neighborhood streets are named to honor nineteenth-century men of action, men of distant fame. Clay. Jackson. Scott. Pierce. Many Victorians in the neighborhood date from before the 1906 earthquake and fire.

Architectural historians credit the gay movement of the 1970s with the urban restoration of San Francisco. Twenty years ago this was a borderline neighborhood. This room, like all the rooms of the house, was painted headache green, apple green, boardinghouse green. In the 1970s, homosexuals moved into black and working-class parts of the city, where they were perceived as pioneers or as block-busters, depending.

Two decades ago, some of the least expensive sections of San Francisco were wooden Victorian sections. It was thus a coincidence of the market that gay men found themselves living within the architectural metaphor for family. No other architecture in the American imagination is more evocative of family than the Victorian house. In those same years—the 1970s—and within those same Victorian houses, homosexuals were living rebellious lives to challenge the foundations of domesticity.

Was "queer-bashing" as much a manifestation of homophobia as a reaction against gentrification? One heard the complaint, often enough, that gay men were as promiscuous with their capital as otherwise, buying, fixing up, then selling and moving on. Two incomes, no children, described an unfair advantage. No sooner would flower boxes begin to appear than an anonymous reply was smeared on the sidewalk out front: KILL FAGGOTS.

The three- or four-story Victorian house, like the Victorian novel, was built to contain several generations and several classes under one roof, behind a single oaken door. What strikes me at odd moments is the confidence of Victorian architecture. Stairs, connecting one story with another, describe the confidence that bound generations together through time—confidence that the family would inherit the earth. The other day I noticed for the first time the vestige of a hinge on the topmost newel of the staircase. This must have been the hinge of a gate that kept infants upstairs so many years ago.

If Victorian houses assert a sturdy optimism by day, they are also associated in our imaginations with the Gothic—with shadows and cobwebby gimcrack, long corridors. The nineteenth century was remarkable for escalating optimism even as it excavated the backstairs, the descending architecture of nightmare—Freud's labor and Engels's.

I live on the second story, in rooms that have been rendered as empty as Yorick's skull—gutted, unrattled, in various ways unlocked—added skylights and new windows, new doors. The hallway remains the darkest part of the house.

This winter the hallway and lobby are being repainted to resemble an eighteenth-century French foyer. Of late we had walls and carpet of Sienese red; a baroque mirror hung in an alcove by the stairwell. Now we are to have enlightened austerity—black-and-white marble floors and faux masonry. A man comes in the afternoons to texture the walls with a sponge and a rag and to paint white mortar lines that create an illusion of permanence, of stone.

The renovation of Victorian San Francisco into dollhouses for libertines may have seemed, in the 1970s, an evasion of what the city was actually becoming. San Francisco's rows of storied houses proclaimed a multigenerational orthodoxy, all the while masking the city's unconventional soul. Elsewhere, meanwhile, domestic America was coming undone.

Suburban Los Angeles, the prototype for a new America, was characterized by a more apparently radical residential architecture. There was, for example, the work of Frank Gehry. In the 1970s, Gehry exploded the nuclear-family house, turning it inside out intellectually and in fact. Though, in a way, Gehry merely completed the logic of the postwar suburban tract house—with its one story, its sliding glass doors, Formica kitchen, two-car garage. The tract house exchanged privacy for mobility. Heterosexuals opted for the one-lifetime house, the freeway, the birth-control pill, minimalist fiction.

The age-old description of homosexuality is of a sin against nature. Moralistic society has always judged emotion literally. The homosexual was sinful because he had no kosher place to stick it. In attempting to drape the architecture of sodomy with art, homosexuals have lived for thousands of years against the expectations of nature. Barren as Shakers and, interestingly, as concerned with the small effect, homosexuals have made a covenant against nature. Homosexual survival lay in artifice, in plumage, in lampshades, sonnets, musical comedy, couture, syntax, religious ceremony, opera, lacquer, irony.

I once asked Byron, an interior decorator, if he had many homosexual clients. "*Mais non,*" said he, flexing his eyelids. "Queers don't need decorators. They were born knowing how. All this ASID stuff —tests and regulations—as if you can confer a homosexual diploma on a suburban housewife by granting her a discount card."

A knack? The genius, we are beginning to fear in an age of AIDS, is irreplaceable—but does it exist? The question is whether the darling affinities are innate to homosexuality or whether they are compensatory. Why have so many homosexuals retired into the small effect, the ineffectual career, the stereotype, the card shop, the florist? *Be gentle with me?* Or do homosexuals know things others do not?

This way power lay. Once upon a time, the homosexual appropriated to himself a mystical province, that of taste. Taste, which is, after all, the insecurity of the middle class, became the homosexual's licentiate to challenge the rule of nature. (The fairy in his blood, he intimated.)

Deciding how best to stick it may be only an architectural problem or a question of physics or of engineering or of cabinetry. Nevertheless, society's condemnation forced the homosexual to find his redemption outside nature. *We'll put a little skirt here.* The impulse is not to create but to re-create, to sham, to convert, to sauce, to rouge, to fragrance, to prettify. No effect is too small or too ephemeral to be snatched away from nature, to be ushered toward the perfection of artificiality. *We'll bring out the highlights there.* The homosexual has marshaled the architecture of the straight world to the very gates of Versailles—that great Vatican of fairyland—beyond which power is tyrannized by leisure.

In San Francisco in the 1980s, the highest form of art became interior decoration. The glory hole was thus converted to an eighteenth-century foyer.

I live away from the street, in a back apartment, in two rooms. I use my bedroom as a visitor's room—the sleigh bed tricked up with shams into a sofa—whereas I rarely invite anyone into my library, the public room, where I write, the public gesture.

I read in my bedroom in the afternoon because the light is good there, especially now, in winter, when the sun recedes from the earth.

There is a door in the south wall that leads to a balcony. The door was once a window. Inside the door, inside my bedroom, are twin green shutters. They are false shutters, of no function beyond wit. The shutters open into the room; they have the effect of turning my apartment inside out.

A few months ago I hired a man to paint the shutters green. I wanted the green shutters of Manet—you know the ones I mean—I wanted a weathered look, as of verdigris. For several days the painter labored, rubbing his paints into the wood and then wiping them off again. In this way he rehearsed for me decades of the ravages of weather. Yellow enough? Black?

The painter left one afternoon, saying he would return the next, leaving behind his tubes, his brushes, his sponges and rags. He never returned. Someone told me he has AIDS.

A black woman haunts California Street between the donut shop and the cheese store. She talks to herself—a debate, wandering, never advancing. Pedestrians who do not know her give her a wide berth. Somebody told me her story; I don't know whether it's true. Neighborhood merchants tolerate her presence as a vestige of dispirited humanity clinging to an otherwise dispiriting progress of "better" shops and restaurants.

Repainted facades extend now from Jackson Street south into what was once the heart of the "Mo"—black Fillmore Street. Today there are watercress sandwiches at three o'clock where recently there had been loud-mouthed kids, hole-in-the-wall bars, pimps. Now there are tweeds and perambulators, matrons and nannies. Yuppies. And gays.

The gay-male revolution had greater influence on San Francisco in the 1970s than did the feminist revolution. Feminists, with whom I include lesbians—such was the inclusiveness of the feminist movement—were preoccupied with career, with escape from the house in order to create a sexually democratic city. Homosexual men sought to reclaim the house, the house that traditionally had been the reward for heterosexuality, with all its selfless tasks and burdens.

Leisure defined the gay-male revolution. The gay political movement began, by most accounts, in 1969 with the Stonewall riots in New York City, whereby gay men fought to defend the nonconformity of their leisure.

It was no coincidence that homosexuals migrated to San Francisco in the 1970s, for the city was famed as a playful place, more Catholic than Protestant in its eschatological intuition. In 1975, the state of California legalized consensual homosexuality, and about that same time Castro Street, southwest of downtown, began to eclipse Polk Street as the homosexual address in San Francisco. Polk Street was a string of bars. The Castro was an entire district. The Castro had Victorian houses and churches, bookstores and restaurants, gyms, dry cleaners, supermarkets, and an elected member of the Board of Supervisors. The Castro supported baths and bars, but there was nothing furtive about them. On Castro Street the light of day penetrated gay life through clear plate-glass windows. The light of day discovered a new confidence, a new politics. Also a new look—a noncosmopolitan, Burt Reynolds, butch-kid style: beer, ball games, Levi's, short hair, muscles.

Gay men who lived elsewhere in the city, in Pacific Heights or in the Richmond, often spoke with derision of "Castro Street clones," describing the look, or scorned what they called the ghettoization of homosexuality. To an older generation of homosexuals, the blatancy of Castro Street threatened the discreet compromise they had negotiated with a tolerant city.

As the Castro district thrived, Folsom Street, south of Market, also began to thrive, as if in contradistinction to the utopian Castro. Folsom Street was a warehouse district of puddled alleys and deserted corners. Folsom Street offered an assortment of leather bars—an evening's regress to the outlaw sexuality of the fifties, the forties, the nineteenth century, and so on—an eroticism of the dark, of the Reeperbahn, or of the guardsman's barracks.

The Castro district implied that sexuality was more crucial, that homosexuality was the central fact of identity. The Castro district, with its ice-cream parlors and hardware stores, was the revolutionary place.

Into which carloads of vacant-eyed teenagers from other districts or from middle-class suburbs would drive after dark, cruising the neighborhood for solitary victims.

The ultimate gay-basher was a city supervisor named Dan White, ex-cop, ex-boxer, ex-fireman, ex-altar boy. Dan White had grown up in the Castro district; he recognized the Castro revolution for what it was. Gays had achieved power over him. He murdered the mayor and he murdered the homosexual member of the Board of Supervisors.

Katherine, a sophisticate if ever there was one, nevertheless dismisses two men descending the aisle at the Opera House: "All so sleek and smooth-jowled and silver-haired—they don't seem real, poor darlings. It must be because they don't have children."

Lodged within Katherine's complaint is the perennial heterosexual annoyance with the homosexual's freedom from childrearing, which does not so much place the homosexual beyond the pale as it relegates the homosexual outside "responsible" life.

It was the glamour of gay life, after all, as much as it was the feminist call to career, that encouraged heterosexuals in the 1970s to excuse themselves from nature, to swallow the birth-control pill. Who needs children? The gay bar became the paradigm for the singles bar. The gay couple became the paradigm for the selfish couple—all dressed up and everywhere to go. And there was the example of the gay house in illustrated life-style magazines. At the same time that suburban housewives were looking outside the home for fulfillment, gay men were reintroducing a new generation in the city—heterosexual men and women—to the complaisancies of the barren house.

Puritanical America dismissed gay camp followers as yuppies; the term means to suggest infantility. Yuppies were obsessive and awk-

ward in their materialism. Whereas gays arranged a decorative life
against a barren state,

> yuppies sought early returns—lives that were not to be all toil and
> spin. Yuppies, trained to careerism from the cradle, wavered in their
> pursuit of the Northern European ethic—indeed, we might now call
> it the pan-Pacific ethic—in favor of the Mediterranean, the Latin, the
> Catholic, the Castro, the Gay.

The international architectural idioms of Skidmore, Owings & Mer-
rill, which defined the skyline of the 1970s, betrayed no awareness of
any street-level debate concerning the primacy of play in San Francisco
or of any human dramas resulting from urban redevelopment. The
repellent office tower was a fortress raised against the sky, against the
street, against the idea of a city. Offices were hives where money was
made, and damn all.

In the 1970s, San Francisco divided between the interests of downtown and the pleasures of the neighborhoods. Neighborhoods asserted
idiosyncrasy, human scale, light. San Francisco neighborhoods perceived downtown as working against their influence in determining
what the city should be. Thus neighborhoods seceded from the idea
of a city.

The gay movement rejected downtown as representing "straight"
conformity. But was it possible that heterosexual Union Street was
related to Castro Street? Was it possible that either was related to the
Latino Mission district? Or to the Sino-Russian Richmond? San Francisco, though complimented worldwide for holding its center, was in
fact without a vision of itself entire.

In the 1980s, in deference to the neighborhoods, City Hall would
attempt a counterreformation of downtown, forbidding "Manhattan-
ization." Shadows were legislated away from parks and playgrounds.
Height restrictions were lowered beneath an existing skyline. Design,
too, fell under the retrojurisdiction of the city planner's office. The
Victorian house was presented to architects as a model of what the
city wanted to uphold and to become. In heterosexual neighborhoods,
one saw newly built Victorians. Downtown, postmodernist prescrip-
tions for playfulness advised skyscrapers to wear party hats, buttons,

comic mustaches. Philip Johnson yielded to the dollhouse impulse to perch angels atop one of his skyscrapers.

I can see downtown from my bedroom window. But days pass and I do not leave the foreground for the city. Most days my public impression of San Francisco is taken from Fillmore Street, from the anchorhold of the Lady of the Donut Shop.

She now often parades with her arms crossed over her breasts in an "X," the posture emblematic of prophecy. And yet gather her madness where she sits on the curb, chain-smoking, hugging her knees, while I disappear down Fillmore Street to make Xerox copies, to mail letters, to rent a video, to shop for dinner. I am soon pleased by the faint breeze from the city, the slight agitation of the homing crowds of singles, so intent upon the path of least resistance. I admire the prosperity of the corridor, the shop windows that beckon inward toward the perfected life-style, the little way of the City of St. Francis.

Turning down Pine Street, I am recalled by the prickly silhouette of St. Dominic's Church against the scrim of the western sky. I turn, instead, into the Pacific Heights Health Club.

In the 1970s, like a lot of men and women in this city, I joined a gym. My club, I've even caught myself calling it.

In the gay city of the 1970s, bodybuilding became an architectural preoccupation of the upper middle class. Bodybuilding is a parody of labor, a useless accumulation of the laborer's bulk and strength. No useful task is accomplished. And yet there is something businesslike about habitués, and the gym is filled with the punch-clock logic of the workplace. Machines clank and hum. Needles on gauges toll spent calories.

The gym is at once a closet of privacy and an exhibition gallery. All four walls are mirrored.

I study my body in the mirror. Physical revelation—nakedness—is no longer possible, cannot be desired, for the body is shrouded in meat and wears itself.

The intent is some merciless press of body against a standard, perfect mold. Bodies are "cut" or "pumped" or "buffed" as on an assembly line in Turin. A body becomes so many extrovert parts. Delts, pecs, lats, traps.

I harness myself in a Nautilus cage.

Lats become wings. For the gym is nothing if not the occasion for transcendence. From homosexual to autosexual . . .

I lift weights over my head, baring my teeth like an animal with the strain.

. . . to nonsexual. The effect of the overdeveloped body is the miniaturization of the sexual organs—of no function beyond wit. Behold the ape become Blakean angel, revolving in an empyrean of mirrors.

The nineteenth-century mirror over the fireplace in my bedroom was purchased by a decorator from the estate of a man who died last year of AIDS. It is a top-heavy piece, confusing styles. Two ebony-painted columns support a frieze of painted glass above the mirror. The frieze depicts three bourgeois graces and a couple of free-range cherubs. The lake of the mirror has formed a cataract, and at its edges it is beginning to corrode.

Thus the mirror that now draws upon my room owns some bright curse, maybe—some memory not mine.

As I regard this mirror, I imagine St. Augustine's meditation slowly hardening into syllogism, passing down through centuries to confound us: evil is the absence of good.

We have become accustomed to figures disappearing from our landscape. Does this not lead us to interrogate the landscape?

With reason do we invest mirrors with the superstition of memory, for they, though glass, though liquid captured in a bay, are so often less fragile than we are. They—bright ovals, or rectangles, or rounds—bump down unscathed, unspilled through centuries, whereas we . . .

The man in the red baseball cap used to jog so religiously on Marina Green. By the time it occurs to me that I have not seen him for months, I realize he may be dead—not lapsed, not moved away. People come and go in the city, it's true. But in San Francisco death has become as routine an explanation for disappearance as Mayflower Van Lines.

AIDS, it has been discovered, is a plague of absence. Absence opened in the blood. Absence condensed into the fluid of passing emotion. Absence shot through opalescent tugs of semen to deflower the city.

And then AIDS, it was discovered, is a nonmetaphorical disease, a disease like any other. Absence sprang from substance—a virus, a hairy bubble perched upon a needle, a platter of no intention served round: fever, blisters, a death sentence.

At first I heard only a few names—names connected, perhaps, with the right faces, perhaps not. People vaguely remembered, as through the cataract of this mirror, from dinner parties or from intermissions. A few articles in the press. The rumored celebrities. But within months the slow beating of the blood had found its bay.

One of San Francisco's gay newspapers, the *Bay Area Reporter*, began to accept advertisements from funeral parlors and casket makers, inserting them between the randy ads for leather bars and tanning salons. The *Reporter* invited homemade obituaries—lovers writing of lovers, friends remembering friends and the blessings of unexceptional life.

Peter. Carlos. Gary. Asel. Perry. Nikos.

Healthy snapshots accompany each annal. At the Russian River. By the Christmas tree. Lifting a beer. In uniform. A dinner jacket. A satin gown.

He was born in Puerto La Libertad, El Salvador.

He attended Apple Valley High School, where he was their first male cheerleader.

From El Paso. From Medford. From Germany. From Long Island.

I moved back to San Francisco in 1979. Oh, I had had some salad days elsewhere, but by 1979 I was a wintry man. I came here in order not to be distracted by the ambitions or, for that matter, the pleasures of others but to pursue my own ambition. Once here, though, I found the company of men who pursued an earthly paradise charming. Skepticism became my demeanor toward them—I was the dinner-party skeptic, a firm believer in Original Sin and in the limits of possibility.

Which charmed them.

He was a dancer.

He settled into the interior-design department of Gump's, where he worked until his illness.

He was a teacher.

César, for example.

César had an excellent mind. César could shave the rind from any assertion to expose its pulp and jelly. But César was otherwise ruled by pulp. César loved everything that ripened in time. Freshmen. Bordeaux. César could fashion liturgy from an artichoke. Yesterday it was not ready (cocking his head, rotating the artichoke in his hand over a pot of cold water). Tomorrow will be too late (Yorick's skull). Today it is perfect (as he lit the fire beneath the pot). We will eat it now.

If he's lucky, he's got a year, a doctor told me. If not, he's got two.

The phone rang. AIDS had tagged a friend. And then the phone rang again. And then the phone rang again. Michael had tested positive. Adrian, well, what he had assumed were shingles . . . Paul was back in the hospital. And César, dammit, César, even César, especially César.

That winter before his death, César traveled back to South America. On his return to San Francisco, he described to me how he had walked with his mother in her garden—his mother chafing her hands as if she were cold. But it was not cold, he said. They moved slowly. Her summer garden was prolonging itself this year, she said. The cicadas will not stop singing.

When he lay on his deathbed, César said everyone else he knew might get AIDS and die. He said I would be the only one spared— "spared" was supposed to have been chased with irony, I knew, but his voice was too weak to do the job. "You are too circumspect," he said then, wagging his finger upon the coverlet.

So I was going to live to see that the garden of earthly delights was, after all, only wallpaper—was that it, César? Hadn't I always said so? It was then I saw that the greater sin against heaven was my unwillingness to embrace life.

César said he found paradise at the baths. He said I didn't understand. He said if I had to ask about it, I might as well ask if a wife will spend eternity with Husband #1 or Husband #2.

The baths were places of good humor, that was Number One; there was nothing demeaning about them. From within cubicles men would nod at one another or not, but there was no sting of rejection, because one had at last entered a region of complete acceptance. César spoke of floating from body to body, open arms yielding to open arms in an angelic round.

The best night. That's easy, he said, the best night was spent in the pool with an antiques dealer—up to their necks in warm water —their two heads bobbing on an ocean of chlorine green, bawling Noël Coward songs.

But each went home alone?

Each satisfied, dear, César corrected. And all the way home San Francisco seemed to him balmed and merciful, he said. He felt weightlessness of being, the pavement under his step as light as air.

It was not as in some Victorian novel—the curtains drawn, the pillows plumped, the streets strewn with sawdust. It was not to be a matter of custards in covered dishes, steaming possets, *Try a little of this, my dear.* Or gathering up the issues of *Architectural Digest* strewn about the bed. Closing the biography of Diana Cooper and marking its place. Or the unfolding of discretionary screens, morphine, parrots, pavilions.

César experienced agony.

Four of his high-school students sawed through a Vivaldi quartet in the corridor outside his hospital room, prolonging the hideous garden.

In the presence of his lover Gregory and friends, Scott passed from this life. . . .

He died peacefully at home in his lover Ron's arms.

Immediately after a friend led a prayer for him to be taken home and while his dear mother was reciting the 23rd Psalm, Bill peacefully took his last breath.

I stood aloof at César's memorial, the kind of party he would enjoy, everyone said. And so for a time César lay improperly buried, unconvincingly resurrected in the conditional: would enjoy. What else could they say? César had no religion beyond aesthetic bravery.

Sunlight remains. Traffic remains. Nocturnal chic attaches to some discovered restaurant. A new novel is reviewed in *The New York Times.* And the mirror rasps on its hook. The mirror is lifted down.

A priest friend, a good friend, who out of naïveté plays the cynic, tells me—this is on a bright, billowy day; we are standing outside —"It's not as sad as you may think. There is at least spectacle in the death of the young. Come to the funeral of an old lady sometime if you want to feel an empty church."

I will grant my priest friend this much: that it is easier, easier on me, to sit with gay men in hospitals than with the staring old. Young men talk as much as they are able.

But those who gather around the young man's bed do not see Chatterton. This doll is Death. I have seen people caressing it, staring Death down. I have seen people wipe its tears, wipe its ass; I have seen people kiss Death on his lips, where once there were lips.

Chris was inspired after his own diagnosis in July 1987 with the truth and reality of how such a terrible disease could bring out the love, warmth, and support of so many friends and family.

Sometimes no family came. If there was family, it was usually Mother. Mom. With her suitcase and with the torn flap of an envelope in her hand.

Brenda. Pat. Connie. Toni. Soledad.

Or parents came but then left without reconciliation, some preferring to say "cancer."

But others came. They walked Death's dog. They washed his dishes. They bought his groceries. They massaged his poor back. They changed his bandages. They emptied his bedpan.

Men who sought the aesthetic ordering of existence were recalled to nature. Men who aspired to the mock-angelic settled for the shirt of hair. The gay community of San Francisco, having found freedom, consented to necessity—to all that the proud world had for so long held up to them, withheld from them, as "real humanity."

And if gays took care of their own, they were not alone. AIDS was a disease of the entire city. Nor were Charity and Mercy only male, only gay. Others came. There were nurses and nuns and the couple from next door, co-workers, strangers, teenagers, corporations, pensioners. A community was forming over the city.

Cary and Rick's friends and family wish to thank the many people who provided both small and great kindnesses.

He was attended to and lovingly cared for by the staff at Coming Home Hospice.

And the saints of this city have names listed in the phone book, names I heard called through a microphone one cold Sunday in Advent as I sat in Most Holy Redeemer Church. It might have been any of the churches or community centers in the Castro district, but it happened at Most Holy Redeemer at a time in the history of the world when the Roman Catholic Church pronounced the homosexual a sinner.

A woman at the microphone called upon volunteers from the AIDS Support Group to come forward. Throughout the church, people stood up, young men and women, and middle-aged and old, straight, gay, and all of them shy at being called. Yet they came forward and assembled in the sanctuary, facing the congregation, grinning self-consciously at one another, their hands hidden behind them.

I am preoccupied by the fussing of a man sitting in the pew directly in front of me—in his seventies, frail, his iodine-colored hair combed forward and pasted upon his forehead. Fingers of porcelain clutch the pearly beads of what must have been his mother's rosary. He is not the sort of man any gay man would have chosen to become in the 1970s. He is probably not what he himself expected to become. Something of the old dear about him, wizened butterfly, powdered old pouf. Certainly he is what I fear becoming. And then he rises, this old monkey, with the most beatific dignity, in answer to the microphone, and he strides into the sanctuary to take his place in the company of the Blessed.

So this is it—this, what looks like a Christmas party in an insurance office, and not as in Renaissance paintings, and not as we had always thought, not some flower-strewn, some sequined curtain call of grease-painted heroes gesturing to the stalls. A lady with a plastic candy cane pinned to her lapel. A Castro clone with a red bandana exploding from his hip pocket. A perfume-counter lady with an Hermès scarf mantled upon her shoulder. A black man in a checkered sports coat. The pink-haired punkess with a jewel in her nose. Here, too, is the gay couple in middle age; interchangeable plaid shirts and corduroy pants. Blood and shit and Mr. Happy Face. These know the weight of bodies.

Bill died.

. . . Passed on to heaven.

. . . Turning over in his bed one night and then gone.

These learned to love what is corruptible, while I, barren skeptic, reader of St. Augustine, curator of the earthly paradise, inheritor of the empty mirror, I shift my tailbone upon the cold, hard pew.

JODI DAYNARD

*J*odi Daynard's work is marked by a sense
of "double-consciousness," a term that
W. E. B. Dubois coined earlier in the century
with regard to black men and women in this
country. In her case, however, this double-
consciousness derives from the uneasy sense that
she fits into neither the Jewish culture of her
heritage nor the suburban culture of her
upbringing. In her essays she often finds herself
an outsider looking in—part with love, part
with horror—at her native terrain. "Suburbia,
USA" is a dark portrait in which Daynard
reveals the bigotry and self-hatred smoldering
behind the stolid doors of 1960s Suburbia. It is
a place that, while comfortable and even
beautiful to a child, suffered from the spiritual
poverty of a materialistic culture, and from
ethnic amnesia, as its newly landed inhabitants
sought to renounce their "unseemly," still-
living heritages.

S U B U R B I A ,
U S A

I WAS BORN IN THE BRONXVILLE HOSPITAL, TWO WEEKS EARLY. IT was a warm morning in August, but I was so cold and small that to keep life and limb together they put me in a straitjacket. My father, needing flowers and finding no store open, stole a heart-shaped wreath of gladioli off the back of a hearse. My mother was not fooled.

My parents took their small bundle of joy back to a custom-built split-level house in Hartsdale, New York. The family had recently moved from a dim tenement apartment on Pelham Parkway in the Bronx, a place so drab and charmless that at the age of six my sister vowed to grow up and surround herself with beautiful objects.

The little house (my mother still rankles at the fact that my father's sister was too cheap to loan them enough for a bigger model) sits atop a hill midway up Caterson Terrace. At the base of that hill close to town, the smaller, seedier families lived. The boys from these homes would come to school in worn white T-shirts and faded Levi jeans. They had pale, freckled faces and frightened eyes, and one always had the sense that their mothers neglected them for drink, and Pall Malls, and vain dreams.

Westchester, Westchester: rolling lawns and tennis courts, Bloomingdales and psychiatrists, and stolid homes behind whose doors alcoholic parents joked about "kikes" and "niggers," homes so cold inside they felt as if no one lived in them. I didn't understand this Westchester in all its bigotry or spiritual impoverishment. Instead, I knew safety and beauty, violence and vulgarity, the suburban child's parameters.

Safety was in my mother's kitchen, whose warm, paneled walls grew the artifacts of my mother's collecting: a rubber jewelry mold, Currier and Ives prints, an old brass lock and key; a bronze harness from her childhood farm, shaped like a pair of wings. I stared at that wall from my mother's arms as she fed me a bottle, and the room seemed as large and dark as the universe.

And beauty was waking up every morning to a pale pink and green room. There, from my bed, I was able to watch the incandescent green leaves of the mock cherry tree shiver and sway outside my window. The light of suburbia was cool and the air soft. Stretched out before me was the discreet wholeness of a suburban day, invisibly circumscribed but full of possibility nonetheless.

At the top of the hill were the newer houses, like ours. They belonged to the Jewish families, ones who had made a little money and were one step out of the Bronx, like us. Down the hill at the other end were the landed Hartsdalians—Gentiles, mostly. Their enormous brick Tudor homes, decked with wreaths and holly during Christmas time, were awesome terrae incognitae. For the longest time I remained in awe of these homes, set back from the street as they were, surrounded by old stone retaining walls. Only later would I come to know their drafty coldness, and the weird, unliving frigidity of their inhabitants.

As one drives up Caterson Terrace, our house is on the left, just past a towering row of privet hedge belonging to our neighbors, the Donsons. They put up the hedge when our house was built, presumably to avoid having to speak to my parents. To this day, my mother accuses the Donsons of having poisoned our pet poodle, Oliver.

This is suburbia, after all. It's not a particularly friendly place. Home is hallowed ground, and its inhabitants defend it like Teutonic tribes. Neighbors look suspiciously at one another, just waiting for a nuisance—a barking dog, the wrong color fence, snow not blown or blown too far—before calling in the cops. Once, our neighbor, annoyed by another neighbor's complaints about her barking dog, placed an advertisement in the real estate section of the paper, listing the complainer's enormous Colonial home for something like

$20,000. The harassed family had to switch to an unlisted number.

In suburbia, one's home is both castle and prison. To leave it, one needs a definite purpose, like shopping. Shopping is the Westchesterite's main hobby, and shop we did: Bloomingdales, Saks, the ever-crowded Loehmans, and the nearby malls. The other purpose was to go to "the club." Everybody belonged to *some* club. Gentiles went to the Westchester Country Club, Jews elsewhere. After a day at the club one shopped some more—for groceries, or an item for the home.

Our home became filled with things: antiques from my mother's collecting, string and keyboard instruments for my father's musical proclivities. Soon after he moved in, my father converted our basement into a nightclub. Life-size cardboard cutouts of chorus girls in sequined bikinis are pinned up behind the trapezoidal stage. There is an electric organ, a synthesizer, and a set of drums. My father glued album covers, set askew, of Herbie Mann and Henry Mancini next to the near-naked girls. He glued glittering gold stars around the ensemble. A twirling red and yellow light above the stage completes the scene.

Looking at this room now, it all seems sad, the worn, tacky remnants of an era when my family had been more alive. As a child, though, this room was magic, a place where music often pounded late into the night and adults, beautiful and glittering in dress-up clothes, danced and laughed, eating on small plates from steaming silver chafing dishes. We had our world, however strange and small.

It is a gossamer spring day in the town of Hartsdale. The year is 1959. My mother has left me in my pram, on the sidewalk in front of the Hartsdale Bakery (alone? with my grandmother?), and I can smell the intense sweetness coming from the shop. In 1959, Hartsdale consisted mainly of a single strip of stores along Hartsdale Avenue, which ended in a cul-de-sac by the old railway station. Everything, and everyone, in the town was split, invisibly, into Jewish and Gentile. I could not say which I thought was better, only that "they" lived in some other world with its own rules and ways completely separate from our own. This never made any sense to me, and it seems that the difference lay in the pure circularity of it always having been so. But to my mother, the differences were real: the Gentiles kept to their own clan, and so were clannish; they were thinner and fairer than we Jews, tighter-lipped. Their food—if one could even call it that—gave them an anemic pallor.

The houses of the Gentiles were larger than ours, and far colder. They drank aperitifs with those mixed sausage and cheese baskets with green plastic straw that one could pick up around holiday time from International Foods. They drank, but not out of sorrow. The Gentiles drank, it seemed, out of sheer, terminal cheeriness.

The stores along Hartsdale Avenue could be separated according to the race of their patrons. The stationery store where I delighted in buying my first school supplies was "Jewish." So was the pharmacist, a taciturn man who already seemed resigned to the death by colon cancer he would not contract for another twenty years. There was the Gentile bookstore, whose owner my mother believed to be an anti-Semite; a disorganized toy store, with whose owner my mother had some long-standing feud and who therefore, although Jewish, had joined, in her mind, the ranks of the Gentiles.

It was always still just light out when my father came home, a suburban twilight that softened the frayed edges of the dozens of husbands making the trek up Caterson Terrace from the train station. I would run to the door, shielding myself behind my mother in case of a bad mood from that tall, mysterious stranger. He would set his feathered hat down on the walnut console, hang up his coat, and walk directly to the kitchen doorway. There, his arm would swing back and forth and I would see his set of keys go flying through the air, clear across the kitchen, where it would land with a clank in a copper pot upon the windowsill. He always smiled at this miraculous success, his talent all the more pleasurable for its uselessness.

My parents were always around; at least, my mother was. But many of my friends seem to have been abandoned, left to wander the caverns of those large Tudor homes like orphans. I remember playing with my friend Paula in her house in Scarsdale. While we played, her mother sat before a mirror in a far-off bedroom, staring at herself in a negligée, puffing on a cigarette. Our voices echoed through the empty house. I never once met Paula's father. Paula wound up in a boarding school for emotionally disturbed children.

Then there was Carrie, a dim girl who lived around the block and whose main claim to fame was to have placed her head in the way of a baseball bat. For months she went to school with a soft, pulsing hollow in her skull. We gaped at the slow, steady pulse that pushed its way through the fragile casing of her scalp. Carrie's brother Curt, the bat-swinger, left Westchester, and some years later put a bullet through his head.

Westchester's children were unhappy—at least, the ones I knew were. Perhaps this was because their mothers were. My image of Westchester's mothers is Paula's mother: sitting alone in their fine silk nightgowns. Plush carpet silences the movement of their feet. Their bodies go neglected, untouched by love or even tenderness. As if sleepwalking, they get up, open packages of frozen vegetables and shrimp egg rolls, or fry pork chops. Absent participants in their own lives, they could not begin to take part in those of their children. They sit smoking, alone and caught up in vague, distant reveries, a cup of instant coffee the only warmth their hands feel.

My best friend Julie's mom never seemed to be home when Julie got home from school—a commonplace now, but nearly unimaginable in the 1960s. Julie's mother, a beautiful opera singer, would be out all day and then come home just long enough to get all dolled up before going out again. Julie's brother seemed chronically depressed, and would wander around their large house in silence, wanting nothing to do with his little sister.

Julie was a big, hulking bully of a girl back then. Once, she almost strangled the life out of me, trying to impress the boy next door with her prowess as she easily tackled me to the ground.

"Bruce! Bruce! Look at this!" she cried, as I sat choking my sobs beneath her.

I didn't speak to Julie for a while after that. But ours was a lonely neighborhood, and one warm spring day I caught sight of her standing down the street, midway between our houses. She looked so lonely, staring up at me. We ran to each other and hugged tight, and the boy next door was—for the time being—forgotten.

There was no limit to the games Julie and I made up together. Our favorite game was to pretend to be The Beatles. We would bounce up and down on her canopy bed with tin-foil microphones, crooning: "Help! I need somebody!"

That game seems telling to me now.

Most of what Julie and I did together got us into trouble. For a while there we were hoodlums just like hoodlums everywhere, except that instead of hubcaps and spray cans we used rotten eggs and Ambesol. It was my idea to dig a trench one time in Julie's yard, fill it with water, and cover it over with dirt, so that hapless Beth, the retarded girl who lived across the street, could trip and fall into it.

We made poor freckle-faced Beth's life miserable. Beth would run toward Julie's house on pink flamingo legs, her face filled with mute, guileless delight. And there we'd be, waiting like twin vampires, with our poisonous concoctions and traps. Once, in our insanity, we mixed together a noxious brew of dirt, Ambesol, and rat poison. We fed it to her, convinced we had discovered the "cure" for her low IQ. We even devised a "test" which we "administered" directly after she had taken her first—and, sagely, last—sip of our concoction. When Beth was subsequently able to answer a few of the questions on our test, we exulted like doctors of the Waffen SS.

Julie's parents never socialized with mine, but they often had cocktails with Carrie's and Beth's parents and other "Gentile" neighbors. They liked to sit around and drink mixed cocktails and eat miniature pretzels, which Julie's father bought in enormous brown tins. Sometimes they told off-color jokes, about Poles and Jews and Blacks. Sometimes when I was with them I would smile at their jokes, too cowardly and confused to say a word.

I wasn't much of a Jew myself, then. When my father moved out of the Bronx, he cut all his ties to Judaism save a strictly cultural one. He changed his name, and for the longest time I thought our family was from Alsace-Lorraine. My father, wanting to spare me any shame at school, had created an entirely fictitious heritage to go along with the new name. In fact, our name is Davidoff, and we come from Kovna, a village in what was then a Lithuanian Pale of Settlement. My grandmother didn't spend her days sipping riesling wine on a snow-capped mountain; she spent them running for her life from Cossacks.

I had my own bout of Jew-hating when my grandma Bobby came to live with us. Bobby had no possessions except for one black bag and the clothes on her body. She had been rendered homeless when city planners in upstate New York evicted her from her farm, to build an airport. They gave her a pittance for each acre, and for the rest of her life she was passed around her three daughters, Gertrude, Molly, and Frances, leaving each as they grew tired of her. As it turns out, Swan Lake never used that airport; it now lies fallow, my grand-mother's wild strawberries growing up through the cracks in the asphalt.

In our house, it seemed, Bobby was least welcome of all. My mother and father used to get into terrible fights about her. My father didn't want her staying with us. Neither did my mother, but she felt too guilty to send her back to Aunt Gertie's. Bobby would appear at our door with her black lizard bag clutched tightly in her wrinkled hands. She had not yet removed her old wool coat when already I could hear my parents' hissing whispers on the stairs:

"No way is she staying six weeks with us."

"She's my mother."

"I don't give a rat's ass. Call Gert and tell her we're sending her back. Next Day Mail."

Bobby spoke a thick, broken English, and her face was as wrinkled and coarse as a walnut shell. Her squat body seemed too slow-moving and massive to walk inside our house, which was filled to bursting with my mother's delicate treasures. Bobby's stockings were always ripped and sagging, and I never saw her put them on or take them off. It seemed to me she never changed them. Her skirt was always some wool plaid remnant with the zipper askew and the hem falling down. I disdained and pitied her, and loved her only in hindsight.

Everyone in Westchester had a Bobby, that sorry relic from their family's recent history, that living reminder of everything they had sought, with such fierce vengeance, to renounce. Of course, in many ways, the suburbs are a pleasant place to live. I live in one now myself, outside of Boston, and feel lucky to do so. But many of our suburbs happened too quickly. People got money in a single generation and moved into fancy, hollow places, leaving their spirits behind in the rush. They didn't entirely trust that what they had bought with all that money was really theirs, and it made them mean. And frightened of losing everything.

Bobby was always losing that precious black bag. We would hear her cry, "Veyah's my poise? Veyah's my poise?" Everything she had to her name was in that purse. Often, after a fight with my mother,

Bobby would root around in the closet for that bag and, finding it, out she'd walk, announcing, "I'm goink! I'm gettin' out of heah and I'm nevah comink back!"

She had no suitcase, no hat, and with only her dignity she would start walking up Caterson Terrace, toward nowhere. My mother always had to go after her. Sometimes, she just sighed and waited a few minutes, enjoying the peace and quiet. Bobby never got very far.

Bobby was coarse, disoriented, and sad. She looked like a poor, uneducated Russian peasant, which is precisely what she was. My sister, who loved her deeply, was also mortified by her. In her diaries from that time she recounts how, once, smooching on the sofa with a boyfriend, she happened to turn around: there was Bobby, lying curled up on the floor behind the couch, sound asleep. Apparently, Bobby had picked a place she thought would be inconspicuous to the young lovers. But Lynne was furious. Why, I always wondered, hadn't Bobby chosen a bed to sleep in? Did she think herself not good enough? There were times in my home that I heard the words "damned Jew kike," though I no longer recall who said them. Was Bobby, to herself, just some "damned Jew kike"?

By the time I knew her, it was hard for Bobby to pick up her feet. The blood of seventy years' farm work had settled into her ankles. Her legs were little more than swollen stumps stuffed into heavy black leather shoes. Her knees wouldn't bend any more, and I hated her because she would shuffle across my pretty room, inevitably crushing some sacred doll or the Addams Family puzzle that I had been working on for months.

By this time I was a young Westchesterite used to tennis games, velvet riding hats, and Bloomingdales. I had a pink velvet custom-built sofa in my room with matching silk curtains, and to me Bobby was a pathetic and altogether foreign intrusion. She hardly seemed of the same species as myself, with her wrinkled, nut brown face and tiny, bright green eyes. When Bobby fought with my mother it was always in Yiddish, a language I didn't understand. But I came to know certain phrases all too well, like "Du gist mir a cup vetik" ("You're giving me a headache," said with hand to left temple and head tilted) and "Don't mitcha me" (hands placed despairingly over solar plexus). Usually, I wanted nothing to do with Bobby.

But I didn't reject her when, late at night as I lay in my bed, she would come over and sit by my side and gently scratch my back with her long, thick fingernails. Nor did I disdain her when she sat next to me behind a white designer chair in the living room, next to a heating vent. In this warm spot Bobby sang me plaintive Yiddish songs, some of them quite theatrical. One began, "Standink on da CAWnah." Full stop. "Minding her own biz-NISS." Stop. "Sadie Green was waiting for a car." Full stop. "Her feet was very TIRED." Stop. "Her head was very dizzi-NESS." Caesura, then, *sotto voce*, "Along came a caw and said, 'Hey, kid, ya goin' FAW?' " Then it had some refrain whose tune I loved although I didn't understand a word of what it meant: "To whom ya talkin' to whom, HA? To whom ya talkin' to whom?"

It was only years later that I developed a conscience about Bobby, and then I got it double for the delay. When we had to visit her in the nursing home, my grief was so great that I would not get out of the car to see her. I grew outwardly cold, and my mother, misunderstanding, said, "You're a cold, unfeeling child." Someday, she said, I would regret my heartlessness.

But I had gone inside that place before, that place they took us to die. Bobby had greeted us in the hallway. She was tied into a wheelchair with a white sheet. At first, she didn't seem to recognize me, but then, with horrifying suddenness, she reached out her arms and uttered a terrible cry: "Veyah, veyah have you been? Vy haven't I seen you?"

I had to turn my face away. This was no way to die, inside white walls, wrapped in a white sheet, with white nurses who wore their uniform smiles as they fed you from spoons—you who were loved no less by them than by your own family, who had moved to Suburbia and therefore, presumably, would never grow old, or senile, or die.

And I didn't get out of the car, either, when they put Bobby into the ground. It was a Jewish cemetery in Hicksville, Long Island. Aunt Gertie was there and Uncle Bernie and all my cousins. The rabbi stood over the hole as a light rain covered the cemetery. He stooped like a black raven in his robes as he said the Kaddish and my aunts and uncles stood in a circle with their heads bowed. I sat a distance away, huddled in one corner of my father's Thunderbird, which still smelled faintly of the vomit I'd ejected on the long trip to the Island and which my father, swearing vocably, had hastily cleaned up. I sat and mourned inside myself, furious at my family. I knew they were all glad to get rid of Bobby, that last sad vestige of who we once were. They would sit *shiva* with the mirrors turned respectfully to the wall, gobbling up Aunt Gertie's copious display of food. Cousin Eddy and I would play Career, or Monopoly. And my world's coldness filled me up a little more.

BRADFORD MORROW

radford Morrow had just finished his third novel, *Trinity Fields*, when approached for an essay. In this novel, Los Alamos serves both as a literal place and as a metaphor for his two protagonists, the emotional "ground zero" of their post-nuclear generation. But Morrow, while finished with *Trinity Fields*, knew that he had not yet finished with Los Alamos. In "The Journey to Trinity," Morrow takes us on a stark, beautiful, devastating journey to the real place, unearthing as he does so an eerie consistency between events that happened there more than a century apart. Morrow's prose, like his fiction, is a rich tapestry of sensual detail, human voices, humor, and awe. "The Journey to Trinity" is a journey not just into Ground Zero, but into the human heart of darkness.

THE
JOURNEY TO
TRINITY

Under a New Mexican morning sky of pale blues and radiant pinks, in the lavender shadows of the Sacramento Mountains, we converged at the northern edge of Alamogordo. We came from all over the world, an incongruous group, hardly a group at all but that we shared this common desire to stand in a place where few have stood—a place where, half a century ago, the world changed forever.

There weren't very many of us, five hundred, perhaps fewer. Families, couples, children, individuals all gathered in the Otero County Fairgrounds parking lot, dressed lightly for the mild autumn weather, which was cool just then, at dawn, but by midday would be baking hot. A solitary motorcyclist in full black leather stared between the high handlebars of his custom chopper, whose gas tank was painted with a grinning skull crowned with thorned wreath and bright red roses. Silent, detached, a congregate of Japanese waited beside their rental. It was impossible not to wonder if any of them were survivors of Hiroshima or Nagasaki. They were about the right age, and could have been among the fortunate schoolchildren who escaped death that morning in August.

We gathered because for our different reasons we wanted to visit Ground Zero, the site where at 5:29:45 Mountain War Time, on July 16, 1945, after a long, rainy night, the physicists who'd worked in secrecy up north of here at Los Alamos witnessed the successful test of their wartime creation, the world's first atomic bomb. We wanted not so much to pay homage but stand in remembrance of just what our forebears had wrought there, that midsummer day, in their hope of bringing a brutal war to a quick conclusion.

Some of us, no doubt, had seen photographs of the site. Out in the middle of the highly restricted White Sands Missile Range, on a truly desolate stretch of desert between the Rio Grande River and the Oscura Mountains, stands an obelisk, fashioned of black malpais lava-stone, that marks where the detonation took place. It is the loneliest monument on earth. And a modest monument, given that what occurred at that first ground zero could be considered the most fearful event in human history, the place where mankind wrested from God the ability to produce the apocalypse. What had traditionally been seen as divine province was now in our own hands. And this was where we were going, to witness where such a catalyst was ushered into the world.

It is not an easy place to visit. Indeed, few if any other national historic landmarks in this country are as inaccessible. None was ever more fraught with ambiguities. Open to the public for only half a dozen hours or so, on the first Saturdays in April and October, the Trinity Site occupies a small part of the forbidding Jornada del Muerto—*the journey of death*, as the conquistadors named it—a flat alkaline basin, hedged by bony mountains, speckled with thorny mesquite and soaptree yucca, with cholla and creosote bushes. One may only enter the range as part of a caravan of cars, escorted by state then military police, having set out from Alamogordo. From the moment the visitors leave Alamogordo—a frontier town founded in 1898 when railroad entrepreneur Charles Eddy bought this land with the idea of laying track across it from El Paso to points north—to the time they depart by Stallion Gate, Trinity pilgrims are closely monitored.

When we make our way this morning toward Tularosa, a small town north of Alamogordo, we will see that those tracks from Eddy's day still carry the old El Paso & Northeastern line. Freight trains a hundred colorful boxcars long will be seen running through here, just as they have all century. Indeed, much of the landscape we cross today will look just as it did long ago. From Tularosa, we will bear west into a parched scratchland where Billy the Kid drove brand-blotted cattle he had rustled out of Mexico and Texas. Pat Garrett's ghost will be out there, still chasing him, as will a spectral pantheon of legendary rawhiders, prospectors, desperadoes, timbermen, muckers, and other lost souls. As uninhabitable as the terrain will seem, generations have made bloody American history on the stoic, timeless back of this desert.

Our convoy set out at eight, the sun fully risen, the skies edged by tawny white clouds at every cardinal point, always frothing and changing shapes. I overheard a man say, when we were told to get into our vehicles and turn on our headlights, "This is gonna look like the darnedest funeral procession you ever seen." Alamogordo Chamber of Commerce volunteers, wearing turquoise sport shirts and jeans, walked cheerfully along the rows of cars, handing out bags that contained literature about the Do's and Don'ts of our journey. As I was riding in the passenger seat, it fell to me to read aloud to the others in our car what was written in these documents.

Dear Trinity Site Visitor, a letter from the Public Affairs Office, Department of the Army, began, *The driving distance from Alamogordo to Trinity Site is about 85 miles. During the drive to the site please follow the directions of the city, state and military police. They are present to insure your safety and protect missile range assets.* Then I turned to a schedule of restrictions all visitors were required to obey. Everyone was bound to stay with the convoy, or risk expulsion. Demonstrations, picketing, sit-ins, political speeches, and other similar activities were prohibited, as well. No one was allowed to eat or drink at Ground Zero, in order to avoid ingestion of radioactive plutonium, traces of which charge the dust that is raised by a breeze or tramping feet. Application of any kind of cosmetics, especially lipstick or balm, is prohibited at the site. No one was to handle Trinitite or remove any fragments of it from the detonation area—Trinitite being the green-black glassy mineral that was created when the sandy floor of the Jornada melted and fused beneath the nuclear fireball. Watch out for rattlesnakes, the list advised, although my companions, who'd made this expedition once before, said that they feared scorpions more than rattlesnakes. Scorpions are harder to see, and give no warning.

Other caveats were listed, too, but above all, this document stated, no one was allowed to take photographs on the way in to Trinity. Anyone caught using a camera would be detained, have his film confiscated, and be conducted back to Tularosa Gate where he would promptly be evicted from the military range. As our caravan moved out onto the highway, police cars with lights flashing ahead of the line and police cars behind, I thought: This is no Mount Rushmore, no Statue of Liberty. There are reasons Trinity Site isn't a component in the visual collective consciousness of the nation.

We passed stark pecan groves, pretty pistachio farms. Eastern hills picked up strands of sunlight along limestone strata and down in fawn alluvial fans. Cottonwoods and Chinese elms quivered in their green gowns. Beyond spikes of cypress washed by saffron light and kinetic shadow were sedimentary cliffs that dated back from Cambrian to Permian eras. We passed mobile home parks with satellite dishes. And in a scrap metal yard, the ruined mixer that once was mounted on a cement truck reminded me of the contour of the Fat Man bomb that razed Nagasaki. This was Route 54 toward Tularosa.

Tularosa, whose name comes from *tular*, a reedy place, harkens back to the days when marshy tracts of cattails embraced by swales of long grass were common here, before herds of thousands of head of cattle were driven northward from Texas, trampling, thus decimating, the delicate ecosystem. What those first colonizers witnessed when they arrived in this sere basin was stark but opulent. Arroyos and washes, now such customary geographic features of the New Mexican land-scape, hardly existed in the terrain before sheep and cattle exposed the fragile, friable soil which for thousands of years lay under the protective inch-deep weave of grass. "Tularosa" no longer makes much sense. The reeds and broad swales of grasses are largely gone, at least those that were indigenous. The migrant settlers who christened this landscape our convoy now crossed, through their very activities of trailblazing and homesteading their Tularosa, rendered meaningless its beautiful name.

Progress was slow along the highway, which gave me the chance to take in the farms and businesses scattered along the roadside. A pickup parked near Tularosa Vineyards caught my eye. Painted on its door was the advertisement, *Ostrich: The Other Red Meat*, and beneath it, the address and phone for a local ostrich farm. What this brought to mind was that Tularosa had always been a place where settlers did well to be creative in their labor to make a living. Little water and much heat has forever reigned in this place. As a result, the first Hispanic and Anglo settlers—not to mention the inhabitants who preceded them by ten thousand years up at Three Rivers—who set down roots in the region all had to display bountiful ingenuity, stubbornness, stamina, and heart essential to survival here, or perish. This was why even now we found ostrich farmers, nut-tree orchard keepers, nuclear weaponry engineers, and Air Force test pilots, all amalgamated here. All eking out their canny existences in a harsh domain.

Half an hour into our journey we reached Higuera Street. The convoy slowed and turned left at Wild Bill's Saddlery. Adobes and low frame houses made up dusty neighborhoods where kids rode bikes and old men sat on porches watching the caravan pass by. Apple trees and white roses prospered along shallow *acequias*. Pastor Chuck Parish's Church of the Nazarene was strung with *ristras* of dark red chilies.

Fences girdled the narrow two-lane road, and soon we reached the outskirts of this sleepy, almost ghost town. It was hard to believe Tularosa had once been a hinterland Sodom where blood feuds over range, water, and other rights were waged year in and out. Where boys like Oliver Lee shot Charles Rhodius over a cattle dispute, and James Smith murdered C. F. Hilton over a land dispute, and François Jean Rochas, known as Frenchy of Cañon del Perro, was murdered by a man named Morrison, over a horse dispute, and so forth. The days of that particular brand of inglorious glory were over, it seemed, though what were we to make of the technological glories that lay up ahead on this road, built to settle grander disputes in grander ways?

In a violent land, as the valley once had been, there was back then one unwritten rule that did obtain. Known as the Rattlesnake Code, it held that if a man deserved to be killed, it was fair to kill him, no matter what reason you had for killing him, just so long as you warned him first of your intention to kill him. You could shoot him in the back, if you so desired, as long as you told him, let him share in the bad news. There are accounts that before Smith murdered Hilton, who was old and unarmed at the time, he did first say, "Hilton, I'm going to kill you." It was a primitive sort of decorum, but decorum nevertheless.

As the first high-tech tracking dome loomed now on the horizon

—resembling a golf ball held at twice arm's length—the contrasts and conundrums of Tularosa Valley began to come into focus. Paradox abounded here. How could I not marvel at the fact that a brief century ago, Tularosans celebrated their first board sidewalk in town with festive huzzahs, pistol shots, dancing, and lots of liquor—the same Tularosans who would have grandchildren who were knocked out of their beds one quiet summer morning when that first atomic blast backlit the San Andres, and sent a massive roiling of radioactive ash into the heavens? While Tularosa seemed to have fallen on hard times again, the vision ahead—not just the proving grounds for the atomic bomb but where cruise and patriot missiles had flown, where Stealth fighters were even now being tested—stood in high relief.

Looking further through the packet of materials distributed back at the fairgrounds, I came upon a document that told more about current activities out on White Sands. Though its language was marked by the upbeat singsong of the sales pitch, what it spoke of struck me as darkly remarkable. "Between the beginning and the end of the test program," it read,

> be it Pershing or solar power, range employees are involved in every operation connected with the customer and his product. The range can and does provide everything from rat traps to telephones, from equipment hoists and flight safety to microsecond timing. We shake, rattle and roll the product, roast it, freeze it, subject it to nuclear radiation, dip it in salt water and roll it in the mud. We test its paint, bend its frame and find out what effect its propulsion material has on flora and fauna. In the end, if it's a missile, we fire it, record its performance and bring back the pieces for post mortem examination.

The caravan had briefly come to a halt, but then started moving forward again. I folded the pamphlet and put it back in the plastic bag, thinking that while the cowboy wars of the nineteenth century were famed for their ferocity, they were but a modest overture to the scenes that would manifest out here in the desert, and beyond, in the century to come. At that moment when Little Boy was dropped from the *Enola Gay*, the humble Rattlesnake Code, absurd and Wild Western as it was, became a comparatively gentle, decorous bit of etiquette from a bygone era.

The Trinity visit was established back in 1971, but most people seem unaware that, however infrequently, Ground Zero is open two days a year to whoever wants to see it. True, the military, who would just as soon not have private citizens caravaning across some of their most intelligence-sensitive terrain, don't go out of their way to advertise the tour. And for many of those who are mindful that the site can be visited, fear of radioactive poisoning or perhaps a distaste for the legacy of the nuclear birthplace deters them from considering a visit.

Such anti-nuke or anti-military sentiments are rarer here in Alamogordo and Tularosa, however. The nerdy culture of aerospace, rocketry, high-tech defense systems has been deeply assimilated into this community. The presence for over half a century of the Army, Navy, and Air Force at White Sands reveals itself in many ways. Earlier this morning, en route to the fairgrounds, for instance, along the main drag from the southern end of town, we passed the Sonic America's Drive-In, Rocket Mobile Homes, 21st Century Hock Shop, the Satellite Inn, and the Star Motel, just to name a few. At night, the blinky neon sign for the Satellite Inn resembles a fifties version of some Jetsons-like spaceship, with pink and silver ellipses flashing in futuristic cartwheels. Many of the buildings along the strip have a nostalgic aura, and at night the blazing light show on either side of White Sands Boulevard puts one in mind of glitzy old Las Vegas— a hollow, honest vulgarity plunked down in the desert.

Indeed, the most prominent building in town, nestled above Alamogordo in the Sacramento foothills, is the International Space Center. Locals call this museum the Golden Cube, because it burns a brilliant tangerine color as its massive windows catch the sunset light. Here one can visit the grave of Ham the chimponaut. America's first primate in suborbital space, Ham had his fifteen (sixteen, actually) minutes of fame in 1961. Here one can see Apollo 11 astronaut Buzz Aldrin's surface visor—its gold globe like a funhouse mirror in which you can see your face contort—and Neil Armstrong's woven stainless-steel glove worn during the first moonwalk, housed in display cases. An old cinetheodolite tracking instrument is displayed at the Center, as are a thousand other early space-age mementos.

The frontier desert that spreads to the horizon below the museum's windows is the birthplace of America's missile and space programs, and a phrase stating this fact is part of the White Sands logo. Back in the forties, V-2 rockets overflew these grounds, and strange objects have coursed across the sky ever since. Is it any wonder that Roswell, due east on the other side of the mountains, is one of the greatest UFO hotspots in the world?

A rainshower began and ended quick as a wink. Sunflowers on stalks that would prove to be as tall as the *malpais* obelisk at Trinity began to glisten now, and the scent of alfalfa mingled with piñon. Jackbottoms stood in the fields, munched orchard grass, and shook their heads. Bright whiteness shimmered in faraway titanic clouds out toward the Oscura range, whose stony slopes hid the bomb tower from detection from over in this part of the basin—hid the tower, that is, and all the equipment there, but certainly not the radioactive cloud and brilliant burst of light that emanated from it.

Now we arrived at a railroad crossing beyond Tularosa. Ten thousand surveyed telemetry, camera, and radar sites lay ahead, most of them mobile, all of them cloaked in secrecy. Instrumentation areas, we could see, loomed on every distant bluff. A sign indicated that cardiac pacemakers may be affected by equipment from this point on.

I recognized the gate and fence from a photograph in the July 16, 1985, issue of the *Albuquerque Journal* that was taken right here. Another range war now came to mind. The photograph was of rancher Pat Withers, who stood in the hard morning sunlight, thumbs hooked in his baggy bluejean pockets, straw Stetson shading his eyes. The look on his seventy-six-year-old face was stubborn if grim, and in the background of the photograph caravan cars passed him on their way into the site that day. Mounted atop the metal fencepost at his side was a skeleton with the upper ribs and shoulder bones hunched up, frustrated, shrugging. A lurid death grimace was drawn on the skeletal face. Under that, writ in a clear hand, was the message: "THIS IS WHAT IS FAST HAPPENING TO THE RANCHERS WAITING FOR THE GOVERNMENT TO PAY THEM FOR THEIR RANCHES."

What the sign referred to was that Pat Withers and a hundred and fifty other ranch families want their property back, claiming the military essentially swindled them out of their lands. Another player in the range wars that defined this part of the world, Pat was, back then, the oldest of that dwindling group of ranchers whose spreads were confiscated by the Army during the last years of World War II in order to make room for the atomic test. The military kept the land for decades, finally bought it for under market value, and ultimately condemned it, so they could continue with their program of hardware testing out here. Forty thousand missiles had been launched over this property in the years that followed. Pat never did get his land back, his death's-head sign proving prophetic.

We entered the range. The convoy halted one last time so that military police could drive by slowly, counting cars and passengers. A breeze made the yellow grasses quiver and stiffly wave. Dead, arid quiet prevailed as a dragonfly perched on a mesquite thorn. Beyond that bush, tiny dunes like ossified puddles of sand came into focus as my eye adjusted to so much pure, saturating light. Looking again, I saw that, no, they were not dunes, but more bunkers and berms and unnatural shelters.

Soon enough the MPs announced by loudspeaker: "Everybody back into your vehicles so we can proceed." A mild northeasterly breeze kicked up—the wind direction on Trinity morning, when the first radioactive cloud in history drifted over the sleepy hamlets of Bingham and Carrizozo not far from here, as crows fly. And as we drove we began to see what the military have done to the landscape. Tula-G Viewing Area overlooked a long mound of pink dirt, one more earthen berm, with tin-roofed bunker behind. Very red clumps grew against the whitish-brown earth, like khaki dipped in cranberry juice. The police raced past the caravan, surveillance against the cameraman, the videographer, the shutterbug—but what in the world, really, was there to photograph here, in the last analysis? I wondered. Given all the "black" programs that were being conducted on the range at any given moment, I supposed my question was rhetorical.

The caravan next serpented past biblical-looking shrubs, past flea-bane with purple flowers and prickly pears. Scattered seemingly at random, though assuredly not, were old observation stations of white concrete with green trim and shutters, bright silvery bowed roofs. We saw blue signs at turnoffs that led into the desert: "*NATO Seasparrow Missile System, Salt Sotim.*" And we saw, way off to the south, an oryx grazing—an African gemsbok with ominous backward-projecting black horns, imported from the Kalahari Desert by the Department of Fish and Game sometime after the war in order to introduce prey more exotic for local hunters than the indigenous mule deer and antelope. The oryx, as it turned out, adapted so successfully to this frontier savannah that they now had developed into a menace, and when provoked could drive their needle-sharp horns through the side of a car. I spotted five others out there, some hundred yards to the north, a small herd, flashing their long black tails in the warming air.

Imagine, for a moment, Oliver Lee and his half brother Perry Altman as they rode from Pecos over into Tularosa Valley with a guide named Cherokee Bill, who had enthused to them about this unsteaded part of the country. Imagine them as they rode past dry Mescalero, over the summit of the blue Sacramentos, and down into a fault-edged rift known as Dog Canyon, whose floor is a clutter of stone and bone.

What they had been looking for was a secluded territory where they could settle, to ranch in absolute peace, having had enough of the populated plains over in Texas where a man couldn't get himself proper elbow room. When he described this valley to the brothers, Cherokee Bill may or may not have exaggerated its lushness, but either way, Oliver and Perry weren't prepared for the austerity of this sun-scorched basin.

Local legend has it Perry turned in the saddle of his thirsty horse to his half brother and said, "Well, Oliver, this country is so damn sorry I think we can stay here a long time and never be bothered by a soul." That was before the great drought of 1889, when, according to one local historian, what little water there was ran speckled with maggots from carcasses of sheep and cattle that lay in streams above.

They lived their lives out not far from here. Dog Canyon was where Frenchy died. Oliver Lee would be involved in the murder of Colonel Albert J. Fountain not too many years later, 1896 or so, out in the snow white reaches of the dunes near where Holloman Air Force Base now sprawls just over the horizon. During a séance down in El Paso, the Colonel's spirit spoke through a spiritualist and confirmed, "I was killed three miles east of the White Sands and within fifteen minutes' ride of Chalk Cliffs. They threw a rope over my head and dragged me some distance." Once a disputatious place always a disputatious place.

High over White Sands, as we moved deep into the missile range now, a formation of jets could be seen, microscopic blots against a cerulean sky. From the plaza of the Space Museum one might look out over this same valley and glimpse the buildings and runways, faint in the heated wavy air, of Holloman. Later today there was to be a ceremony to induct Soviet cosmonaut Sergei Krikalev, who spent more than a year in outer space during his career, into the Hall of Fame. As part of the inaugural festivities a fly-over of a Stealth fighter was scheduled. I mentioned to the others in our car, now an hour out of Alamogordo, that I hoped we would be able to get back in time for the festivities. It wasn't every day one could see a Stealth making a low pass over a friendly audience.

Unfortunately, a brief but furious rainstorm caused the airshow to be canceled.

We were now far enough into the desert that past and present seemed to become one and the same. Past Rhodes Canyon Range Center, white buildings were clustered near where the road abruptly turned north, having gone thirty miles straight west. Out the car window, old electrical poles zipped by, wireless and weathered gray-brown, their clear glass insulators glimmering, poles and crossbeams—some cradling hawks' nests in their wooden arms—looking like ideograms against the subtly polychromatic geology. In the foreground were acres of alkalite waterflats, dry frost on the pink-brown floor. Feral horses ran down in a draw; roan, gray-mottled. The mountains, a long stone curtain, were dappled by cloud shadows.

Now we reached the conventional-payload impact areas. Another of the paradoxes of Trinity: Is there anywhere on earth where the overwhelming natural beauty—stark, serene, venerable, magisterial—comes more fully into appositive contact with the darker ambitions of mankind? In the normal course of things, mountains erode into mesas, mesas erode into buttes, buttes into towers, towers into spires, and spires into soil, until volcanic thrust creates new mountains. Here, the probabilities for fast-forwarding nature by means of explosives changed forever the definition of normalcy.

Denver we neared next, but not *that* Denver. More tracking points, more anonymous-looking buildings out on the recumbent field. Signs on both sides of the roads, painted red and black on white back-ground, read: "DANGER UNEXPLODED MUNITIONS KEEP OUT—*Peligro Prohibido Municiones Explosivas.*" Unknown quantities of lost, unex-ploded ordnance may be dispersed across the landscape. And yet it seemed impossible to lose airborne munitions, given all the observa-tories set on white steel-girder platforms which house super-high-speed optical tracking cameras that follow the trajectories of each launched object as it flies over startled coyotes and spooked oryx. I'm told, though, that even after survey and clean-up, the danger exists. More signs at dusty turnoffs, for back roads that would take you to sites like Burris Wells and impact areas with curious names such as Pup and Zumwalt (Bat) Test Track. We turned off KZZX Alamo-gordo Country Radio 105.5 and listened to the country music of crickets and wind.

When we reached Mockingbird Gap, I knew we were close. This was a landmark I'd read about, a spot where scientists and others had hunkered down to watch the detonation through tinted welder's glass. The road ascended into the foothills and after some minutes we emerged into a high desert plain, where we saw for the first time the Jornada itself, where the atomic blast occurred.

The world seemed different over here. Far paler, yellowed, less de-fined than the Tularosa basin, somehow bleaker. The Oscura Moun-tains, which ran like a spine between the Jornada and Tularosa, now curved away to the right. Below us, more bunkers dotted the scape. One road sign read: "*Hardhat Area Beyond This Point,*" and then an-other: "*High Explosive Test Area.*" Uneasiness settled over me, as we passed vintage observation bunkers, Quonsetesque structures bull-dozed under half a century ago and all but buried in red sandy soil, like toy train tunnels. Firing and instrumentation bunkers were sim-ilarly constructed, here and there, with shedlike frames buried under earth, into which dozens of communication lines once fed, from low T-poles that webbed the terrain. Some observation towers that likely were used during the test still endured, wobbly on their rotted pins, way off to the southeast. Wild oat grasses in virginal stands caught gusts of wind and flinched, as we drove farther into the Jornada. Globemallow, small coral flowers on soft green stalks, decorated the road shoulder, and out desertward was a tamarisk grove. Tiny birds, black-throated sparrows, bounded over their habitat, free of the history of their home.

By eleven we neared the MacDonald Ranch House. This was the place where Trinity began, really. In this old stone and stucco dwelling they assembled the core of the bomb—the Gadget, as it was called —painstakingly inserting the initiator between two hemispheres of marvelously warm alpha-dispersing plutonium, then fitting the unit, a nickel sphere, into a plug of tamper, deep in the center of a highly explosive shell. The pit-assembly team, in dusty white lab coats, gathered over there on Friday the 13th, July 1945. Once the Gadget was assembled, it was transported, slowly, carefully, from the ranch house over to a tower, and hoisted above ground into final position. As we passed the last observation bunker before reaching Ground Zero itself, I couldn't help but remember how, back in 1945, just after detonation, while the mushroom cloud rose heavenward, Trinity Project director Kenneth Bainbridge turned to Manhattan Project director J. Robert Oppenheimer and made his well-known remark, "Now we are all sons of bitches."

One wonders what thoughts were running through the scientists' minds during those several days *before* critical mass was achieved in the ugly metal contraption fixed atop that tower near here, when none of them could be certain whether the test would fizzle or else ignite the atmosphere and destroy all life on earth. The hard reality of finally arriving at the Trinity site, and this disquietude I could not avoid, it seemed, surely gave me some grasp of the tenor of those unknowable thoughts.

Later, an Army bus would take us the short distance from Ground Zero to the restored MacDonald Ranch House. Its Aeromotor windmill, its timeworn stables, the watertank where Project personnel swam, all stand in tranquil abandonment. Walking along the trail to the house with White Sands public relations director Jim Eckles, I will mention we are only two miles from Ground Zero and ask, "How did the ranch house survive the blast?"

"Well, some of the windows were blown out," is what he says.

"From all the footage I've ever seen of atom bombs, I'd have thought the shock wave would have blown this place to smithereens."

A tall, lean, affable man, Eckles says to me, "Well, it wasn't *that* big an atom bomb."

Trinity site, where the Manhattan Project came to fruition. We are finally here. The military police direct us to park in rows—more rows, rows again—on the flats outside a fenced area. Next to a concession stand and a long, yes, row of latrines lies a rusty iron cylinder, twelve feet in diameter and over twenty feet long. This is Jumbo, which was to be used as a containment device to recover precious plutonium if the test failed. It cost millions upon millions of dollars to fabricate and transfer here, and now it lies on its side, a broken piece of junk, desert breezes flowing back and forth through its hollow center.

All sun, not a tree in sight. Hot now and weirdly quiet, the sound swallowed by the engulfing desert. We walk through the first gate, past a triangular weather-faded *"Danger Radioactive Materials"* sign. Two women hike ahead with pastel parasols, odd splashes of Impressionist color against the powdery beige and sage. Our procession is suddenly so grave, hushed. It reminds me of Good Friday on the road to Chimayó, up north of Santa Fe, though rather than thirty thousand believers making a religious pilgrimage, here we number in the hundreds and the quiet is not worshipful.

A chill sensation of melancholy stabs through me. I can't be the only one who feels this, the pure enormity of the *thing itself* which is now so powerfully present. Something about the sheer desolation, the pure glorious vast forsaken emptiness of the desert, sharpens one's perception of our shared mortality. One overhears a clichéd joke like, "I'm going to glow in the dark to*night*"—sure—but the eavesdropper also hears the confessional words, "My life is kind of twisting me around," as we all walk down the dusty wide straight track, bounded by sturdy barbed wire on each side, toward the place where the tower once stood. When a baby on her father's shoulders begins to cry and squirm, her father asks her, "What're you nervous?" Her mother says to him in a scolding voice, "Oh, she doesn't know where she's gonna be," and though she might not, I wonder whether the solemnity of we walkers hasn't alarmed her.

Halfway there, a hundred yards or so along, you see it, the blunt crown of the obelisk, where it rises into view from the declivity of the wide, shallow crater. The black monolith in the movie 2001—

that moment when Stanley Kubrick's astronauts venture down into the blindingly illuminated moon excavation—comes to mind. An imaginative, visual image of the bomb's effect I try with only modest success to superimpose on this tranquil scene. A melon butterfly with black underwing wafts by as if to taunt my efforts.

Ground Zero stands within a circular enclosure of two chain-link fences and barbed wire. A makeshift lean-to off the tailgate of a Chevy van is parked by the entrance. On a card table they have assembled a little display—science-fair style—with Geiger counter, chunks of Trinitite, and other objects. We are invited to pass the copper tube of the Geiger counter over an orange Fiestaware plate, and when we hear the clicking increase, we're told that to get this particular shade of orange, the Fiestaware makers used lead and uranium in the finish. It clicks with equal insistence when held above the sparkling, grainy, green chunks of Trinitite.

I tie my jacket around my waist and walk through the last gate into a circular fenced enclosure, toward the obelisk, which stands off to the right of center. Dead ahead is a flatbed with a replica of Fat Man, brownish-red, riddled by rust. To the left is a low shelter, through whose dusty windows you can see the original crater floor as it was after the blast. Bulldozers and wind have long since buried the highly radioactive Trinitite crust, though bits and pieces of it blink beneath our feet. Attached to the fence, off behind the iron mannequin, are some thirty photographs showing the sequence of the first nuclear explosion. We walk over to look, my companions and I, at this sequence of shots.

First we see the dome of pure light at 0.006 seconds, already enveloped in apocalyptic fire over a hundred meters of area. Next, at 0.016 seconds, a ruffled skirt around the bottom of the scalding dome appeared, and the diameter of the fireball had expanded to three hundred meters. A mere 0.053 seconds after detonation, and this torrid, searing periphery embraced over a quarter mile. All of us strolling here this morning would have long since been vaporized by thermal radiation, transmuted in the shocking spew of heat, light, neutrons, gamma rays. Not one cell of our bodies would have escaped a fiery conversion at the hypocenter of the nuclear storm. As it is, only a small twisted bit of one of the four concrete-and-steel footings of the tower survived the blast.

Vegetation is sparse within the compound, but twinkling in the fine dust are those many specks of Trinitite. I kneel, stare at a little chunk, and against my better judgment, not to mention the rules set forth in that document I read back in Alamogordo, I reach down and take it up into my hand. It sparkles, a twentieth-century mineral, another of the many fantastic progeny our age has spawned.

Huge white puffy clouds populate the sky. The hard beauty, the majesty of the Jornada, rimmed by silent blue mountains, is overwhelming. It invokes the proper scale of man in nature, and strips away in me for one silent moment just at noon any sense of time. As I stand now beside this obelisk at Ground Zero, and reach out to rest my palm against the pocked, charcoal stone of the monument, I notice that spiders have woven webs in crevices of the mortar. I step back and discover that, indeed, the obelisk is decorated with many such nests. Indomitable life goes on, I marvel, even on the very face of what might well be seen as a premature yet surely cautionary gravestone, this cenotaph for mankind and all our fellow creatures, if ever it came to pass that what this place saw first was used again in war.

SCOTT RUSSELL SANDERS

ne of the foremost American essayists living today, Scott Russell Sanders has an uncanny knack for transforming complaint into art. Although Sanders has written on a wide variety of subjects, he often returns to the importance of place, not just in terms of spirit and imagination but in the more concrete terms of our survival as a species. In everything Sanders writes, however, the starting point seems to be some nagging discomfort, like a grain of sand worried from all angles, until the pearl is formed. "Mountain Music," about a Colorado river-rafting trip with his son, is thematically complex. It explores the conflicts between landscape and human character, between father and son, and finally, between the warring sides of the author himself: the pessimist who cannot accept the blind march of "civilization," and the father who wishes to give the son he loves the gift of optimism.

M O U N T A I N
M U S I C

ON A JUNE MORNING HIGH IN THE ROCKY MOUNTAINS OF COLO-
rado, snowy peaks rose before me like the promise of a world without
grief. A creek brimful of meltwater roiled along to my left, and to
my right an aspen grove shimmered with freshly minted leaves. Blue-
birds kept darting in and out of holes in the aspen trunks. Butterflies
flickered beside every puddle, tasting the succulent mud. Sun glazed
the new grass and licked a silver sheen along the boughs of pines.

With all of that to look at, I gazed instead at my son's broad back,
as he stalked away from me up the trail. Sweat had darkened his gray
T-shirt in patches the color of bruises. His shoulders were stiff with
anger that would weight his tongue and keep his face turned from
me for hours. Anger also made him quicken his stride until I could
no longer keep up. I had forty-nine years on my legs and heart and
lungs, while Jesse had only seventeen on his. My left foot ached from
old bone breaks and my right knee creaked from recent surgery. Used
to breathing among the low, muggy hills of Indiana, I was gasping
up here in the alpine air, a mile and a half above sea level. Jesse
would not stop, would not even slow down unless I asked; and I was
in no mood to ask. So I slumped against a boulder beside the trail
and let him rush on ahead.

The day, our first full one in Rocky Mountain National Park, had
started out well. I woke at first light, soothed by the roar of a river

foaming along one edge of the campground, and I looked out from our tent to find half a dozen elk, all cows and calves, grazing so close by that I could see the gleam of their teeth. Just beyond the elk, a pair of ground squirrels loafed at the lip of their burrow, noses twitching. Beyond the squirrels, a ponderosa pine, backlit by sunrise, caught the wind in its ragged limbs. The sky was a blue slate marked only by the curving flight of swallows.

Up to that point, and for several hours more, the day was equally unblemished. Jesse slept on while I sipped coffee and studied maps and soaked in the early light. We made our plans over breakfast without squabbling: Walk to Bridal Veil Falls in the morning, raft on the Cache la Poudre River in the afternoon, return to camp in the evening to get ready for backpacking the next day up into Wild Basin. Tomorrow we would be heavy-laden, but today we carried only water and snacks, and I felt buoyant as we hiked along Cow Creek toward the waterfall. We talked easily the whole way, joking and teasing, more like good friends than like father and son. Yet even as we sat at the base of the falls, our shoulders touching, the mist of Bridal Veil cooling our skin, we remained father and son, locked in a struggle that I could only partly understand.

For the previous year or so, no matter how long our spells of serenity, Jesse and I had kept falling into quarrels, like victims of malaria breaking out in fever. We might be talking about soccer or supper, about the car keys or the news, and suddenly our voices would begin to clash like swords. I had proposed this trip to the mountains in hopes of discovering the source of that strife. Of course I knew that teenage sons and their fathers always fight, yet I sensed there was a deeper grievance between us, beyond the usual vexations. Jesse was troubled by more than a desire to run his own life, and I was troubled by more than the pain of letting him go. I wished to track our anger to its lair, to find where it hid and fed and grew, and then, if I could not slay the beast, at least I could drag it into the light and call it by name.

The peace between us held until we turned back from the waterfall and began discussing where to camp the following night. Jesse wanted to push on up to Thunder Lake, near eleven thousand feet, and pitch our tent on snow. I wanted to stop a thousand feet lower and sleep on dry dirt.

"We're not equipped for snow," I told him.

"Sure we are. Why do you think I bought a new sleeping bag? Why did I call ahead to reserve snowshoes?"

I suggested that we could hike up from a lower campsite and snowshoe to his heart's content. He loosed a snort of disgust.

"I can't believe you're wimping out on me, Dad."

"I'm just being sensible."

"You're wimping out. I came here to see the backcountry, and all you want to do is poke around the foothills."

"This isn't wild enough for you?" I waved my arms at the view. "What do you need, avalanches and grizzlies?"

Just then, as we rounded a bend, an elderly couple came shuffling toward us, hunched over walking sticks, white hair jutting from beneath their straw hats. They were followed by three toddling children, each one rigged out with tiny backpack and canteen. Jesse and I stood aside to let them pass, returning nods to their cheery hellos.

When they had trooped by, Jesse muttered, "We're in the wilds, huh, Dad? That's why the trail's full of grandparents and kids." Then he quickened his pace until the damp blond curls that dangled below his billed cap were slapping against his neck.

"Is this how it's going to be?" I called after him. "You're going to spoil the trip because I won't agree to camp on snow?"

He glared around at me. "You're the one who's spoiling it, you and your hang-ups. You always ruin everything."

With that, he swung his face away and lengthened his stride and rushed on ahead. I watched his rigid shoulders and the bruise-colored patches on the back of his T-shirt until he disappeared beyond a rise. That was when I gave up on chasing him, slumped against a boulder, and sucked at the thin air. Butterflies dallied around my boots and hawks kited on the breeze, but they might have been blips on a screen, and the whole panorama of snowy peaks and shimmering aspens and shining pines might have been cut from cardboard, for all the feeling they stirred in me.

The rocks that give these mountains their name are ancient, nearly a third as old as the earth, but the Rockies themselves are new, having been lifted up only six or seven million years ago, and they were utterly new to me, for I had never seen them before except from airplanes. I had been yearning toward them since I was Jesse's age, had been learning about their natural and human history, the surge of stone and gouge of glaciers, the wandering of hunters and wolves. Drawn to these mountains from the rumpled quilt of fields and forests in the hill country of the Ohio Valley, I was primed for splendor. And yet, now that I was here, I felt blinkered and numb.

What we call landscape is a stretch of earth overlaid with memory, expectation, and thought. Land is everything that is actually *there*, independent of us; landscape is what we allow in through the doors of perception. My own doors had slammed shut. My quarrel with Jesse changed nothing about the Rockies, but changed everything in my experience of the place. What had seemed glorious and vibrant to me when we set out that morning now seemed bleak and bare. It was as though anger had drilled a hole in the world and leached the color away.

I was still simmering when I caught up with Jesse at the trailhead, where he was leaning against our rented car, arms crossed over his chest, head sunk forward in a sullen pose I knew too well, eyes hidden beneath the frayed bill of his cap. Having to wait for me to unlock the car no doubt reminded him of another gripe: I had the only set of keys. Because he was too young to be covered by the rental insurance, I would not let him drive. He had fumed about my decision, interpreting it as proof that I mistrusted him, still thought of him as a child. That earlier scuffle had petered out with him grumbling, "Stupid, stupid. I knew this would happen. Why did I come out here? Why?"

The arguments all ran together, playing over and over in my head as we jounced, too fast, along a rutted gravel road toward the highway. The tires whumped and the small engine whined up hills and down, but the silence inside the car was louder. We had two hours of driving to our rendezvous spot for the rafting trip, and I knew that Jesse could easily clamp his jaw shut for that long, and longer. I glanced over at him from time to time, looking for any sign of detente. His eyes were glass.

We drove. In the depths of Big Thompson Canyon, where the road swerved along a frothy river between sheer rockface and spindly guard rail, I could bear the silence no longer. "So what are my hang-ups?" I demanded. "How do I ruin everything?"

"You don't want to know," he said.

"I want to know. What is it about me that grates on you?"

I do not pretend to recall the exact words we hurled at one another after my challenge, but I remember the tone and thrust of them, and here is how they have stayed with me:

"You wouldn't understand," he said.

"Try me."

He cut me a look, shrugged, then stared back through the windshield. "You're just so out of touch."

"With what?"

"With my whole world. You hate everything that's fun. You hate television and movies and video games. You hate my music."

"I like some of your music. I just don't like it loud."

"You hate advertising," he said quickly, rolling now. "You hate billboards, lotteries, developers, logging companies, and big corporations. You hate snowmobiles and jet skis. You hate malls and fashions and cars."

"You're still on my case because I won't buy a Jeep?" I said, harking back to another old argument.

"Forget Jeeps. You look at any car, and all you think is pollution, traffic, roadside crap. You say fast food's poisoning our bodies and TV's poisoning our minds. You think the Internet is just another scam for selling stuff. You think business is a conspiracy to rape the earth."

"None of that bothers you?"

"Of course it does. But that's the *world*. That's where we've got to live. It's not going to go away just because you don't approve. What's the good of spitting on it?"

"I don't spit on it. I grieve over it."

He was still for a moment, then resumed quietly, "What's the good of grieving if you can't change anything?"

"Who says you can't change anything?"

"You do. Maybe not with your mouth, but with your eyes." Jesse rubbed his own eyes, and the words came out muffled through his cupped palms. "Your view of things is totally dark. It bums me out. You make me feel the planet's dying, and people are to blame, and nothing can be done about it. There's no room for hope. Maybe you can get along without hope, but I can't. I've got a lot of living still to do. I have to believe there's a way we can get out of this mess. Otherwise, what's the point? Why study, why work, why do anything if it's all going to hell?"

That sounded unfair to me, a caricature of my views, and I thought of many sharp replies; yet there was too much truth and too much hurt in what he said for me to fire back an answer. Had I really deprived my son of hope? Was this the deeper grievance, the source of our strife—that I had passed on to him, so young, my anguish over the world? Was this what lurked between us, driving us apart, the beast called despair?

"You're right," I finally told him. "Life's meaningless without hope. But I think you're wrong to say I've given up."

"It seems that way to me. As if you think we're doomed."

"No, buddy, I don't think we're doomed. It's just that nearly everything I care about is under assault."

"See, that's what I mean. You're so worried about the fate of the earth, you can't enjoy anything. We come to these mountains, and you bring the shadows with you. You've got me seeing nothing but darkness."

Stunned by the force of his words, I could not speak. If my gloom cast a shadow over the creation for my son, then I had failed him. What remedy could there be for such a betrayal?

Through all the shouting and then talking and then painful hush, our car hugged the swerving road, yet I cannot remember steering. I cannot remember even seeing the stony canyon, the white mane of the Big Thompson whipping along beside us, the oncoming traffic. Somehow we survived our sashay with the river and cruised into a zone of burger joints and car-care emporiums and trinket shops. I realized how often, how relentlessly I had groused about just this sort of commercial dreck, and how futile my complaints must have seemed to Jesse.

He was caught between a chorus of voices telling him that the universe was made for us, that the earth is an inexhaustible warehouse, that consumption is the goal of life, that money is the road to delight—and the stubborn voice of his father saying none of this is so. If his father was right, then most of what humans babble every day—in ads and editorials, in sitcoms and song lyrics, in thrillers and market reports and teenage gab—is a monstrous lie. Far more likely that his father was wrong, deluded, perhaps even mad.

We observed an unofficial truce for the rest of the way to the gas station north of Fort Collins, where we met the rafting crew at noon. There had been record rain and snowfall in the Rockies for the previous three months, so every brook and river tumbling down from the mountains was frenzied and fast. When local people heard that we meant to raft the Cache la Poudre in this rough season, they frowned, advised against it, recounting stories of broken legs, crushed skulls, deaths. Seeing that we were determined to go, they urged us to sign up for the shorter trip that joined the river below the canyon, where the water spread out and calmed down. But Jesse had his heart set on taking the wildest ride available, so we had signed up for the twelve-mile trip through the boulder-strewn canyon.

I was relieved to see a crowd of twenty or so, including scrawny kids and rotund parents, waiting at the rendezvous point. If the outfitters were willing to haul such passengers, how risky could the journey be? The sky blue rafts, stacked on trailers behind yellow vans, looked indestructible. The guides seemed edgy, however, as they told us what to do if we were flung into the river, how to survive a tumble over rocks, how to get out from under a flipped raft, how to drag a flailing comrade back on board.

Jesse stood off by himself and listened to these dire instructions with a sober face. I could see him preparing, gaze focused inward, lips tight, the way he would concentrate before taking his place in goal at a soccer game.

When the time came for us to board the vans, he and I turned out to be the only customers for the canyon run; all the others, the reedy kids and puffing parents, were going on the tamer trip. Our raft would be filled out by three sinewy young men, students at Colorado State, who were being paid to risk their necks: a guide with a year's experience and two trainees.

The water in Poudre Canyon looked murderous, all spume and standing waves and suckholes and rips. Every cascade, every low bridge, every jumble of boulders reminded the guides of some disaster, which they rehearsed with gusto. It was part of their job to crank up the thrill, I knew that; but I also knew from talking with friends that most of the tales were true.

At the launching spot, Jesse and I wriggled into our black wetsuits, cinched tight the orange flotation vests, buckled on white helmets. The sight of my son in that armor sent a blade of anxiety through me again. What if he got hurt? Lord God, what if he were killed?

"Hey, Dad," Jesse called, hoisting a paddle in his fist, "you remember how to use one of these?"

"Seems like I remember teaching you," I called back.

He flashed me a grin, the first sign of communion since we had sat with shoulders touching in the mist of Bridal Veil Falls. That one look restored me to my senses, and I felt suddenly the dazzle of sunlight, heard the river's rumble and the fluting of birds, smelled pine sap and wet stone.

One of the trainees, a lithe wisecracker named Harry, would guide our run. "If it gets quiet in back," he announced, "that means I've fallen in and somebody else better take over."

We clambered into the raft—Jesse and I up front, the veteran guide and the other trainee in the middle, Harry in the stern. Each of us hooked one foot under a loop sewn into the rubbery floor, jammed the other foot under a thwart. Before we hit the first rapids, Harry made us practice synchronizing our strokes, as he hollered: "Back paddle! Forward paddle! Stop! Left turn! Right turn!" The only other command, he explained, was "Jump!" Hearing that, the paddlers on the side away from some looming boulder or snag were to heave themselves *toward* the obstruction, in order to keep the raft from flipping.

"I know it sounds crazy," said Harry, "but it works. And remember: from now on, if you hear fear in my voice, it's real."

Fear was all I felt over the next few minutes, a bit for myself and a lot for Jesse, as we struck whitewater and the raft began to buck. Waves slammed against the bow, spray flew, stone whizzed by. A bridge swelled ahead of us, water boiling under the low arches, and Harry shouted, "Duck!", then steered us between the lethal pilings and out the other side into more rapids, where he yelled, "Left turn! Dig hard! Harder!"

He kept barking orders, and soon I was too busy paddling to feel anything except my own muscles pulling against the great writhing muscle of the river. I breathed in as much water as air. The raft spun and dipped and leapt with ungainly grace, sliding through narrow flumes, gliding over rocks, kissing cliffs and bouncing away, yielding to the grip of the current and springing free. Gradually I sank into my body.

The land blurred past. Sandstone bluffs rose steeply along one shore, then the other, then both, hundreds of feet of rock pinching the sky high above into a ribbon of blue. Here and there a terrace opened, revealing a scatter of junipers and scrub cedars, yet before I could spy what else might be growing there it jerked away out of sight. I could tell only that this was dry country, harsh and spare, with dirt the color of scrap iron gouged by erosion. Every time I tried to fix on a detail, on bird or flower or stone, a shout from Harry yanked me back to the swing of the paddle.

The point of our bucking ride, I realized, was not to see the canyon but to survive it. The river was our bronco, our bull, and the land through which it flowed was no more present to us than the rodeo's dusty arena to a whirling cowboy. Haste hid the country, dissolved the landscape, as surely as anger or despair ever did.

"Forward paddle!" Harry shouted. "Give me all you've got! We're coming to the Widowmaker! Let's hope we come out alive!"

The flooded Poudre, surging through its crooked canyon, was a string of emergencies, each one christened with an ominous name. In a lull between rapids, I glanced over at Jesse, and he was beaming. The helmet seemed to strain from the expansive pressure of his smile. I laughed aloud to see him. When he was little, I could summon that look of unmixed delight into his face merely by coming home, opening my arms, and calling, "Where's my boy?" In his teenage years, the look had become rare, and it hardly ever had anything to do with me.

"Jump!" Harry shouted.

Before I could react, Jesse lunged at me and landed heavily, and the raft bulged over a boulder, nearly tipping, then righted itself and plunged on downstream.

"Good job!" Harry crowed. "That was a close one."

Jesse scrambled back to his post. "You okay?" he asked.

"Sure," I answered. "How about you?"

"Great," he said. "Fantastic."

For the remaining two hours of our romp down the Poudre, I kept stealing glances at Jesse, who paddled as though his life truly depended on how hard he pulled. His face shone with joy, and my own joy was kindled from seeing it.

This is an old habit of mine, the watching and weighing of my son's experience. Since his birth, I have enveloped him in a cloud of thought. How's he doing? I wonder. Is he hungry? Hurting? Tired? Is he grumpy or glad? Like so many other exchanges between parent and child, this concern flows mainly one way; Jesse does not surround *me* with thought. On the contrary, with each passing year he pays less and less attention to me, except when he needs something, and then he bristles at being reminded of his dependence.

Before leaving for Colorado, I had imagined that he would be able to meet the Rockies with clear eyes, with the freshness of his green age. So long as he was in my company, however, he would see the land through the weather of my moods. And if despair had so darkened my vision that I was casting a shadow over Jesse's world—even here among these magnificent mountains and tumultuous rivers—then I would have to change. I would have to learn to see differently. Since I could not forget the wounds to people and planet, could not unlearn the dismal numbers—of pollution and population and poverty—that foretold catastrophe, I would have to look harder for antidotes, for medicines, for sources of hope.

Tired and throbbing from the river trip, we scarcely spoke during the long drive back to our campground in the national park. This time the silence felt easy, like a fullness rather than a void.

In that tranquility I recalled our morning's hike to Bridal Veil Falls, before the first quarrel of the day. No matter how briskly I walked, Jesse kept pulling ahead. He seemed to be in a race, eyes focused far up the trail, as though testing himself against the rugged terrain. I had come to this high country for a holiday from rushing. A refugee from the tyranny of deadlines and destinations, I wished to linger, squatting over the least flower or fern, reading the Braille of bark with my fingers, catching the notes of water and birds and wind. But Jesse was just as intent on covering ground. Although we covered the same ground, most of the time we experienced quite different landscapes, his charged with trials of endurance, mine with trials of perception. Then every once in a while the land brought us together—in the mist of the falls, on the back of the river—and it was as if, for a moment, the same music played in both of us.

Without any quarrel to distract me, I watched the road faithfully as we swerved up through Big Thompson Canyon. We entered the park at dusk and a rosy light glinted on the frozen peaks of the Front Range.

I was driving slowly, on the lookout for wildlife, when a coyote loped onto the road ahead of us, paused halfway across, then stared back in the direction from which it had come. As we rolled to a stop, a female elk came charging after, head lowered and teeth bared. The coyote bounded away, scooted up a bank on the far side of the road, paused, then peered back over its bony shoulder. Again the elk charged; again the coyote pranced away, halted, stared. Jesse and I watched this ballet of taunting and chasing, taunting and chasing, until the pair vanished over a ridge.

"What was that all about?" he asked when we drove on.

"She was protecting a calf, I expect."

"You mean a coyote can eat an elk?"

"The newborns they can."

When I shut off the engine at the campground and we climbed out of the car, it was as though we had stepped back into the raft, for the sound of rushing water swept over us. The sound lured us downhill to the bank of a stream and we sat there soaking in the watery music until our bellies growled. We made supper while the full moon chased Jupiter and Mars up the arc of the sky. The flame on our stove flounced in a northerly breeze, promising cool weather for tomorrow's hike into Wild Basin.

We left the flap of our tent open so we could lie on our backs and watch the stars, which burned fiercely in the mountain air. Our heads were so close together that I could hear Jesse's breath, even above the shoosh of the river, and I could tell he was nowhere near sleep.

"I feel like I'm still on the water," he said after a spell, "and the raft's bobbing under me and the waves are crashing all around."

"I feel it too."

"That's one of the things I wanted to be sure and do before things fall apart."

I rolled onto my side and propped my head on an elbow and looked at his moonlit profile. "Things don't have to fall apart, buddy."

"Maybe not." He blinked, and the spark in his eyes went out and relit. "I just get scared."

"So do I. But the earth's a tough old bird. And we should be smart enough to figure out how to live here."

"Let's hope." There was the scritch of a zipper and a thrashing of legs and Jesse sprawled on top of his new sleeping bag, which was too warm for this fifty-degree night. "I guess things could be scarier," he said. "Imagine being an elk, never knowing what's sneaking up on you."

"Or a coyote," I said, "never knowing where you'll find your next meal."

A great horned owl called. Another answered, setting up a duet across our valley. We listened until they quit.

"You know," said Jesse, "I've been thinking, maybe we don't need to sleep on snow. Maybe we can pitch camp in the morning at North St. Vrain, where there ought to be some bare ground, then we can snowshoe on up to Thunder Lake in the afternoon."

"You wouldn't be disappointed if we did that? Wouldn't feel we'd wimped out?"

"Naw," he said. "That's cool."

"Then that's the plan, man."

The stars burned on. The moon climbed. Just when I thought he was asleep, Jesse murmured, "How's that knee?"

"Holding up so far," I told him, surprised by the question, and only then did I notice the ache in my knee and foot.

"Glad to hear it. I don't want to be lugging you out of the mountains."

When he was still young enough to ride in a backpack, I had lugged him to the tops of mountains and through dripping woods and along the slate beds of creeks and past glittering windows on city streets, while he burbled and sang over my shoulder; but I knew better than to remind him of that now in his muscular youth. I lay quietly, following the twin currents of the river and my son's breath. Here were two reasons for rejoicing, two sources of hope. For Jesse's sake, and for mine, I would get up the next morning and hunt for more.

PHILLIP LOPATE

hillip Lopate's prose is a disarming combination of crabby, "get out of my face" Manhattan toughness and an almost classically pure elegance. Lopate has written often about his life in Manhattan. "Manhattan, Floating World" shows an artist experimenting with his form, expanding the linear boundaries of the conventional essay. Part reminiscence, part diatribe, part urban history, Lopate's essay captures Manhattan past and present in all its harried, beautiful, insane guises. "Manhattan, Floating World" is both an unsentimental celebration of Manhattan and a relieved wave of good-bye to it.

MANHATTAN, FLOATING WORLD

MANHATTAN IS SHAPED LIKE AN OCEAN LINER OR LIKE A LOZENGE or like a paramecium (the protruding piers its cilia) or like a gourd or like some kind of fish, a striped bass, say, but most of all like a luxury liner, permanently docked, going nowhere.

The Japanese of the late seventeenth and early eighteenth centuries had a word, *ukiyo*, for the "floating world" of courtesans, actors, rich merchants and their spoiled sons and daughters who made up the town's most visible element. Manhattan is a floating world, too: buoyant as balsa, heavy as granite. The reason skyscrapers developed so readily on this spit of earth, I once heard, is that its foundation stone was strong enough to take any amount of drilling. You can still bruise your ego against Manhattan's rocky cheek. Like other island city-states, Crete, Rhodes, Venice, or Hong Kong, it has a brash, arrogant energy far disproportionate to its size, and an uneasiness about domination by larger forces which it always tries to conceal.

Lewis Mumford has written tenderly about the approach to Manhattan from the water: "Those wonderful long ferry rides! Alas for a later generation that cannot guess how they opened the city up, or how the change of pace and place, from swift to slow, from land to water, had a specially stimulating effect upon the mind."

Myself, I first began coming to Manhattan on foot from Brooklyn. My whole family would walk across the Williamsburg Bridge at sundown on a Saturday night, to mark the Sabbath's end with a meal at a Manhattan dairy restaurant, usually Ratner's or Rappaport's. Not that my parents were such observant Jews; but, living in a Hasidic area, they adapted somewhat to their neighbors' customs. Later, I took to walking across the bridge myself, a poeticizing adolescent mesmerized by motes in air. These motes, *which only I could see, thanks to my precocious genius,* floating before the solid brick housing projects that already walled off the Lower East Side's edge from the river's beauty, represented to me the possibility of a transcendent escape from the ghetto and the manure pile I took to be my life. Not motes but money, I came to see later, was the ticket out.

The look of Manhattan, its aesthetic destiny, was sealed in 1811 with the approval of the grid plan. This arrangement set forth "a basis for the orderly sale and development of land in Manhattan between 14th Street and Washington Heights by establishing a rectangular grid of streets and property lines without regard to topography," notes *The Encyclopedia of New York City.* The prevailing wisdom today among planners and architects is that it is important to honor the land's contours, which just goes to show how visionary New York's city fathers were. They created an "intentional city," like St. Petersburg, a madly rational scheme imposed on nature. "Convinced that simple rectangular houses and lots were best, the commissioners avoided the addition of circles, ovals, and other features" popular in European capitals, adds the encyclopedist. The city fathers loved the ninety-degree angle, the forthright, manly plod of the rectangle extended indefinitely. They would have gridded the stars if given a chance.

The Manhattan grid is a mighty device, existential metaphor, Procrustean bed, call it what you will, a thing impossible to overpraise. I realize it is fashionable in left-wing academic circles to speak of the grid disparagingly as merely a capitalist scheme for real estate speculation. For instance, Richard Sennett wrote about Manhattan in his book, *The Conscience of the Eye,* "The grid has been used in modern times as a plan that neutralizes the environment. It is a Protestant sign for the neutral city." This glib semiotic reading fails to account for the famous vitality of Manhattan's streets; overlooks the power of this particular grid to generate meaning, clarity, resonance, and joy through its very repetitions; ignores the role of Broadway as a diagonal "rogue" street creating event and drama with its triangulations wherever it intersects an avenue (such as at 72nd Street, 59th Street, 42nd Street, 34th Street, 23rd Street); and omits the variations in street size within the grid, which differentiate the petite, elegantly trifling blocks of the Upper East Side, say, from the long dour treks between avenues on the Upper West Side.

"Before him, then, the slope stretched upward, and above it the brilliant sky, and beyond it, cloudy and far away, he saw the skyline of New York. He did not know why, but there arose in him an exultation and a sense of power, and he ran up the hill like an engine, or a madman, willing to throw himself headlong into the city that glowed before him."

This passage, taken from James Baldwin's *Go Tell It on the Mountain*, epitomizes a whole literature about sensitive provincials from the outer boroughs or Harlem approaching midtown Manhattan with a lump in their throats. I do not propose to add my own lump. Rather, let me fast-forward through adolescence, Columbia, a premature first marriage at twenty, conjugal cocooning in Washington Heights, divorce at twenty-five, a California-runaway period; skip ahead to my late twenties, when I returned to live on the Upper East Side, and to search out, as an avid bachelor this time, Mannahatta, Whitman's "City of orgies, walks and joys."

I walked. How I walked! In midtown Manhattan you walk as though on a conveyor belt, the grid pulling you along. It is not a restful sensation, true. There are none of those piazzas as in Rome where you can cool your feet in a sidewalk café and stare across at a fountain. You keep moving, you feel purposeful, wary, pointed, athletic. You can gauge your progress to an appointment (a block takes roughly a minute on foot), and given the vagaries of the subway system and traffic jams, walking is often the most reliable as well as most economical transportation option. Meanwhile, the grid is a reassuring compass always orienting you. It pulls your eye straight up the street, to long, unimpeded vistas; left or right, if you are anywhere near the waterfront, you can catch a peripheral glimpse of river or sunset (made more beautiful by the atmosphere's pollutants); and so your eye keeps adjusting astigmatically between long distance and middle range. And all the time there is so much coming at you that you have to attend to the immediate surround, dodging bodies and seizing opportunities. You take in the street by layers: this guy with the hat stepping too close to your shoulder; the storefront signs and displays, prompting impulse purchases; the stone-cut ornaments just above your head (cornices, cherubs, lions) and sometimes a whole second-story tier of retail; the wall posters selling movies, politicians, rock shows; and finally, the tops of buildings, for which the best touches are often saved—Babylonian roof gardens, green copper domes, castle turrets, Greek columns, Mayan setback fantasias, and all sorts of pointy symbols for the heavenward needle of commerce.

I loved the ability of Manhattan's public spaces to absorb without fuss a mix of classes, races, ethnicities, sexual orientations. For the moment, at least, everyone in the pedestrian swirl is assigned the same human value: You are either in my way or not.

Here I began to appreciate the performance art of pedestrianism. Each New Yorker is like a minor character actor who has honed his or her persona into a sharp, three-second cameo. I would have only an instant to catch the passer-by's unique gesture or telltale accessory: a cough, an insouciant drawing on a cigarette, hair primped, a nubby scarf, some words muttered under the breath, an eyebrow squinched in doubt, the sigh-filled lifting of a shopping cart. Diane Arbus used to say that in that split-second she looked for the *flaw*. I would say I look for the self-dramatizing element. On the one hand, the streets bring out a pure solipsism in New Yorkers, a self-absorption unembarrassed by myriad witnesses; on the other hand, their furrowed brows bespeak a secret religious conviction that they are being watched by higher powers, and their anxious eyes all seem to ask: My God, why hast Thou forsaken me?

It so happens I was then under the tutelage of a Jungian shrink who tried to get me to attend to the present moment—a hopeless proposition, in the long run; but for a while, I schooled myself to the concrete (the opposite of motes), to the one-thing-after-another world of the streets. A therapist alone could not have gotten me to attend to the present, but this was also a general recipe among poets, and I wanted to be a poet. I had in mind writing a proudly urban verse, inspired by Frank O'Hara's *Lunch Poems*, which captured the ironic, *jolie-laide* simultaneities of Manhattan sidewalks. My other urban gurus were Jane Jacobs, with her wisdom about everyday life and mixed uses in city neighborhoods; Walter Benjamin, with his analyses of *flâneurs* and his approach to the city as a cabbalistic text; and Charles Reznikoff, with his eavesdropping, anecdotal poems about chance street encounters.

A few entries from my past diaries should convey the spirit of that experiment, when I told myself: "You need not seek, the streets deliver all in due time."

In front of Carnegie Hall near the Russian Tea Room, there was a crazy man screaming his lungs out, something about "Man is an animal!"—in any case, not very interesting from the viewpoint of language or ideas. People were swerving away from him, but he was tyrannizing the whole street with his insane yelling. Finally I had had enough: I said, "Oh, shut up!" Straightaway he got a happy gleam in his eye. I made a beeline for the coffee shop across the street and sat down at a table, but he came in right after me, and in front of the cash register man and a dozen customers on stools, he began poking his finger at me. I realized now that he was much taller than I had thought. I started making the motion with my hand of patting the waves, the now-wait-a-minute-buddy-calm-down gesture.

"You want me on your back?" he yelled with satisfaction. "Huh? You want ME ON YOUR BACK, *Mister?!" I had to admit that he had a point.*

A New York snow turns to slush in the rain, and every pedestrian navigates to find some footing, as a river opens at each crossing. They watch a pioneer test the snow, to see if it is good for footing or has a false crust. I see a beautiful young woman in a mouton coat and elegant reddish-brown, ringletted hairdo hesitate at the corner, then plunge in with her black leather shoes, like ballet slippers, resigned to getting wet. An old black woman seems to be remembering country skills as she attempts a crossing.

I was in Fairway Supermarket on the Upper West Side, which is always crowded like mad, and I wanted to buy a few rolls, but an elderly, well-combed woman was pausing interminably before the bagels and bialys section with the customer prongs in her hand.

"Excuse me for taking so long," she said. "My eyes aren't good, I have cataracts."

I nodded. We all have our problems.

"I really can't see very well, they tell me I have cataracts," she continued, "and I don't want the ordinary bagels, I want the brown pumpernickel ones."

Lady, I thought to myself, if you have cataracts maybe you shouldn't be so picky.

She knocked her prongs through the bin a while without much conviction, then said, like someone used to ordering servants, "Could you find them for me?"

I had lost the duel of wills. "Sure."

"You know, those pumpernickel ones with the seeds," she added, as though I were the grocery boy. I snapped to it, just to see what it felt like, imagining myself in a white apron, all eyes on me.

I must have done a realistic job, because afterwards someone came up to me to ask where she could find the tomato paste.

Today I am walking down Broadway and 72nd Street and a police car screams by. I pay it no attention. Two more police cars pull up. Must be a shootout, I think. Another squad car; cops are yelling, "Get back! Clear the streets!" Must be a big *shootout: burglars trapped in a holdup? Hostages? Now I'm tempted to backtrack just to find out. Ah well (I walk on, thinking), can't interrupt my life for every crime. This is the exaggerated picture of New York that the rest of the world takes from Hollywood movies—police sirens running, cars converging. It's actuality today. I ask some people what's going on: they don't know. Suddenly a dozen motorcycle cops roar down the street. "It's the President!" I hear people say around me. "It's Carter!" The motorcycle squad is followed by one black limousine after another, bing bing bing. Which one's the Prez? They're driving by too fast to see. In the fifth or sixth limo I see a white hand on the bulletproof windowpane, palm up in greeting. The crowd murmurs, That must be him! That's all, just a little white hand. Our President.*

The truncated anecdote: so often this is what I brought home from my walks and tried to work up into something literary. I was trying to squeeze the sidewalks for free entertainment. Often enough, they obliged. Urbanists are fond of comparing the streets of a metropolis to a theater set. This turns out to be a tricky metaphor and, by now, a tiresome one. The American theater being what it is today, the streets are probably more reliable as a source of diversion. But what they give you, for the most part, are curtain-raisers.

In addition to spending hours each day walking and observing, I began reading more about town planning and New York history. I tried to understand the aesthetic secrets behind the pleasure I got from the streets. The Manhattan skyline, I came to discover, is unique in its juxtaposition of so many disparate architectural styles and eras, unapologetically cheek by jowl—and the fact that somehow they all work together. What makes them cohere visually is the Manhattan tradition of the unbroken street-wall, which democratizes every building by keeping it in its place, starting as far back from the sidewalk as its neighbors. The continuous street-wall, a by-product of the grid plan, has become as important as the grid itself in maintaining the dense, vertical look of Manhattan.

It was also Manhattan's good fortune to have been built up, for the most part, before the present era of jumbo tower technology, with its ugly one-building-per-block sprawl. Earlier skyscrapers were more svelte; even the Empire State Building, built as the tallest in the world, had to take its place like a good citizen alongside the other edifices along 34th Street between Fifth and Sixth Avenues.

While undergoing this unsystematic education in the urban landscape, I discovered I was not alone in my preoccupation. From the late seventies onward, almost every Manhattanite seemed to be developing into an amateur urbanologist. This fad may have been triggered by a sense of impending loss attendant on the city's 1975 brush with bankruptcy. The default scare made New Yorkers acutely worried—and self-conscious—about the preservation of a way of life they had been taking for granted.

This fascination with the city's web continued in the gentrifying eighties, when we came to see how any architectural grace note from the past could be framed and exploited for maximum commercial value. The eighties' resurgence in the city's fortunes—a foreign investment–driven, artificial boom—paradoxically led to a housing shortage, and a sharp increase in homelessness and street begging. It was no longer easy to write humorous sketches about loonies encountered on walks, now that their plight was revealed as part of a wider socioeconomic misery.

Gentrification produced a whole generation savvy about restoration, land use, city history. This was particularly true in Manhattan, with its extremely finite boundaries. Manhattan is a chessboard whereon everyone knows the value and provenance of each square. It can't expand (except through landfill), so it cannibalizes itself and reinvents itself in place. At prime locations, such as Times Square, Columbus Circle, Battery Park, nothing new can transpire without controversy and the screaming of ghosts.

Take the example of Madison Square Garden. The first arena was built, appropriately enough, on Madison Square, as a successor to P. T. Barnum's Hippodrome. This was knocked down and replaced by a much more distinguished version—a lavish, minareted affair designed by Stanford White, of the great New York architectural firm of McKim, Mead & White. When the New York Life Insurance Company bought the property and decided to raze the arena and build its own headquarters, Madison Square Garden trudged off to 50th Street and Eighth Avenue. There it lumbered through countless circuses and prizefights and Knicks games, until the early sixties, when the arena was moved again, this time as anchor to a huge speculative development on Seventh Avenue between 31st and 34th Streets. This was certainly a prime location, housing as it did that priceless architectural masterpiece, Pennsylvania Station, also by McKim, Mead & White. We know the rest: Penn Station was torn down, replaced by a tacky Madison Square Garden and a squalid underground railway juncture. The destruction of Pennsylvania Station changed the mentality of New Yorkers forever, from an amnesiac populace confidently, if blindly, embracing Progress, to a haunted band of nostalgics evicted from Eden, haunted by the corpse they could never revive.

Try telling Manhattanites about any proposed neighborhood change; they already know it. They know it because information is the plasma of New York, and because real estate ventures are well reported in the local press, and because they can see the transformations at street level. There is something particularly frustrating about this high degree of sophistication, combined as it is with a powerlessness to disarm evil or promote the civic good. Unless you are a "player"—a powerful developer, politician, union leader, community activist, realty lawyer—you are reduced to the role of spectator, elegiac in advance.

I was no player, but an increasingly elegiac appreciator. I walked, I walked. In cold weather I appreciated the chestnut sellers, the Christmas trees in Rockefeller Center. Various tall buildings were suddenly

competing to illuminate their crowns; I appreciated the chalky elephant gray lighting of Radio City and the NBC Building. In hot
weather I became a connoisseur of halter tops and sidewalk book
vendors.

There is about this vanity of walking, in cases like mine, the insular
smell of a maleness unable to break out of itself: solitary, literary,
onanistic, cerebral, boastful, defensive, and melancholy (like most
flirtations with the infinite). I walked as though hunting for erotic
adventure. Though I never actually picked up anyone on these pere-
grinations, they were all taken under the sign of Venus. The Manhattan street, with its ethnic variety, purveys a succession of women
whose beauty is heartstopping in different ways: this one because of
her elegant legs, that one because of her eloquent, ferocious face, the
next, her bright red hair, or something indefinably pleasing in the
ensemble. . . . I was not looking to find romance so much as to be
invaded by sharp, fleeting glimpses of feminine grace, to take back
home with me and muse over in bittersweet solitude. It seemed to
me I could achieve happiness with so many of these women. That
such naive optimism was contradicted by my extensive experience as
a bachelor never succeeded in rooting out the utopian dream of he-
donism which the street proffered.

Then I fell in love in my late forties, and remarried. I wondered,
worried, since the aesthetic response to beauty never dies, if the streets
of Manhattan might pose a continuous challenge to my fidelity, men-
tally if not physically. Of course I still look, but the main result of
marriage was that I found myself walking less. Manhattan, that mecca
for singles, became less fascinating to me now that the hunt was over.
It was also perhaps that, at fifty, age had finally caught up with me,
wearing out the enthusiasm, driven by longing, of my earlier, street-
besotted self.

These days, most of the time, I do not really see the city. I walk
around Manhattan in a muted blur, taking in only what I need in
order to navigate its streets. At times I'll even read a book as I walk,
espying only as much of the streetscape as peripheral vision around
the page's borders will allow. I resent the pressure (which I've put on
myself—nobody asked me to!) to find grace in the old gargoyles and
brickwork and water towers, the physiognomies of my fellow citizens.
Yes, New York is amazing, but must I always pay it homage? So

often in my youth, I conned myself into being programmatically astounded by this, my native city, even pretending it was someplace foreign and exotic, like Budapest or Buenos Aires or Prague, and making believe I was a tourist seeing it for the first time when I looked up at, say, the turn-of-the-century buildings in the Flatiron district. No more. If it is going to astonish me, it had better do so without my lifting a finger.

It still does, even if the astonishment is milder. In late May, I love to walk around Greenwich Village in the afternoon and see the three o'clock sun on the facades of town houses, red brick or painted white. I think there's some mystery to the light at this time of year, but then I realize it's only that the trees are in bloom, and I'm seeing the light filtered through and softened by erose leaves, which cast delicate shadows against the building walls. Also, there's a perfect correspondence in scale: one tree, one town house. An equivalence, a relationship. You can only get that in a few Manhattan neighborhoods, like the Village or parts of Chelsea, where the buildings are smaller. By July, you are so used to the fullness of the trees that you don't notice the light any more—you notice the heat. And of course in winter the sun is dimmer and the trees are bare. But there really is something miraculous about the sun-licked facades of Federal-style town houses at that time of year. And your energy is higher, because it's fun to walk around in the sun with a nip still in the air.

Built into literary discourse about Manhattan, it seems, is a movement from object of desire to disenchantment. F. Scott Fitzgerald, in "My Lost City," remembers his feelings as a young man that "New York had all the iridescence of the beginning of the world," and later, his dyspeptic conviction that "Whole sections of the city had grown rather poisonous. . . . The city was bloated, glutted, stupid with cake and circuses. . . . And with the awful realization that New York was a city after all and not a universe, the whole shining edifice . . . came crashing to the ground." He concluded: ". . . I have lost my splendid mirage. Come back, come back, O glittering and white!"

Joan Didion echoes his sentiments in her essay "Goodbye to All That." Initially, she writes, "New York was no mere city. It was instead an infinitely romantic notion, the mysterious nexus of all love and money and power, the shining and perishable dream itself. . . .

I still believed in possibilities then, still had the sense, so peculiar to New York, that something extraordinary would happen any minute, any day, any month." In the end she leaves, of course; "the golden dream was broken, and I am not that young any more. The last time I was in New York was in a cold January, and everyone was ill and tired."

American writers seem to associate New York with a good place to be young, and then blame it for the fact that it is not elixir enough to let them hold onto their youth. They project their own awareness of mortality onto it: hence, they always see New York as dying. French writers are fond of personifying Paris as a faithless trollop. In a sense, Manhattan has always remained true, faithful to its nature, and it is the writers who have proved faithless. I am no exception: true, in my twenties I hardly shared the cocktail party life of newcomers like Fitzgerald and Didion, and my journey from Brooklyn to Manhattan was shorter and more mundane. But I, too, romanticized the place, falsely identifying my own youthful, Whitmanesque, lyrically colonizing energy with the island's, then turned on it when I began to slow down.

If growing older means losing Manhattan—or the El Dorado it has signified—that loss of innocence may be more than compensated for by a gain in worldly stoicism. It would do well for writers like myself to follow the advice Cavafy gives in his great poem "The God Abandons Antony":

> say goodbye to her, to the Alexandria who is leaving.
> Above all, don't fool yourself, don't say
> it was a dream, your ears deceived you:
> don't degrade yourself with empty hopes like these.
> As one long prepared, and full of courage,
> as is right for you who were given this kind of city,
> go firmly to the window
> and listen with deep emotion,
> but not with the whining, the pleas of a coward;
> listen—your final pleasure—to the voices,
> to the exquisite music of the strange procession,
> and say goodbye to her, to the Alexandria you are losing.

Meantime, I have moved back to Brooklyn.

GRETEL EHRLICH

When it first appeared in 1984, Gretel Ehrlich's *The Solace of Open Spaces* became an important prototype for many subsequent contemporary writings about places. In this chapter taken from the book, as in everything she writes, Ehrlich displays a masterful ability to combine science, history, geography, and personal narrative, leaping from one to the other as gracefully as a figure skater. "The Solace of Open Spaces" is about Wyoming life, and the life Ehrlich herself was able to reinvent there after the death of a loved one. It is an elegant meditation upon the saving power of landscape, and of open space itself.

THE SOLACE

OF OPEN

SPACES

IT'S MAY AND I'VE JUST AWAKENED FROM A NAP, CURLED AGAINST sagebrush the way my dog taught me to sleep—sheltered from wind. A front is pulling the huge sky over me, and from the dark a hailstone has hit me on the head. I'm trailing a band of two thousand sheep across a stretch of Wyoming badlands, a fifty-mile trip that takes five days because sheep shade up in hot sun and won't budge until it's cool. Bunched together now, and excited into a run by the storm, they drift across dry land, tumbling into draws like water, and surge out again onto the rugged, choppy plateaus that are the building blocks of this state.

The name Wyoming comes from an Indian word meaning "at the great plains," but the plains are really valleys, great arid valleys, sixteen hundred square miles, with the horizon bending up on all sides into mountain ranges. This gives the vastness a sheltering look.

Winter lasts six months here. Prevailing winds spill snowdrifts to the east, and new storms from the northwest replenish them. This white bulk is sometimes dizzying, even nauseating, to look at. At twenty, thirty, and forty degrees below zero, not only does your car not work, but neither do your mind and body. The landscape hardens into a dungeon of space. During the winter, while I was riding to find a new calf, my jeans froze to the saddle, and in the silence that such cold creates I felt like the first person on earth, or the last.

Today the sun is out—only a few clouds billowing. In the east, where the sheep have started off without me, the benchland tilts up in a series of eroded red-earthed mesas, planed flat on top by a million years of water; behind them, a bold line of muscular scarps rears up ten thousand feet to become the Big Horn Mountains. A tidal pattern is engraved into the ground, as if left by the sea that once covered this state. Canyons curve down like galaxies to meet the oncoming rush of flat land.

To live and work in this kind of open country, with its hundred-mile views, is to lose the distinction between background and foreground. When I asked an older ranch hand to describe Wyoming's openness, he said, "It's all a bunch of nothing—wind and rattlesnakes—and so much of it you can't tell where you're going or where you've been and it don't make much difference." John, a sheepman I know, is tall and handsome and has an explosive temperament. He has a perfect intuition about people and sheep. They call him "Highpockets," because he's so long-legged; his graceful stride matches the distances he has to cover. He says, "Open space hasn't affected me at all. It's all the people moving in on it." The huge ranch he was born on takes up much of one county and spreads into another state; to put a hundred thousand miles on his pickup in three years and never leave home is not unusual. A friend of mine has an aunt who ranched on Powder River and didn't go off her place for eleven years. When her husband died, she quickly moved to town, bought a car, and drove around the States to see what she'd been missing.

Most people tell me they've simply driven through Wyoming, as if there were nothing to stop for. Or else they've skied in Jackson Hole, a place Wyomingites acknowledge uncomfortably because its green beauty and chic affluence are mismatched with the rest of the state. Most of Wyoming has a "lean-to" look. Instead of big, roomy barns and Victorian houses, there are dugouts, low sheds, log cabins, sheep camps, and fence lines that look like driftwood blown haphazardly into place. People here still feel pride because they live in such a harsh place, part of the glamorous cowboy past, and they are determined not to be the victims of a mining-dominated future.

Most characteristic of the state's landscape is what a developer euphemistically describes as "indigenous growth right up to your front door"—a reference to waterless stands of salt sage, snakes, jackrabbits, deerflies, red dust, a brief respite of wildflowers, dry washes, and no trees. In the Great Plains the vistas look like music, like Kyries of grass, but Wyoming seems to be the doing of a mad architect— tumbled and twisted, ribboned with faded, deathbed colors, thrust up and pulled down as if the place had been startled out of a deep sleep and thrown into a pure light.

I came here four years ago. I had not planned to stay, but I couldn't make myself leave. John, the sheepman, put me to work immediately. It was spring, and shearing time. For fourteen days of fourteen hours each, we moved thousands of sheep through sorting corrals to be sheared, branded, and deloused. I suspect that my original motive for coming here was to "lose myself" in new and unpopulated territory. Instead of producing the numbness I thought I wanted, life on the sheep ranch woke me up. The vitality of the people I was working with flushed out what had become a hallucinatory rawness inside me. I threw away my clothes and bought new ones; I cut my hair. The arid country was a clean slate. Its absolute indifference steadied me.

Sagebrush covers 58,000 square miles of Wyoming. The biggest city has a population of fifty thousand, and there are only five settlements that could be called cities in the whole state. The rest are towns, scattered across the expanse with as much as sixty miles between them, their populations two thousand, fifty, or ten. They are fugitive-looking, perched on a barren, windblown bench, or tagged onto a river or a railroad, or laid out straight in a farming valley with implement stores and a block-long Mormon church. In the eastern part of the state, which slides down into the Great Plains, the new mining settlements are boomtowns, trailer cities, metal knots on flat land.

Despite the desolate look, there's a coziness to living in this state. There are so few people (only 470,000) that ranchers who buy and sell cattle know one another statewide; the kids who choose to go to college usually go to the state's one university, in Laramie; hired hands work their way around Wyoming in a lifetime of hirings and firings. And despite the physical separation, people stay in touch, often driving two or three hours to another ranch for dinner.

Seventy-five years ago, when travel was by buckboard or horseback, cowboys who were temporarily out of work rode the grub line— drifting from ranch to ranch, mending fences or milking cows, and receiving in exchange a bed and meals. Gossip and messages traveled this slow circuit with them, creating an intimacy between ranchers who were three and four weeks' ride apart. One old-time couple I know, whose turn-of-the-century homestead was used by an outlaw gang as a relay station for stolen horses, recall that if you were traveling, desperado or not, any lighted ranch house was a welcome sign. Even now, for someone who lives in a remote spot, arriving at a ranch or coming to town for supplies is cause for celebration. To emerge from isolation can be disorienting. Everything looks bright, new, vivid. After I had been herding sheep for only three days, the sound of the camp tender's pickup flustered me. Longing for human company, I felt a foolish grin take over my face; yet I had to resist an urgent temptation to run and hide.

Things happen suddenly in Wyoming, the change of seasons and weather; for people, the violent swings in and out of isolation. But good-naturedness is concomitant with severity. Friendliness is a tradition. Strangers passing on the road wave hello. A common sight is two pickups stopped side by side far out on a range, on a dirt track winding through the sage. The drivers will share a cigarette, uncap their thermos bottles, and pass a battered cup, steaming with coffee, between windows. These meetings summon up the details of several generations, because, in Wyoming, private histories are largely public knowledge.

Because ranch work is a physical and, these days, economic strain, being "at home on the range" is a matter of vigor, self-reliance, and common sense. A person's life is not a series of dramatic events for which he or she is applauded or exiled but a slow accumulation of days, seasons, years, fleshed out by the generational weight of one's family and anchored by a land-bound sense of place.

In most parts of Wyoming, the human population is visibly outnumbered by the animal. Not far from my town of fifty, I rode into a narrow valley and startled a herd of two hundred elk. Eagles look like small people as they eat car-killed deer by the road. Antelope, moving in small, graceful bands, travel at sixty miles an hour, their mouths open as if drinking in the space.

The solitude in which westerners live makes them quiet. They telegraph thoughts and feelings by the way they tilt their heads and listen; pulling their Stetsons into a steep dive over their eyes, or pigeon-toeing one boot over the other, they lean against a fence with a fat wedge of Copenhagen beneath their lower lips and take in the whole scene. These detached looks of quiet amusement are sometimes cynical, but they can also come from a dry-eyed humility as lucid as the air is clear.

Conversation goes on in what sounds like a private code; a few phrases imply a complex of meanings. Asking directions, you get a curious list of details. While trailing sheep I was told to "ride up to that kinda upturned rock, follow the pink wash, turn left at the dump, and then you'll see the water hole." One friend told his wife on roundup to "turn at the salt lick and the dead cow," which turned out to be a scattering of bones and no salt lick at all.

Sentence structure is shortened to the skin and bones of a thought. Descriptive words are dropped, even verbs; a cowboy looking over a corral full of horses will say to a wrangler, "Which one needs rode?" People hold back their thoughts in what seems to be a dumbfounded silence, then erupt with an excoriating perceptive remark. Language, so compressed, becomes metaphorical. A rancher ended a relationship with one remark: "You're a bad check," meaning bouncing in and out was intolerable, and even coming back would be no good.

What's behind this laconic style is shyness. There is no vocabulary for the subject of feelings. It's not a hangdog shyness, or anything coy—always there's a robust spirit in evidence behind the restraint, as if the earth-dredging wind that pulls across Wyoming had carried its people's voices away but everything else in them had shouldered confidently into the breeze.

I've spent hours riding to sheep camp at dawn in a pickup when nothing was said; eaten meals in the cookhouse when the only words spoken were a mumbled "Thank you, ma'am" at the end of dinner. The silence is profound. Instead of talking, we seem to share one eye. Keenly observed, the world is transformed. The landscape is engorged with detail, every movement on it chillingly sharp. The air between people is charged. Days unfold, bathed in their own music. Nights become hallucinatory; dreams, prescient.

Spring weather is capricious and mean. It snows, then blisters with heat. There have been tornadoes. They lay their elephant trunks out in the sage until they find houses, then slurp everything up and leave. I've noticed that melting snowbanks hiss and rot, viperous, then drip into calm pools where ducklings hatch and livestock, being trailed to summer range, drink. With the ice cover gone, rivers churn a milk-shake brown, taking culverts and small bridges with them. Water in such an arid place (the average annual rainfall where I live is less than eight inches) is like blood. It festoons drab land with green veins; a line of cottonwoods following a stream; a strip of alfalfa; and, on ditch banks, wild asparagus growing.

I've moved to a small cattle ranch owned by friends. It's at the foot of the Big Horn Mountains. A few weeks ago, I helped them deliver a calf who was stuck halfway out of his mother's body. By the time he was freed, we could see a heartbeat, but he was straining against a swollen tongue for air. Mary and I held him upside down by his back feet, while Stan, on his hands and knees in the blood, gave the calf mouth-to-mouth resuscitation. I have a vague memory of being pneumonia-choked as a child, my mother giving me her air, which may account for my romance with this windswept state.

If anything is endemic to Wyoming, it is wind. This big room of space is swept out daily, leaving a bone yard of fossils, agates, and carcasses in every stage of decay. Though it was water that initially shaped the state, wind is the meticulous gardener, raising dust and pruning the sage.

I try to imagine a world in which I could ride my horse across un-charted land. There is no wilderness left; wildness, yes, but true wil-derness has been gone on this continent since the time of Lewis and Clark's overland journey.

Two hundred years ago, the Crow, Shoshone, Arapaho, Cheyenne, and Sioux roamed the intermountain West, orchestrating their move-ments according to hunger, season, and warfare. Once they acquired horses, they traversed the spines of all the big Wyoming ranges—the Absarokas, the Wind Rivers, the Tetons, the Big Horns—and win-tered on the unprotected plains that fan out from them. Space was life. The world was their home.

What was life-giving to Native Americans was often nightmarish to sodbusters who had arrived encumbered with families and ethnic pasts to be transplanted in nearly uninhabitable land. The great distances, the shortage of water and trees, and the loneliness created unexpected hardships for them. In her book *O Pioneers!*, Willa Cather gives a settler's version of the bleak landscape:

> The little town behind them had vanished as if it had never been, had fallen behind the swell of the prairie, and the stern frozen country received them into its bosom. The homesteads were few and far apart; here and there a windmill gaunt against the sky, a sod house crouching in a hollow.

The emptiness of the West was for others a geography of possibility. Men and women who amassed great chunks of land and struggled to preserve unfenced empires were, despite their self-serving motives, unwitting geographers. They understood the lay of the land. But by the 1850s the Oregon and Mormon trails sported bumper-to-bumper traffic. Wealthy landowners, many of them aristocratic absentee landlords, known as remittance men because they were paid to come West and get out of their families' hair, overstocked the range with more than a million head of cattle. By 1885 the feed and water were desperately short, and the winter of 1886 laid out the gaunt bodies of dead animals so closely together that when the thaw came, one rancher from Kaycee claimed to have walked on cowhide all the way to Crazy Woman Creek, twenty miles away.

Territorial Wyoming was a boy's world. The land was generous with everything but water. At first there was room enough, food enough, for everyone. And, as with all beginnings, an expansive mood set in. The young cowboys, drifters, shopkeepers, schoolteachers, were heroic, lawless, generous, rowdy, and tenacious. The individualism and optimism generated during those times have endured.

John Tisdale rode north with the trail herds from Texas. He was a college-educated man with enough money to buy a small outfit near the Powder River. While driving home from the town of Buffalo with a buckboard full of Christmas toys for his family and a winter's supply of food, he was shot in the back by an agent of the cattle barons who resented the encroachment of small-time stockmen like him. The wealthy cattlemen tried to control all the public grazing land by restricting membership in the Wyoming Stock Growers Association, as if it were a country club. They ostracized from roundups and brandings cowboys and ranchers who were not members, then denounced them as rustlers. Tisdale's death, the second such cold-blooded murder, kicked off the Johnson County cattle war, which was no simple good-guy–bad-guy shootout but a complicated class struggle between landed gentry and less affluent settlers—a shocking reminder that the West was not an egalitarian sanctuary after all.

Fencing ultimately enforced boundaries, but barbed wire abrogated space. It was stretched across the beautiful valleys, into the mountains, over desert badlands, through buffalo grass. The "anything is possible" fever—the lure of any new place—was constricted. The integrity of the land as a geographical body, and the freedom to ride anywhere on it, were lost.

I punched cows with a young man named Martin, who is the great-grandson of John Tisdale. His inheritance is not the open land that Tisdale knew and prematurely lost but a rage against restraint.

Wyoming tips down as you head northeast; the highest ground—the Laramie Plains—is on the Colorado border. Up where I live, the Big Horn River leaks into difficult, arid terrain. In the basin where it's dammed, sandhill cranes gather and, with delicate legwork, slice through the stilled water. I was driving by with a rancher one morning when he commented that cranes are "old-fashioned." When I asked why, he said, "Because they mate for life." Then he looked at me with a twinkle in his eyes, as if to say he really did believe in such things but also understood why we break our own rules.

In all this open space, values crystalize quickly. People are strong on scruples but tenderhearted about quirky behavior. A friend and I found one ranch hand, who's "not quite right in the head," sitting in front of the badly decayed carcass of a cow, shaking his finger and saying, "Now, I don't want you to do this ever again!" When I asked what was wrong with him, I was told, "He's goofier than hell, just like the rest of us." Perhaps because the West is historically new, conventional morality is still felt to be less important than rockbottom truths. Though there's always a lot of teasing and sparring, people are blunt with one another, sometimes even cruel, believing honesty is stronger medicine than sympathy, which may console but often conceals.

The formality that goes hand in hand with the rowdiness is known as the Western Code. It's a list of practical do's and don'ts, faithfully observed. A friend, Cliff, who runs a trapline in the winter, cut off half his foot while chopping a hole in the ice. Alone, he dragged himself to his pickup and headed for town, stopping to open the ranch gate as he left, and getting out to close it again, thus losing, in his observance of rules, precious time and blood. Later, he commented, "How would it look, them having to come to the hospital to tell me their cows had gotten out?"

Accustomed to emergencies, my friends doctor each other from the vet's bag with relish. When one old-timer suffered a heart attack in hunting camp, his partner quickly stirred up a brew of red horse liniment and hot water and made the half-conscious victim drink it, then tied him onto a horse and led him twenty miles to town. He regained consciousness and lived.

The roominess of the state has affected political attitudes as well. Ranchers keep up with world politics and the convulsions of the economy but are basically isolationists. Being used to running their own small empires of land and livestock, they're suspicious of big government. It's a "don't fence me in" holdover from a century ago. They still want the elbow room their grandfathers had, so they're strongly conservative, but with a populist twist.

Summer is the season when we get our "cowboy tans"—on the lower parts of our faces and on three fourths of our arms. Excessive heat, in the nineties and higher, sends us outside with the mosquitoes. In winter we're tucked inside our houses, and the white wasteland outside appears to be expanding, but in summer all the greenery abridges space. Summer is a go-ahead season. Every living thing is off the block and in the race: battalions of bugs in flight and biting; bats swinging around my log cabin as if the bases were loaded and someone had hit a home run. Some of summer's high-speed growth is ominous: larkspur, death camas, and green greasewood can kill sheep—an ironic idea, dying in this desert from eating what is too verdant. With sixteen hours of daylight, farmers and ranchers irrigate feverishly. There are first, second, and third cuttings of hay, some crews averaging only four hours of sleep a night for weeks. And, like the cowboys who in summer ride the night rodeo circuit, nighthawks make daredevil dives at dusk with an eerie whirring sound like a plane going down on the shimmering horizon.

In the town where I live, they've had to board up the dance-hall windows because there have been so many fights. There's so little to do except work that people wind up in a state of idle agitation that becomes fatalistic, as if there were nothing to be done about all this untapped energy. So the dark side to the grandeur of these spaces is the small-mindedness that seals people in. Men become hermits; women go mad. Cabin fever explodes into suicides, or into grudges and lifelong family feuds. Two sisters in my area inherited a ranch but found they couldn't get along. They fenced the place in half. When one's cows got out and mixed with the other's, the women went at each other with shovels. They ended up in the same hospital room but never spoke a word to each other for the rest of their lives.

After the brief lushness of summer, the sun moves south. The range grass is brown. Livestock is trailed back down from the mountains. Water holes begin to frost over at night. Last fall Martin asked me to accompany him on a pack trip. With five horses, we followed a river into the mountains behind the tiny Wyoming town of Mee-teetse. Groves of aspen, red and orange, gave off a light that made us look toasted. Our hunting camp was so high that clouds skidded across our foreheads, then slowed to sail out across the warm valleys. Except for a bull moose who wandered into our camp and mistook our black gelding for a rival, we shot at nothing.

One of our evening entertainments was to watch the night sky. My dog, a dingo bred to herd sheep, also came on the trip. He is so used to the silence and empty skies that when an airplane flies over he always looks up and eyes the distant intruder quizzically. The sky, lately, seems to be much more crowded than it used to be. Satellites make their silent passes in the dark with great regularity. We counted eighteen in one hour's viewing. How odd to think that while they circumnavigated the planet, Martin and I had moved only six miles into our local wilderness and had seen no other human for the two weeks we stayed there.

At night, by moonlight, the land is whittled to slivers—a ridge, a river, a strip of grassland stretching to the mountains, then the huge sky. One morning a full moon was setting in the west just as the sun was rising. I felt precariously balanced between the two as I loped across a meadow. For a moment, I could believe that the stars, which were still visible, work like cooper's bands, holding together everything above Wyoming.

Space has a spiritual equivalent and can heal what is divided and burdensome in us. My grandchildren will probably use space shuttles for a honeymoon trip or to recover from heart attacks, but closer to home we might also learn how to carry space inside ourselves in the effortless way we carry our skins. Space represents sanity, not a life purified, dull, or "spaced out," but one that might accommodate intelligently any idea or situation.

From the clayey soil of northern Wyoming is mined bentonite, which is used as a filler in candy, gum, and lipstick. We Americans are great on fillers, as if what we have, what we are, is not enough. We have a cultural tendency toward denial, but, being affluent, we strangle ourselves with what we can buy. We have only to look at the houses we build to see how we build *against* space, the way we drink against pain and loneliness. We fill up space as if it were a pie shell, with things whose opacity further obstructs our ability to see what is already there.

KATHLEEN NORRIS

When first approached to write an essay for *The Place Within*, Kathleen Norris was silent for a while. "Well, there is this *tree* I like quite a bit . . ." It did not seem an auspicious subject for an essay, but, having read Norris's *Dakota: A Spiritual Journey*, the editor should have had more faith. Like many of the connected essays in *Dakota*, "Dreaming of Trees" begins with one small subject, only, moments later, to fly toward far bigger ones. In "Dreaming of Trees," the author meditates not just on the scarcity of trees in her Dakota landscape but on the interplay between the material and the spiritual worlds, between the cozy consolation of things and the freedom of space.

D R E A M I N G

O F

T R E E S

I have noticed in my life that all men have a liking for some special animal, tree, plant, or spot of earth. If men would pay more attention to these preferences and seek what is best to do in order to make themselves worthy . . . they might have dreams which would purify their lives. . . .

—BRAVE BUFFALO, SIOUX
in *By the Power of Their Dreams*

JIM BURDEN, THE NARRATOR OF WILLA CATHER'S *MY ANTONIA*, says of the Nebraska prairie to which he has moved from Virginia that "trees were so rare in that country, and they had to make such a hard fight to grow, that we used to feel anxious about them, and visit them as if they were persons." He adds, "It must have been the scarcity of detail in that tawny landscape that made detail so precious."

Burden is speaking of the American frontier at the end of the nineteenth century, but his words ring true for a prairie dweller one hundred years later. The small town where I live, like most towns in the western Dakotas, was plunked down on a treeless plain. Settlement followed the path of railroad lines, not rivers, and nearly all of the trees, like all the buildings, had to be planted. Photographs of our backyard taken in the 1920s, when my mother was a child, offer a view of buttes, a stark horizon. No houses. No trees. Even now, standing in the dirt alley to the east of our house, I can look north, down a three-block length of hedges and trees, to open country.

My mother can remember when most of the trees on our street, and in the town itself, were mere saplings. My husband and I had to take down a lovely cottonwood a few years ago—it was crowding a basement wall—and a neighbor came by to mourn with us. He was five years old when that tree was planted; he's now in his seventies. It was strange to think that we were erasing a part of his childhood. My husband says that destroying that tree still makes him sad, that he imagined it to be like killing an elephant, something larger, wiser, and more mysterious than himself. I miss the tree for the marvelous play of light and shade it made on our kitchen windows in the late afternoon.

But it's folly to miss trees here, where as one friend says, out of a hundred things that can happen to a tree, ninety-nine of them are bad. A lengthy drought in the 1980s killed off many of the aging shelter belts around farmhouses, as well as windbreaks in cropland that were first planted, with government assistance, in the 1930s. Though it's been a good conservation practice, I doubt that there will be money available to replant them. Like so many human institutions of the western plains, these rows of trees will simply fade away.

Even the monks at a nearby monastery, who have planted and tended trees here for nearly a hundred years, tend to be fatalistic about it. They work hard—one monk I know says that in his nineteen years at the monastery he's planted nearly a hundred trees—and on hot summer days it's a common sight to see a monk on a small tractor hauling a home-rigged tank that holds thirteen hundred gallons to water trees in the cemetery, the orchard, the western ridge. But the monks also know that to care for a tree in western Dakota is to transcend work; it becomes a form of prayer, or as St. Paul said, a "hope in things unseen." Maybe that's why they're so good at it, so persistent in their efforts.

I marvel at the fecundity of a crabapple tree that my grandmother planted at the north edge of our backyard that has drawn four generations of children to its branches and tart, rosy fruit. I worry about the two elms just south of the garden plot, weakened by drought and then disease. Will we have the energy, the hope, to replace them? Maybe with cottonwoods, the Siouxland variety developed for this harsh climate. But most of all, when I dream of trees here, when I visit them, they are the trees out in the open, trees I can take no responsibility for, but consider to be my friends.

One of my favorites stands at the edge of a large pasture on the outskirts of Mandan, North Dakota. A young, small tree—what kind I don't even know, but from the highway it looks like a burr oak—nudges a fence, its branches straddling the barbed wire. There it has persisted for God knows how long with one half of it in vigorous leaf, the other rubbed bare by cattle. There are no other trees in that pasture. This tree, like a tough little juniper that emerges from the lodgepole pines of the Slim Buttes, far to the south, to stand alone on a limestone outcropping, reminds me of an elegantly carved figurehead on a sailing ship's prow, riding magnificently the dry prairie winds that will one day help to tear it down.

Many such glimpses abide: a tall, leafy locust split down the middle by a lightning strike; a lone Russian olive standing like a sentry near a pasture gate, its black branches vivid beneath the shimmery leaves. I picture the large burr oak in a ranch family's yard; it's been pruned and shaped to a striking perfection, and is the one tree I know of here that would not look out of place on a New England village common. And I mourn what I think of as the political trees, an eerie landscape of waterlogged dead and dying trees just west of Mobridge and the Missouri River, casualties of the Oahe Dam. They make me treasure all the more the profusion of trees—willow, box elder, elm, cottonwood, wild plums, in the vast Missouri bottomland at Fort Yates, Cannonball, and Bismarck.

The immensity of land and sky in the western Dakotas allows for few trees, and I love the way that treelessness reveals the contours of the land, the way that each tree that remains seems a message bearer. I love what trees signify in the open country. The Audubon field book describes the burr oak as "a pioneer tree, invading the prairie grassland," and I try to listen to what these "volunteers" have to say about persistence, the strength of water, seeds, and roots, the awesome whimsy of birds scattering seed in their excrement, casting not only oak but small groves of Russian olive in their wake. Cottonwoods need more water; their presence signifies groundwater, or the meanderings of a creek. Sometimes, in the distance, you glimpse what looks like a stand of scrub brush or chokecherry bushes. But if you turn off the asphalt two-lane highway onto a gravel road, you find that what you've seen is the tops of tall cottonwoods standing in glory along a creek bottom, accompanied by willows.

Nearly every morning I pass by a young tree—some sort of locust—that signifies survival against all odds. Most likely it was stripped bare in its earliest years, when every summer a farmer mowed the roadside ditch for hay. But it lived on, a leaf or two surviving each year, until the farmer noticed it and decided to mow around it. It's now nearly seven feet tall, a clever tree standing alone at the very bottom of the shallow ditch, catching what moisture it can. It feels natural for me to converse with it, in any season, in the light just before dawn.

I share with this tree years of mornings, a moonset so enormous and red I mistook it for a fire in the distance, an ice storm with winds so sharp I couldn't keep walking westward and had to return home. Years of painterly skies at dawn. Foxes on the run, cats on the hunt. For much of my walk I am as treeless as the land around me, but on my way back into town I pass a large grove, an entrance to a drive-in movie theater, long since gone. If the wind is up, the trees roar like the ocean. Sometimes sheep are grazing there, and even though I expect to see them, they startle me with their cries, which sound remarkably like those of a human infant. This past summer the grove was the haunt of kestrels, and I often watched them maneuvering in the sky, wondering what it would feel like to ride backwards, forwards, sideways on the currents of air.

Our trees, our treelessness, are, as so much in life, a matter of perspective. One summer both my father-in-law and my mother were visiting. He was raised in New York State, and couldn't get over the lack of trees. I think he found it terrifying, as many easterners do. My mother kept telling him that there were many more trees here now than when she was a girl, so many that the countryside seemed luxuriant. Maybe trees are a luxury here; the question then becomes, how many do we need?

My mother has told me that she first encountered the notion of a forest from the illustrations in Grimms' fairy tales. She wanted so badly to see a forest, any forest, that she would crawl under the lilac bushes that her mother had planted by the front door and pretend she was in the Black Forest. I used to pretend—I can no longer remember what—with the honeysuckle bushes in the first backyard I remember, in Arlington, Virginia. I spent a lot of time with them, watching from my two-seat glider swing. The one great tree in that backyard, an elm, was a powerful symbol for me, a tree of family myth, because when I was five and my brother nine, he had used it to run away from home. Climbing out his second-story bedroom window to get away from a baby-sitter he disliked, he'd spent an afternoon at a neighborhood drugstore, reading comic books. I remember looking up at that tree, after the great event, trying to imagine that freedom. I also examined the branches from the upstairs window, and doubted that I'd ever have the nerve to make the leap.

We left Virginia when I was seven, and moved to Illinois. I lost the honeysuckle, and the other trees of my early childhood—dogwood, magnolia, sassafras, sycamore, and the enormous weeping willow and white oak of a nursery school in the countryside where my mother had enrolled me. I have only faint memories of the fabled cherry trees of Washington, D.C., and suspect that what I recall of the blossoms comes mainly from having been told about them, and looking at family photographs.

Beach Park, Illinois, just north of Waukegan, was still rural in 1954; I walked to a four-room country school. We lived in a small, new suburb on acre lots, where the trees were saplings. But across the street was a plowed field with an island of tall trees in the center. Oak, elm, aspen. Although it was good to know that the trees were there, a brooding, comforting presence, I never ventured into them. I much preferred what was close at hand, the stands of pussy willow in the roadside ditch.

The trees of northern Illinois were lost to me when we moved to Honolulu in 1959, and I learned a new vocabulary: Banyan. Hala. Koa. Bamboo. My favorite tree on all of Oahu was (and is) the magnificent spreading monkeypod of Moanalua Gardens. Even the stench and incessant roar of traffic on an encroaching freeway doesn't diminish its beauty. The other tree I came to love in Honolulu is the eucalyptus that stands by the wooden stairway of Old School Hall on my high school campus, a building erected in the 1860s. It made me happy to study English in a building that had stood when Emily

Dickinson was alive, and the stately tree, its bark variegated like a fragile nineteenth-century endpaper, seemed a suitable companion in that happiness.

I recall testing an ancient legend on the slopes of Kilauea, on the Big Island, with some high school girlfriends. We picked several sassy, fringed blooms of the native lehua tree, and sure enough, were sprinkled with rain on our hike back to our lodge. I also recall harvesting bananas in our backyard, a process that involved arming myself with a machete and cutting down the entire tree—it is in fact a form of grass, a thick and pulpy weed. I shook out the spiders and let the tiny bananas, over twenty pounds worth, ripen in a paper sack. They're much sweeter than anything you can buy in a grocery store. Years later, that experience rescued me. At a cocktail party in New York City, a man recently returned from Brazil declared that the trouble with America was that you couldn't buy a decent machete. While I had no idea if the family machete was a good one or not, I was the only person in the group who'd actually used one, and what had been a dreary, sodden literary gathering became more interesting.

By the time I went to college, in Vermont, I had lost the language of deciduous trees. People had to name for me the maple, oak, sumac, and beech. I recognized birches from photographs, and poems. As fine and fabled as it is, now that I've been on the Plains for over twenty years, New England foliage seems profligate to me, too showy. Here, in the fall, the groves of ash and poplars planted as windbreaks glow in a golden, Italianate light, and I feel as if I am in a painting by Giotto, or Fra Angelico. A dusty, spare, but lovely place in Tuscany, or western Dakota.

Each December I visit my family in Honolulu, traveling from the wintry Plains to what I call the green world. It is profligate to the extreme; in a yard not much bigger than my own is an enormous mango tree, and also lime, tangerine, pomengranate, pomelo, mountain apple, lichee, hibiscus, hala, lehua, plumeria, and Norfolk Island pine. Like many Hawaii residents, we often top a pine to make a Christmas tree.

After all of that, I find it an odd joy to return to winter, to a stark white world. And I dream of trees, wondering if sometimes I would rather dream of trees than have so many close at hand. Even when it means adjusting to a temperature more than 100 degrees colder than in Hawaii, it's the dryness of the Plains that most affects me. My face and hands turn to tree bark. In the heart of winter the green world is dormant, not yet hoped-for. Moisture is scarce—even our snow is dry—and the vast space around the bare branches of trees is all the more a presence.

This brings me back to where I began, with Jim Burden's reflection on scarcity. If scarcity makes things more precious, what does it mean to choose the spare world over one in which we are sated with abundance? Is this the spiritual dimension that Brave Buffalo leads us to? Does living in a place with so few trees bring with it certain responsibilities? Gratitude, for example? The painful acceptance that underlies Psalm 16's "Welcome indeed the heritage that falls to me"?

Monastic men and women tell me that one question that bites pretty hard in their early years in the monastery is why anyone would choose to live this way, deprived of the autonomy and abundance of choices that middle-class Americans take for granted. We're taught all our lives to "keep our options open," but a commitment to monastic life puts an end to that. It is not a choice but a call, and often the people who last in a monastery are those who struggle through their early years reminding themselves of that fact. One sister told me that it wasn't until she had entered monastic formation that the words of Jesus in John 15:16 had any significance in her life: "Ye have not chosen me, but I have chosen you. . . ."

Stark words in a stark environment. A monk in his early thirties once told me that he'd come to the monastery not realizing what a shock it would be to suddenly not have to compete for the things that young men are conditioned to compete for in American society, in his words, "a good salary, a cool car, and a pretty girlfriend." "When all of that was suddenly gone," he added, "and held of no account, I felt as if my whole life were a lie. It took me years to find out who God wanted me to be."

What does it mean to become simple? I think of the abbey of New Mellary in Iowa, the walls of its church long plastered over, until the architectural consultant they had hired to help them remodel discovered that underneath the plaster were walls of native stone. The monks themselves did the work of uncovering them, and now the church is a place where one can sit and wait and watch the play of sunlight and shadow, a place made holy by the simple glory of light on stone.

What would I find in my own heart, if the noise of the world were silenced? Who would I be? Who will I be, when loss or crisis or the depredations of time take away the trappings of success, of self-importance, even personality itself? Could the trees of my beloved Plains, or the lack of them, help me to know? The first monks read the earth as the work and word of God, a creation that was spoken into being. "Study fish," advises St. Gregory of Nazianzus. "In the water they fly, and they find the air they need in the water. They would die in our atmosphere, just as we would die in the water. Watch their habits, their way of mating and procreating their kind, their beauty, their permanent homes and their wanderings." Look, Gregory says, "at the bees and the spiders. Where do their love of work and their ingenuity come from? Can you explain it and arrive at an understanding of the wisdom they point to?"

The wisdom of the few, struggling trees on the Plains, and the vast spaces around them, are a continual reminder that my life is cluttered by comparison. At home, an abundance of books and papers overlays the heavy furniture I inherited from my grandparents. A perfectly simple room, with one perfect object to meditate on, remains a dream until I step outside, onto the Plains. A tree. A butte. The sunrise. It always makes me wonder: What is enough? Are there enough trees here? As always, it seems that the more I can distinguish my true needs from my wants, it is a shock to realize how little *is* enough.

On a summer night, between 2:00 and 3:00 A.M., a front moves in and I awake. A fierce wind has stirred the trees. It's been hot for so long, I go outdoors to luxuriate in the newly cooled air. A friend from far away is sleeping in my studio, and I want to say the prayers that will protect him, give him needed rest. I want my husband's sleep to help him heal from the pain of recent surgery. The trees that fan me are the fruit of others' labor, planted by an earlier generation of plains dwellers who longed for trees to shelter them. The land resisted, but let them have these few. I am startled by something flashing through the trees—it is the Pleiades, all seven of them plainly visible with the naked eye. This is another's work, and a mystery. And it is enough.

GERALD EARLY

erald Early's essays reveal the brilliantly arch
mind of an intellectual in the best—and
increasingly rare—sense of this word. Whether
writing about high culture or pop culture,
literature or boxing, Early's essays pander to no
one. With a wry humor and a critical eye,
Early's work continually seeks truth in
observation rather than in ideology, always
subverting notions of what a contemporary
black intellectual "should" think. In "St. Louis:
The Midwestern Long Good-bye," Early turns
his eye toward the city he has called home
since 1982. It is a sometimes humorous, always
ironic portrait of an outwardly comfortable,
self-sufficient city. In particular, Early's essay
captures the "odd angle of Being" for the city's
black inhabitants, who have never quite known,
despite their long history here, whether this
place is truly "home."

ST. LOUIS:
THE MIDWESTERN
LONG GOOD-BYE

PART ONE: EMBARRASSED SPLENDOR

It is a curious, if not altogether unusual, fact about St. Louis that there is a tendency for at least a certain class of its citizens to apologize for having what appears to them the bland misfortune of living here. This is almost exclusively true of people who are not natives, that is, were not born in St. Louis, especially those born in other major American cities, although I do hear it from time to time from a few who have spent their entire lives here. This singular feeling of inadequacy does not arise from the fact that St. Louis, in spying its downtown skyline, does not seem as relentlessly modernist, as extravagantly Art Deco, as some other cities. It is not a place of many imposing skyscrapers or an overly done up downtown that is like a movie set through which tourists can move with a supremely untroubled sense of distraction (although our waterfront district, Laclede's Landing, has all the Yuppie, faked "authenticity" of Memphis's Beale Street, the contrived spectacle of nineteenth-century gentility without the slave pens and the wharves and the rats and the life-threatening dives, in short, without the stuff that made nineteenth-century St. Louis, for better and for worse, a real place).

St. Louis has a certain modesty in its outline that belies a true richness in its architecture and a kind of subtle beauty in its westward sprawl from the Mississippi. True, on its most ordinary days, the river seems little more than a toxic waste dump. "What's so great about this river?" my oldest daughter said just a year ago as we were standing at a pier on an afternoon, waiting for my mother, who was buying souvenirs in one of the shops. "It looks horrible and it smells bad." I don't recall ever going to Mississippi simply to see the river because there is, normally, nothing to see, although to take visiting friends and relatives on the River Road to Pere Marquette is scenic enough, indeed, a strikingly lyrical ride. But when the river floods, as it has done twice in the last five years, it seems a muddy magnificence, as mythic and merciless, as grandiose in its apostrophized fury and holy indifference, as Twain's river in *Huckleberry Finn*, as Faulkner's river in "Old Man," as Wright's river in "Down by the Riverside." During the last flood, I was flying back from New York and as the plane circled St. Louis, the river seemed everywhere, certainly everywhere in Illinois and upstate, everything overturned, unmoored, submerged, and uprooted, as if, were God to grant a new heaven and a new earth, then this might be it; a sight of both dread and absurdity, of tragedy and resignation, of suffering and renewal. Not the end of everything is it, but surely the end of some things. And I felt especially as if I were being reminded that, after all, nature is nature and we are, well, what we are, both a part of nature and apart from it. Nothing reminds one of this so well as the flooding Mississippi.

St. Louis possesses a set of charms that make it a city far more worthwhile to see than, say, Kansas City or Milwaukee or Cincinnati. The most compelling man-made landmark in the United States is the St. Louis Gateway Arch, a startling engineering feat, finished in 1965 after seven years of construction. It stands at 632 feet from base to apex. It is, perhaps, as a spectacle the great American rune, an ineffable symbol of the enigma of the great American adventure, the linchpin of East and West that defines what the Middle West is. "That's my middle west," writes Fitzgerald in *The Great Gatsby*, "not the wheat or the prairies or the lost Swede towns, but the thrilling returning trains of my youth. . . ." And my Middle West is that inverted tuning fork pointed straight in the St. Louis sky, humming with a strange running current of subterranean energy, the hieroglyphic of eminence of the Middle West's youthfulness. To go up in the Arch—a crazy elevator ride where one goes both up and sideways, and once reaching the top, tries to see St. Louis from a set of small windows that on crowded days are impossible to get to, and at less frequented times seem a bit of a disappointment—this excursion is pointless. For the splendor of the Arch, the silver metal looking almost liquidly transparent in the sun, opaque as an ancient ruin in the rain, the experience of this technical marvel, is standing outside and looking up at it. It was once claimed that only Lenin's Tomb and the two Disney theme parks drew more tourists than the Arch. Still, some of us in St. Louis demur.

I remember once talking to a colleague of mine who works at a prestigious school on the East Coast. "So, you're still out there, heh?" he said, with a shake of the head as if I might feel better to know that he was pitying rather than patronizing me. And I found myself being apologetic: "Well, you know, St. Louis is not such a bad place." I am not sure if this apology, abject and unseemly as it was, resulted from a natural timidity to contradict the stupid and the arrogant, or was the cowering acknowledgment of a paralyzing sense of civic inferiority. I was born and reared in Philadelphia, so perhaps my life here since 1982 has been a long period of cultural slumming, so to speak, in the great American outback. Admittedly, when I first came to St. Louis, I thought it to be a barbaric place for two reasons principally: first, it had no public transportation worthy of the name; and second, it was a town that was impossible to walk in. For the first few years here, I felt imprisoned by my need for a car, which, frankly, I considered to be unnatural and a cause of considerable anxiety. But I have learned since my earliest days here that certain stretches of neighborhood are quite walkable, even if the city as a whole is not.

The Hill, for instance, reminds me of the Little Italy of my native South Philadelphia, and when I lived in an apartment in University City, I used walk around the area quite often. Indeed, I used to frequently walk to work as the university was close by. Later, when I moved to Olivette, a community just west of University City, I used to walk and run in the park there all the time. Getting a dog after moving to Webster Groves has forced me to walk over a good portion of this town, past Webster University, Eden Seminary, the shops of Old Webster, the Hawken House, the YMCA, much to my pleasure, perhaps the sole pleasure I have discovered in owning a dog. Also, because its public transportation, despite the recent opening of the Metro Link—an elevated train which my very eastern mother refers to as "one-half of one line of a decent train system"—is still not very well developed, the city has taken on, for me, a certain quaint stillness or still quaintness that seems a positive relief whenever I return here from a sojourn in the East, where people seem utterly murderous in their attempt to get somewhere.

It is almost a pleasure to drive in St. Louis, probably in no small measure because there is a strong possibility that one will be able to park one's car upon arriving somewhere. I certainly never felt that way back east. I no longer feel I have lost anything or sacrificed anything to live here. There is no need for me to feel that way, since others have decided to feel that way for me. I have, regrettably and regularly, encountered from people from either coast the sense that it must be a great grief, a wide, wild sorrow to have to live in the Middle West, and even greater the tragedy not to live in Chicago, apparently the sole midwestern location that people on either coast take seriously.

For people in St. Louis, a city once described by former Missouri senator Thomas Eagleton,* who, at the time, was heading an effort to get us a new professional football team, as "a raucous Des Moines," their apologies take many forms. The progressives, leftists, radicals, and liberal elements always talk about how "conservative" the city is, as if to imply that their great self-righteous efforts to make us all better human beings would not be like so many seeds scattered on barren soil if they lived where the population was not so backward and "rich, white men did not run everything." This apology is of course the progressive's own confession that he or she is nothing more than a second-rate leftist; otherwise he or she wouldn't be stuck in this political roadshow called St. Louis where the local wrangling seems downright genteel compared to Chicago or any major East Coast city; where they can scarcely mount a good street demonstration; and where the police do not have nearly the reputation for beat-

---

* Senator Eagleton is a fine man and was a capable, skilled politician during his days in public office. However, to the world outside Missouri he will simply be remembered as the "nutcase" that George McGovern selected as his running mate in the 1972 presidential election. Eagleton was kicked in unceremonious and cowardly fashion from the ticket after an outcry about his having been given electro-shock treatment many years earlier, and replaced by Sargent Shriver. McGovern went down in ignominious and deserved defeat at the hands of Richard M. Nixon.

ing the crap out of people that they do in other places. (Indeed, when I first moved to St. Louis, I thought the police here needed lessons from the cops in Philadelphia in how to intimidate and brutalize citizens in a fruitless effort to control crime, although I am sure there are many who can testify to the fact, as we have no shortage of police brutality claims and accusations, that the police in St. Louis are no kindness, or as Raymond Chandler so aptly put it, "[no] way has yet been invented to say good-bye to them.")

Now, the rich, white men who run St. Louis are collectively called Civic Progress, and progress civically we surely do under the guidance of these wonderful and wise patricians of our order. Most of them are either the leading CEOs—St. Louis has an extraordinary number of corporate headquarters here, including McDonnell-Douglas, TWA, Anheuser-Busch, Ralston-Purina, and Monsanto—or the old St. Louis money families, or both.* As a ruling class goes, it is no better or worse than the ruling classes of rich, white men who run everything that is worth running in the United States, despite the strenuous efforts of our most committed leftists and multiculturalists at least to give us, if not a ruling class at all, a ruling class "that looks like America." Some of the blacks who live here will also complain about

---

* St. Louis lost its professional football team, the Cardinals, because its owner, Bill Bidwell, was not permitted to join Civic Progress. Indeed, he was snubbed by the ruling class here. The poor man actually saw his team as a business, not a hobby, and needed his income from it. In any case, in 1988, Bidwell moved his team to Phoenix, where, presumably, the local ruling class will not snub him. In 1995, St. Louis acquired a new professional team, the former Los Angeles Rams. Presumably, too, its owner, Georgia Frontiere, the hotsy-totsy sixty-something-year-old blonde who grew up here, although she never gave the town a passing thought for nearly her entire adult life until we prostrated ourselves in front of her like a cash cow begging to be bilked, will not be snubbed by our ruling class—saviour that she is by being willing to come here to grow richer instead of some other sexier place, and thus save our civic pride. (Professional sports team owners resemble no one so much in our cultural history as southern plantation owners.) We have built an indoor stadium, the TWA Dome, another civic tribute to business mismanagement as TWA is virtually bankrupt, to the tune of nearly $300 million in her honor and to serve as a better romper room for her football players. When the ruins of this are uncovered five thousand years from now, it may be thought by the inhabitants then that we, in simpler times, prayed to decidedly lesser gods. I am sure our new football owner will be a part of the Veiled Prophets' Ball, some odd, slightly Masonic, faintly racist (although black people now attend in fairly representative numbers and surely some black girl will one day soon be named Veiled Prophet Queen), decidedly atavistic, social register event of the ruling class, where it seems to take both itself and its amusements seriously.

the "conservatism," compared to those bastions of African American political disruption on the East and West Coasts. This too merely reflects that they feel themselves second-raters. Otherwise, they would be where the action supposedly is. The leftists and the African Americans felt a great deal better about themselves when finally, in 1993, a black, Freeman Bosley, Jr.—a man for whom politics is something like the family business, and who combines all the inevitability of a political hack with all the public expectancy of something approaching leadership—was elected mayor of the city. It was embarrassing for them to have a city that is over 40 percent black and not have a black mayor. To have that symbol of progressive change pass us by for so many years *really* made the place seem like a backwater. "We're so conservative, we can't even elect a black mayor," they said. Indeed, the major political offices of the city—the mayor, the police chief, and the city comptroller—are all in the hands of blacks. It is nice for the progressives and the blacks to know that mediocre black leadership can have equal access to the paltry patronage that's left, and that mediocre white leadership controlled for so long.

I must explain a small but important feature of St. Louis's political geography before I go on. The city of St. Louis, with its huge black population (mostly located in North St. Louis, which I will discuss a bit more momentarily), its overwhelmingly black public schools (wretched places, naturally), its high crime ("I try to avoid the city at night except if I'm going to a concert or a ball game," say your average suburban residents), and its eroding tax base (middle-class whites and blacks are fleeing with abandon), is a distinct entity from St. Louis County, although residents here will often refer to the entire region as "St. Louis" in a generic way. As most people who live here have intercourse with and carry on their lives almost daily traveling between both the city and the county, both constitute the identity of the place called St. Louis. The county cannot be seen simply as the suburbs or mere bedroom communities. It consists of independent municipalities, with their own mayors, police forces, fire departments, schools, and the like. Some of them, like Ladue (where some of our richest and most famous citizens live), Clayton (which has our best, our richest public school system), and Frontenac (where our local Neiman-Marcus and Saks Fifth Avenue are located) are lily-white and very exclusive.

Some, like Webster Groves, where I live, boast a considerable history and families who go back many generations. Some, like Kinloch and Wellston, are all-black, very crime-ridden, and very poor, which is, of course, no news as this seems the chronic condition of a significant number of blacks in America. University City prides itself on its diversity—the most rabbinical schools and Afrocentric bookstores—and the fact that it has the closest thing to Harvard Square in an area called the Loop, a mere few blocks from Washington University, the most renowned school in Missouri. Richmond Heights can claim the area's busiest and biggest mall, the Galleria, and one of the principal seminaries. (Webster Groves has the other.) Crève Coeur has the craziest zoning and Kirkwood the best comic book store. Chesterfield may have the hottest real estate development, while Town and Country may have the cleanest streets. The vast majority of people who make up the region known as St. Louis live in the county, over two million. (Considerably less than a million live in the city of St. Louis.) If there is one side of America's political reality in Civic Progress and the existence of an upper-crust ruling class, this bewildering array of townships, this multiplicity of municipal identities is another side of that same reality, the contending, contentious middle-level groups.

People who live in the city assert this with a certain pride as if they, at least, are not abandoning *their* civic duty by running off and leaving the poor behind like the modern-day lepers everybody knows the poor really are.* The great advantage that those who live in the city have are these: they live in the area of the most compelling and original architecture, and of all the cultural institutions. All professional baseball, football, and hockey are played downtown. The sym-

---

* I am told by several friends and acquaintances, both black and white, that as a middle-class black and, of course, a role model (apparently a professional activity, although I do not know it), I ought to be living in the city instead of the golden triangle of Webster Groves. To those blacks who feel that way, I say that I owe it to the memory of Martin Luther King, Jr., and the continued success of Affirmative Action to integrate wherever and whenever I can. To those whites who feel that way, I say that I have had, after all, the experience of living with and among black folk for many years, having in the process learned their cultural ways and habits to such a degree that I might be said to have some ethnographic expertise about them. "I think you should try living among them now," I say, "as I am sure you will find it as enriching and valuable as I did. There are a good many vacant places going begging in North St. Louis." Nothing follows this but silence.

phony performs there, as do two of our three major theater companies. Most major concerts are held there, and virtually any jazz worthy of the name can only be heard there. The zoo, the art museum, the history museum, and our outdoor musical theater—the Muny—are all located in Forest Park, which is in the city. Indeed, Forest Park, dedicated in 1876, is one of our major parks. The other major park, Tower Grove Park, was donated to the city by Henry Shaw, the founder of the Botanical Gardens. And the Botanical Gardens, among the most beautiful places to visit in St. Louis, and the one of the finest gardens of their type anywhere in the world, are also in the city. In short, the residents of the county need the city if they want the standard cultural amenities that make suburban living bearable, in fact, that make suburban living possible.

This brings up another way that people apologize for St. Louis: conjuring up this cultural life. All cities and towns do this sort of boosterism, naturally, but there is a certain pitch of desperation in St. Louis's push for cultural relevance. In the Loop area of University City is the St. Louis Walk of Fame, where there is concerted effort to memorialize in concrete every famous, noteworthy person who seemingly ever so much as ate a meal in the environs of St. Louis. I say environs because in our lust for an impressive roster of cultural figures, people who are actually connected to East St. Louis (which is across the river in Illinois and totally unconnected to St. Louis), like dancer Katherine Dunham, track star Jackie Joyner Kersee, and trumpeter Miles Davis, are included. I am not sure if singer Leon Thomas, also of East St. Louis, is included. If not, he will be eventually.

These people played in clubs in St. Louis or competed in St. Louis, so they are connected to the city in some way, I suppose. As with any big city, a fair share of significant people have come from here: Chuck Berry, Tennessee Williams, T. S. Eliot, Dick Gregory, Kate Chopin, Michael and Leon Spinks,* John Goodman. Scott Joplin lived

---

* The emergence of the Spinks brothers as a result of the 1976 Olympics proved a bit of an embarrassment to St. Louis as they both grew up in the Pruitt-Igoe housing project, a disastrously failed experiment in public housing. Pruitt-Igoe consisted of thirty-three eleven-story buildings with a combined capacity for three thousand families. The first units opened in 1954 and 1955. It was one of the largest public housing projects of its kind and was meant to solve the problem of low-cost housing for the poor. By 1965, the projects were unlivable, plagued by crime and vandalism; there was little public transportation, no rec-

here for a brief spell, and Stan Musial came, never to leave. Howard Nemerov and Stanley Elkin died here. Charles Lindbergh's backers were St. Louisans and the plane that crossed the Atlantic was called the *Spirit of St. Louis*. But it was certainly not their St. Louis connection that made these people noteworthy. Indeed, St. Louis played very little role in their fame and some might say that, in certain cases, St. Louis was nearly an inimical force. What drove them to be what they became, in many instances, was their sheer hatred of the place. This is not unusual in the case of a great many famous people no matter where they are from, but I believe we in St. Louis feel a bit sheepish about providing such a negative impetus for so many. This might be particularly true for the noteworthy blacks who have come from here. Few ever liked the place, feeling stifled by the powerful tentacles of both black and white provincialism.* Hardly any returned to live here once they achieved fame.

PART TWO: THE ODD ANGLE OF BEING

My wife was just elected president of the St. Louis Chapter of the Junior League. She had been a member since 1988. This is historic because my wife is the first black woman ever to be president of this chapter. The first blacks ever to do anything in white America are always historic, although I doubt that it should be so, and one might expect, as integration is still a relatively new mode of social interaction (or engineering, depending on how one sees it) among us, that we will have our share of Jackie Robinsons for some many years yet. I wish my wife well as she embarks on this two-year enterprise. (As

---

reational space, no shopping, and no health services. By 1971, only seventeen of the thirty-three buildings were occupied. By 1975, the entire project was dynamited (shown repeatedly on national television during the Spinks brothers' rise to boxing glory). As historian James Neale Primm put it: ". . . the empty and sterile seventy acres became a stark reminder of good intentions gone wrong."

* Of course, the whites who write and promote the city's black heritage can find much white provincialism but no black provincialism for as far as the eye can see. All they see with blacks are "forms of resistance" and "courageous building of cultural institutions." These whites project their own fantasies of escaping their own white provincialism through the cultural hardiness and charisma of blacks. They do not have black skins and have never known black experience from the inside out. I have. And there is more soul-killing black provincialism than one can possibly imagine.

many black women in the area have decided to place the entire burden of the success of integration in the Junior League on my wife's shoulders, I am sure that the symbolic weight of all this is something she'd prefer not to have in addition to doing everything else all the white past presidents have normally had to do.) Indeed, as I am fond of several of the women in the Junior League, I wish the entire organization well. It is an exciting time for all of them.

The irony is that the headquarters of the Junior League is located in Frontenac where, a few years ago, I had my infamous run-in with local law enforcement and racist presumption while attending a Junior League Christmas Bazaar. A jewelry store owner in the mall where the bazaar took place saw me, the only black man, walking around among a number of white men and women who were also roaming about, and decided I was going to rob his store and rape his clerk. This might have been droll had it not been a dramatization of something very painful in American life for both blacks and whites. I provide a full account of that incident in a book I wrote called *Daughters: On Family and Fatherhood.* What is striking about the incident is that it seems to have a life of its own in St. Louis, where it became a major story at the time, November 1991. As recently as the latest Martin Luther King, Jr., holiday (January 15, 1996), I was interviewed about it. I was more than a little nonplussed as I could not possibly imagine that St. Louis has had no such incidents occur in the last five years. This must be a provincial place if such a relatively minor incident (I was not arrested or beaten by the police or even treated discourteously by them) is still news. "You make a wonderful story because you are the big-shot black professor at the big-shot university. There was no ambiguity in this case. You weren't some sixteen-year-old black kid with a couple of arrests wrongly accused of stealing a shirt from Sears," my wife said. "I just wish the news people would stop mentioning the Earlys with the incident in Frontenac. I'm not in a permanent state of protest against the town of Frontenac. We've been out there many times since the incident and nothing has happened."

I wonder how often the story of the Earlys' attempt to get an apology from Frontenac will come up during my wife's tenure as president of Junior League. It will doubtless be a period of adjustment for the Junior League itself as it discovers that wonderful note of complexity that the presence of Negroes adds to virtually every aspect of American life, for we blacks wind up relating to things in slightly odd angles, a bit in the manner that Thelonious Monk struck chords on the piano. I must admit that going to Frontenac, especially at night, as a black man, fills me with an intense degree of foreboding. The husbands of the other Junior League women, I am sure, never think about this. Oddly, I have experienced far less racism in St. Louis than in any other place I have ever lived.

When we first came to St. Louis, my wife decided, in order to get to know some people, to become very active in the local chapter of her college sorority, Alpha Kappa Alpha. This gave her an automatic entree to black St. Louis that I certainly never had and about which I was a bit envious. She became well acquainted with North St. Louis, and with black St. Louis life by slow stages (she was an outsider and so did not easily penetrate social circles long established by high school and church ties), particularly an area called the Ville where many of her sorority sisters lived. This was a remarkable neighborhood, run-down, defeated, a ghetto, but with the imprint of cultural self-sufficiency and pride. I was not necessarily impressed to learn that blacks like Dick Gregory and Chuck Berry came from this neighborhood. But I was overwhelmed by the number of institutions, functioning and defunct, that the neighborhood contained: all manner of businesses, from funeral homes to insurance companies, from groceries to barbershops, from real estate developers to newspaper offices.

Sumner High School, located in this area, was the first black high school west of the Mississippi. Most people acquainted with black American cultural history have heard of Madame C. J. Walker and her hair-products empire, but Annie Malone of St. Louis amassed a fortune nearly as great selling much the same stuff. She also started the Poro Beauty College in this area, an institution that did far more than merely train beauticians. A children's home in the area now bears the name of this industrious "race" woman. North St. Louis came to my consciousness as a political entity shortly after my arrival because of the huge fight over the fate of the Homer G. Phillips Hospital, which eventually closed in 1984. Blacks began to push for a full-service health facility as early as 1915, according to historian George Lipsitz. Black lawyer and northside leader Homer G. Phillips led the fight for the hospital. One year after his death (which seemed suspiciously like murder) in 1931, construction began on the "colored" hospital that bore his name, after years of agitation, broken promises, and not-so-benign neglect.

The protests to keep the hospital open were not so much for practical reasons as for emotional ones. The hospital was part of the identity of black St. Louis, a symbol of its struggle for recognition and fair treatment (despite the fact that the hospital was always a second-rate, underfunded facility where newborn babies, for instance, were kept in something resembling chicken coops, a clear intention of the policy of segregation whereby whites made sure that blacks never enjoyed the "normal" amenities of any aspect of American life). I understood as soon as I arrived in St. Louis that black people stood at a rather odd angle to the history of the place, as they do to virtually any place. If they were provincial, they were no more so than any other black folk I had ever met or lived with. For I was both moved and frightened by the Ville, a place that was at once so enormously and courageously self-supporting and so terribly self-contained and removed. The worst sort of social cliques are those of the oppressed ethnics, the worst sort of old-boy network is that of the oppressed elite. Always with such groups, merit doesn't count as much as who you're related to, who you know, or, in the case of black folk, how light your skin is.

The ethnics are always mightily aggrandized by ludicrous claims to petty power. The worst ruling class is the one with no real power or authority to rule. It's just like the Little Italy of my boyhood, I thought, which had seemed to me such a remarkable place. The only thing a sensible Italian American could want to do is to get out of this, I thought as a young man. This neighborhood is like being embalmed by your own terrors of what lies beyond it. It is everything as a black person you wish to embrace and escape simultaneously in a contradictory madness that almost always seems as if it will rip you in two. This has often made me wonder what blacks think of the ordinary symbols of our culture, of our American endeavor, in which they share. One day, while standing at the Arch with my youngest daughter (we had just left a Cardinal baseball game at Busch Memorial Stadium, a few blocks away, the place I remember as a boy watching on television a handsome, grim-faced black man named Bob Gibson mow down Red Sox and Tiger batters in the 1967 and 1968

World Series),* I asked her what she thought of it. "Well, it's the Gateway to the West, right?" she said. "I just can't figure out if it means you're supposed to stop here or go on. I can't figure out if it's saying hello to you or good-bye." Perhaps that is the mystery for blacks in St. Louis as well as they look at what life has meant to them in this city through its greatest symbol: Is it saying hello to me or good-bye?

---

* When Bob Gibson mowed down Yankee batters in the 1964 World Series, the Cardinals were still playing at the old ball field, Sportsman's Park. The Cardinals moved into Busch Memorial Stadium, a kind of all-purpose park meant to accommodate both baseball and football with its shape and artificial playing surface, in 1965. It is a decent place to see a ball game but lacks personality. Its inability to accommodate the capacity necessary for professional football led to the departure of the football Cardinals. At the 1966 All-Star game, played at Busch, New York Mets manager Casey Stengel remarked on how well the playing surface held the heat. My youngest daughter, who played in a high school marching band competition at the stadium on a very warm day last fall, agreed with that assessment.

WILLIAM KITTREDGE

When Bill Kittredge submitted "Taking Care of Our Horses" to *The Place Within*, it was with the apology, "Well, it's about Oregon—again." Kittredge, one of America's leading essayists, has written often about the MC ranch in southeastern Oregon where he grew up and continued to work until the age of thirty-five. What keeps drawing him back, it seems, is the mystery inherent in his own life: How did a buckaroo born straddling a horse manage to break away and become a writer? And did he truly break away? "Taking Care of Our Horses" is a moving tale not just about Oregon but about the universal relationship between fathers and sons, rebellion and return.

TAKING
CARE OF
OUR HORSES

AFTER HORSES WERE DOMESTICATED ON THE HIGH STEPPES OF Central Asia some four thousand years ago, a couple of different kinds of cultures evolved. One was made up of farming people who stayed home to tend crops—their villages evolved into cities and kingdoms and all that. The others were horse people who followed herds through the seasons, and never had a true home—they became warriors, employed by the kingdoms, inhabiting a horseback, traveling version of the right life.

The horseman's world where I grew up was without much in the way of law but ran inside the constraints of ironbound traditions. Days and work were ordered by a mostly unspoken but widely accepted code, which centered, at least as I understood it as a boy, on an utter refusal to admit fraility or defeat; weakness was to be suffered in silence.

At the end of the 1930s, in our sagebrush corner of the Great Basin, cowhands still thought of themselves as warriors, for hire, and rootless. In my boyhood I had a brush with initiation into their society.

Before I could read, I had learned to revere horsemen and cowhorses and pay attention to cookhouse manners. When I was maybe thirteen, after some seasons of imitating those men on the high sagebrush and lavarock deserts of southeastern Oregon with my grandfather's chuck-wagon buckaroo outfit, riding camp to camp with the branding crew,

I was given the high privilege of helping drive thirty or so saddle horses from the MC Ranch Remuda over the Warner Mountains to Lakeview, some thirty-five miles, for the Labor Day Rodeo (everybody who was capable of sitting a horse went in and at least rode in the parades).

The best part of that horse drive came when we cantered down out of a small canyon onto the asphalt streets through the little business center of Lakeview on our way to the stockyards. People lined the sidewalks as we clattered along, townspeople and men and women in off the ranches; and kids—that was the part I liked—kids, who were jealous of a boy like me, horseback with three or four MC buckaroos: an old man called John the Swede who would spend most of his weekend in the bordellos out back of the rodeo grounds; and a couple of young bucks like Rossie Dollarhide and Casper Gunderson who would, if there was any justice in the world, be facing off in the saddle bronc finals come Monday afternoon.

We unsaddled and grained our horses, then went up to the bars, where a boy like me was served a bottle of beer without anybody making any fuss about it as long as he was with such men. For that little while I could deceive myself into believing that I was destined to be a buckaroo.

But it was not to actually be. I was an owner's kid; buckaroos were wandering men who'd quit a job just to see what was down the road. Their most powerful opinion was an ancient traditional disdain for settlers, those who settle, townspeople and farmers. We went our ways.

At daybreak on the high deserts of eastern Oregon, my father and some other men who are dead now eased into a round willow-walled coral where sixty or so spooky geldings were circling counterclockwise around the rock-solid juniper center post. My father was, in those distant times, a lean, gray-eyed man who loved stories and any sporting sociability you could think of, but now he would turn momentarily serious and flip his rawhide riata in an effortless way and drop the loop over the head of his roping horse, a quick stocking-footed bay, and I would watch as he eased down the taut rope toward the trembling animal. I don't know who I was; I have dim photographs my mother took—that soft-faced boy, his face shaded by a floppy old hat, his shirttail out, leading a colt out the gate of a willow-walled corral. Those moments from fifty years ago string together in my memory like a run of dreams.

On the deserts of southeastern Oregon and northern Nevada we were not cowboys. Cowboys came up the trails from Texas to the east side of the Rockies in the 1880s with irrational Texas traditions, like roping with their seagrass ropes tied hard and fast to the saddle horn.

Only a crazy person would tie hard and fast. I once saw a big rosin-jawed Texan mistakenly catch a twelve-hundred-pound four-year-old steer when they were both heading different directions at top speed. Accidents happen.

This one was a considerable wreck. Tied hard and fast, there was no way for the Texan to cut loose. The steer hit the end of the rope, the Texan's horse went down sideways, the cinch broke, and saddle came free, to sail off through the greasewood behind that steer. Our Texan was left on the ground with three broken ribs, a horse that was never to trust him again, and some old hands laughing at him behind his back.

We were buckaroos. Our traditions were stylish and Spanish, brought north to southeastern Oregon out of California in the 1870s. When we were roping, with our home-braided rawhide riatas, we took *dallys*, a set of quick wraps around the saddle horn, so we could cast off in time of trouble. We thought dallying was a pretty skill to watch.

The summer I turned four my father began catching an old gelding called Moon, lifting me to the saddle, and leading me to the plow-ground along the irrigation ditch at the head of our garden, where he would instruct me in the arts of horseback. If I came unseated, he'd knock the dust off my shirt and lift me up again.

Childish crying was unthinkable. This was my start at being part of who we were in my family. The processes of coming to understand what it meant to act like a horseman in our part of the outback West involved a lot of great pretending. We learned a lot of theater at an early age; we learned to be who we were supposed to be.

By the time I was seven I was riding with a sort of cruel Spanish spade bit, the silver-mounted side bars shaped to the form of a woman's thigh, knee, and calf. I could draw blood from my horse's mouth with that Spanish bit. But I caught hell if I ever did it.

There were proper ways to live, and the most proper involved taking care of your horses. This was not because our rules had much of anything to say about kindness or compassion, but rather for reasons of utility. We cherished our horses if we had any sense. Without good horses we weren't much of anybody, and our world wouldn't function. It was high praise to say a man was "easy on his horses." A man who didn't take care of his horses was regarded as close to useless. His horses were bound to be no good; a man with sorry horses was less than a man.

My father was legendary for his fairness, and his drinking and poker. "Playing with Oscar," one of his friends told me, "you were in with one of the boys who made up the game." Life was most of the time easiest to think about if considered a sport, with clear rules. Its inherent unfairnesses were best ignored.

Men like my grandfather and father came to the country and took what they wanted. They believed they deserved what they got because they worked and suffered for their rewards, because they had earned them. They took care of their people and did not much believe in sympathy or handouts. They could be pitiless in the way they despised the weak, or those who whined and talked too much. My father and grandfather were certain their purposes were profound; they were willing to take enormous risks in the interests of realizing those purposes.

Theirs was a way of proceeding that often led to coldheartedness. It's easy to fault such men for lacking the humanity to find certain injustices intolerable; old men and women worked until they couldn't work any more and were often left to die alone in third-rate hotels. My father had no use for the unemployed, but the men who worked for him stayed, and he loaned them money, bought them whiskey, hired them back after the drunk was run, and never allowed for an instant that they were his equals. He loved and respected two fine women, but he was quite willing to claim that women had no place in politics and should never have been given the vote. "They're not fit for it," he would say, and he was not altogether joking.

What he was speaking of was for him a sensible distinction. As he saw it, women played a compassionate game. Women lived by rules of the house and of childrearing, of giving and solace. Those were fine, even necessary rules for women, but disastrous in business and politics where power, never love, called the shots.

It's an argument that sounds simple-minded these days (as no doubt it always did), intent on preserving prerogatives, driven by selfishness. It is so easy to disdain that we are in danger of forgetting the virtues which came West with those old boys in the days when theirs was the radical energy loose in the land. They came bringing vivid intelligence and great force of will to the task of realizing independence, and new lives in a fresh land. They believed absolutely in the non-negotiable value of the individual. They understood freedom as the prime source of political possibility. Those are hard notions to fault. They yearned for a simple paradise, as we do. Some of them, for a while, thought they had found it.

Men like my grandfather and father came to believe that the world was made to be used, and could be owned. They came to believe absolutely in property as the source of identity, and in family as property—but by this time they had crossed the line; they had become farmers, settlers, owners. They were only once in a while horseback, for ceremonies like the Lakeview Rodeo. Ordinarily, they rode around in Cadillacs, on paved roads.

The smell of coffee rolling to boil before sunrise comes back to me with the ringing clarity of steel struck by steel. The fire reeked of sage; the tarpaulin over the bedding where I'd slept in all my clothing except for my boots (they were under the blankets with me) was stiff with frost.

Sixty or so saddle horses were cantering toward the willow-walled corral, come from the mists along the slough in the meadow, fresh horses splashing through the tiny creek at Catnip Springs out in the high desert distances of southeastern Oregon. I was thirteen and ready to go myself. I sat up, shivering in the chill, and put on my dusty gray hat, and my warm boots. I knew how to live this way; I was not a child any more.

Catching horses was the beginning of things. We'd get them saddled, ride them out, and get them used to the idea that this was a day of work, then feed them a dash of oats and go to our own breakfast. By sunup we'd be gone from camp.

Without taking my hat off I'd splash my face with cold water and sip at a cup of that bitter coffee. The horses in the corral would circle clockwise and then turn back. A fine cloud of manure dust would be stirring.

Each rider had his own string of horses, long-legged desert traveling horses and quick little roping horses—ours to care for in every way. A couple of young bucks were drawing ten bucks a month extra for breaking a few three-year-olds into the rhythms of the work—it was called "riding the rough string."

I'd be carrying a hackamore of hard woven rawhide and my Spanish-bit bridle, both rigs tied together with one of those short horsehair ropes called a *mecate*. It was more rig than any sensible person would need on the kind of middle-aged horse I was going to be riding, but I was at that stage of boyish expertise when gear meant a lot.

One of those mornings before sunrise when we were camped at Catnip Springs, I made a humiliating mistake. I asked for an easy-traveling dark bay named Snuffy. The man doing the roping misunderstood and caught me a sour-spirited bad boy named Tuffy. They looked much alike, and I didn't catch the difference until I was lazily swinging into the saddle, where I didn't stay very long.

Tuffy made a couple of quick energetic moves, and I was gone over his head in a high arc to land like a sack of flour in a thicket of greasewood. The wind was knocked out of me, my hat was gone, and I was hurting to the point of nausea. There was a couple of whoops, Tuffy bucked a few more times, just working out the kinks, surprised he'd got rid of me so easily. Then there was silence.

One of the most central rules in our code said you had to get back on soon as you caught your wind. A little bowlegged man named Cecil Dixon caught Tuffy and led him to me, studied me, and said, "Shit, kid."

Cecil took pity, pulled off my saddle, dropped it on the ground, and led Tuffy back to the corral. "That kid don't think he wants this Tuffy horse," Cecil said.

There was a few snorts of laughter, but he was right. They caught me my Snuffy horse, who was sweet as a pet when I got him saddled. He wanted his oats. My ribs ached, and I couldn't eat breakfast.

It was clear I should have climbed back on the horse that bucked me off; I should have buckled on some spurs and given Tuffy another go-round, no matter the consequences. But I was thirteen and a child. I didn't even offer to make such a move, and I was sick with shame.

Maybe that was where I began learning that getting the work done was more significant than surviving humiliation. It's taken decades, but I've come to see that effort to preserve the communality of our lives in that eastern Oregon valley, which for so long I was so willing to underestimate, was what most of our buckaroo attitudinizing was truly about. The stories we inhabit—like the one about horsemen—are our common defenses against chaos, like barricades.

But any code of behavior, pushed far enough, turns into nonsense. Cecil Dixon knew it when he said, "That kid don't think he wants this Tuffy horse." Those men knew it. If he'd been there that morning, my father would have likely grinned at me and said in his soft, gray-eyed and ironic sort of way, "Maybe that woke you up."

It would have been his way of opening a door between us. Then he would have turned to his breakfast. Theater and pretending stood between us for a long time.

But ultimately we made contact. Twenty years later, my own family broken, wife and children gone away to another life in California, the ranch sold—at that moment of great difficulty, on a cold morning, windows opaque with frost, my father sipped a glass of Jack Daniel's and asked me what I was going to do with myself.

When I told him I was going back to college, with the idea of trying to learn how to be a writer, I didn't know how he would react. I halfway expected him to shake his head and laugh. Such runaway career moves, at that time, were not considered even remotely appropriate for ranch men in southeastern Oregon. What I was telling him—that trying to write seemed like my one chance to turn into someone I wanted to be—reeked even in my mind of a secret agenda, failure, and my need to escape.

What I wasn't telling him, which he must have known anyway, was that I didn't want to be like him and end up giving my life to a commercial enterprise I didn't in any long run seem capable of particularly valuing.

There were a lot of things I didn't like about ranching: the way we exploited laboring men and women, the ways we drained the waterfowl swamps for our barley fields, then sprayed them with killer chemicals, the indifference with which we allowed our thousands of cattle to tromp fragile high desert streamsides to dust.

But those weren't lines of thought I could articulate in my father's presence. I was willing to pretend I felt like a fool who was confessing to weakness. I would have been happy, I think, playing that role. But my father didn't give me a chance. He took me seriously. "Do what you want," he said. "That's my idea. I've done things I hated all my life. I sure as hell wouldn't recommend that."

My story of myself, and who I should be, rolled over. My father— through what was for me an utterly unanticipated act of the imagination—was giving me permission he must have known I needed, to go into the world and be whatever I could manage. He believed, absolutely, that we are sustained by our willingness to chance the results of freedom.

Some of us in the West sorrow for a lost world where we were raised. We came to understand our lives inside a story that people like my father taught us, about independence and demanding your fair share of the world. But those old people are mostly gone, and we're on our own. We can't go on living in a world they made for us. We have to invent our own.

Think of a young boy bringing a half dozen cows and calves out the rimrocks toward his father's home fields in the vast isolations of the sun-blasted summertime country north of the Black Rock Desert in Nevada, the way he dreams of girls down by the Humboldt River in Winnemucca and stays with his slow work anyhow. Imagine a red-headed woman in her kitchen while the snow blows across that highland country, feeding juniper firewood to a stove made of a fifty-five-gallon fuel barrel and listening to zydeco music on National Public Radio while she braids a perfect rawhide riata.

Think of that woman and her husband growing a huge garden the next summer, and the woman trucking the produce to some town and just giving the food away. She will make rough signs that say: "FREE—FREE FOOD."

That red-headed woman from the backlands of Nevada, and the boy who is helping her, stand there before cardboard boxs of snap-beans and corn and carrots and beets in the dusty light of a Saturday morning on the streets of Lovelock, and the people in that western town study them like they might be crazy and dangerous.

Imagine some other woman, maybe a schoolteacher or a single mother run away from San Diego, risking the craziness and coming forward to accept a dozen free ears of corn, accepting a gift that has meaning primarily because it is a gift and a way of adding to the beauty of things. One act of the imagination, one freedom, then another. Think of shattering, the faraway sounds of ice beginning to break.

S U S A N   P O W E R

*I*n her first novel, *The Grass Dancer*, Susan Power
returns to the Dakota Sioux reservation of her
mother's upbringing, a world shimmering with
spirit, legend, and awesome magic powers.
Although "a city Indian," as she calls herself,
raised in Chicago and schooled at Harvard,
Power's writing reveals the unmistakable traces
of her mother's heritage. In "Chicago Waters,"
Power displays her growing respect for the
fearsome animus of the natural world. It is a
tender story of a modern girl growing up in
freedom but in whose ear remain the warning
voices of her ancestors. It's a story, too, about
the joy of accepting the contradictions inherent
in who we are.

CHICAGO
WATERS

MY MOTHER USED TO SAY THAT BY THE TIME I WAS AN OLD WOMAN, Lake Michigan would be the size of a silver dollar. She pinched her index finger with her thumb to show me the pitiful dimensions.

"People will gather around the tiny lake, what's left of it, and cluck over a spoonful of water," she told me.

I learned to squint at the 1967 shoreline until I had carved away the structures and roads built on landfill, and could imagine the lake and its city as my mother found them in 1942 when she arrived in Chicago. I say "the lake and its city" rather than "the city and its lake" because my mother taught me another secret: the city of Chicago belongs to Lake Michigan.

But which of my mother's pronouncements to believe? That Chicago would swallow the midwestern sea, smother it in concrete, or that the lake wielded enough strength to outpolitick even Mayor Richard J. Daley?

Mayor Daley, Sr., is gone now, but the lake remains, alternately tranquil and riled, changing colors like a mood ring. I guess we know who won.

When my mother watches the water from her lakeside apartment building, she still sucks in her breath. "You have to respect the power of that lake," she tells me. And I do now. I do.

I was fifteen years old when I learned that the lake did not love me or hate me, but could claim me, nevertheless. I was showing off for a boy, my best friend, Tommy, who lived in the same building. He usually accompanied me when I went for a swim, but on this particular day he decided the water was too choppy. I always preferred the lake when it was agitated because its temperature warmed, transforming it into a kind of Jacuzzi.

Tommy is right, I thought, once I saw the looming swells which had looked so unimpressive from the twelfth floor. Waves crashed against the breakwater wall and the metal ladder that led into and out of the lake, like the entrance to the deep end of a swimming pool.

I shouldn't do this, I told myself, but I noticed Tommy watching me from his first-floor window. "I'm not afraid," I said to him under my breath. "I bet you think that I'll chicken out just because I'm a girl."

It had been a hot summer of dares, some foolish, some benign. Sense was clearly wanting. I took a deep breath and leapt off the wall into the turmoil since the ladder was under attack. How did I think I would get out of the water? I hadn't thought that far. I bobbed to the surface and was instantly slapped in the face. I was beaten by water, smashed under again and again, until I began choking because I couldn't catch my breath.

I'm going to die now, I realized, and my heart filled with sorrow for my mother, who had already lost a husband and would now lose a daughter. I fought the waves, struggled to reach the air and the light, the sound of breakers swelling in my ears, unnaturally loud, like the noise of Judgment Day. *Here we go,* I thought. Then I surprised myself, becoming unusually calm. I managed a quick gasp of breath and plunged to the bottom of the lake, where the water was a little quieter. I swam to the beach next door, remaining on the lake floor until I reached shallow waters. I burst to the surface then, my lungs burning, and it took me nearly five minutes to walk fifteen feet, knocked off balance as I was by waves that sucked at my legs. This beach now belongs to my mother and the other shareholders in her building, property recently purchased and attached to their existing lot. But in 1977 it was owned by someone else, and a barbed-wire fence separated the properties. I ended my misadventure by managing to climb over the sharp wire.

I remained downstairs until I stopped shaking. Tommy no longer watched me from his window, bored by my private games, unaware of the danger. I didn't tell my mother what had happened until hours later. I was angry at myself for being so foolish, so careless with my life, but I was never for a moment angry at the lake. I didn't come to fear it either, though it is a mighty force that drops 923 feet in its deepest heart. I understand that it struck indifferently; I was neither target nor friend. My life was my own affair, to lose or to save. Once I stopped struggling with the great lake, I flowed through it, and was expelled from its hectic mouth.

My mother still calls Fort Yates, North Dakota, home, despite the fact that she has lived in Chicago for nearly fifty-five years. She has taken me to visit the Standing Rock Sioux Reservation where she was raised, and although a good portion of it was flooded during the construction of the Oahe Dam, she can point to hills and buttes and creeks of significance. The landscape there endures, outlives its inhabitants. But I am a child of the city, where landmarks are man-made, impermanent. My attachments to place are attachments to people, my love for a particular area only as strong as my local relationships. I have lived in several cities and will live in several more. I visit the country with curiosity and trepidation, a clear foreigner, out of my league, and envy the connection my mother has to a dusty town, the peace she finds on a prairie. It is a kind of religion, her devotion to Proposal Hill and the Missouri River, a sacred bond that I can only half-understand. If I try to see the world through my mother's eyes, find the point where my own flesh falls to earth, I realize my home is Lake Michigan, the source of so many lessons.

As a teenager I loved to swim in the dark, to dive beneath the surface where the water was as black as the sky. The lake seemed limitless and so was I, an arm, a leg, a wrist, a face, indistinguishable from the wooden boards of a sunken dock, from the sand I squeezed between my toes. I always left reluctantly, loath to become a body again and feel more acutely the oppressive pull of gravity.

It was my father who taught me to swim, with his usual patience and clear instructions. First he helped me float, his hands beneath my back and legs, his torso shading me from the sun. Next he taught me to flutter-kick, and I tried to make as much noise as possible. I dog-paddled in circles as a little girl, but my father swam in a straight line perpendicular to shore, as if he were trying to leave this land forever. Just as he had left New York State after a lifetime spent within its borders, easily, without regret. His swim was always the longest, the farthest. Mom and I would watch him as we lounged on our beach towels, nervous that a boat might clip him. It was a great relief to see him turn around and coast in our direction.

"Here he comes," Mom would breathe. "He's coming back now."

My father also showed me how to skip a stone across the water. He was skillful, and could make a flat rock bounce like a tiny, leaping frog, sometimes five or six hops before it sank to the bottom. It was the only time I could imagine this distinguished, silver-haired gentleman as a boy, and I laughed at him affectionately because the difference in our years collapsed.

My mother collects stones in her backyard—a rough, rocky beach in South Shore. She looks for pebbles drilled with holes, not pits or mere scratches, but tiny punctures worn clear through the stone.

"I can't leave until I find at least one," she tells me.

"Why?" I ask. I've asked her more than once because I am forgetful.

"There are powerful spirits in these stones, trying to tunnel their way out."

Ah, that explains the holes. What I do not ask is why she selects them, these obviously unquiet souls, why she places them in a candy dish or a basket worn soft as flannel. What good can it do them? What good can it do her to unleash such restless forces on the quiet of her rooms?

I finger my mother's collection when I'm home for a visit. I have even pressed a smooth specimen against my cheek. The touch is cool, I believe it could draw a fever, and the object is mute and passive in my hand. At first I think there is a failing on my part, I cannot hear what my mother hears, and then I decide that the spirits caught in these stones have already escaped. I imagine them returning to the lake, to the waves that pushed them onto the beach and washed their pebble flesh, because it is such a comfort to return to water.

And then I remember my own weightless immersion, how my body becomes a fluid spirit when I pull myself underwater, where breath stops. And I remember gliding along the lake's sandy bottom as a child, awed by the orderly pattern of its dunes. Lake Michigan is cold, reliably cold, but occasionally I passed through warm pockets, abrupt cells of tepid water that always came as a surprise. I am reminded of cold spots reputedly found in haunted houses, and wonder: Are these warm areas evidence of my lost souls?

A young man drowned in these waters behind my mother's building some years ago. Mom was seated in a lawn chair, visiting with another tenant on the terrace. They sat together facing the lake so they could watch its activity, though it was calm that day, uninteresting. A young man stroked into view, swimming parallel to the shore and headed north. He was close enough for them to read his features; he was fifteen feet away from shallow depths where he could have stood with his head above water. He called to them, a reasonable question in a calm voice. He wanted to know how far south he was. The 7300 block, they told him. He moved on. A marathon swimmer, the women decided. But eventually my mother and her friend noticed his absence, scanned the horizon unable to see his bobbing head and strong arms. They alerted the doorman, who called the police. The young man was found near the spot where he'd made his cordial inquiry.

"Why didn't he cry for help? Why didn't he signal his distress?" my mother asked the response unit.

"This happens all the time with men," she was told. "They aren't taught to cry for help."

So he is there too, the swimmer, a warm presence in cold water or a spirit in a stone.

I have gone swimming in other places—a chlorinated pool in Hollywood, the warm waters of the Caribbean, the Heart River in North Dakota—only to be disappointed and emerge unrefreshed. I am too used to Lake Michigan and its eccentricities. I must have cold, fresh water. I must have the stinking corpses of silver alewives floating on the surface as an occasional nasty surprise, discovered dead and never alive. I must have sailboats on the horizon and steel mills on the southern shore, golf balls I can find clustered around submerged pilings (shot from the local course), and breakwater boulders heavy as tombs lining the beach. I must have sullen lifeguards who whistle to anyone bold enough to stand in three feet of water, and periodic arguments between wind and water which produce tearing waves and lake-spattered windows.

When I was little, maybe seven or eight, my parents and I went swimming in a storm. The weather was mild when we first set out, but the squall arrived quickly, without warning, as often happens in the Midwest. I remember we swam anyway, keeping an eye on the lightning not yet arrived from the north. There was no one to stop us since we were dipping into deep water between beaches, in an area that was unpatrolled. The water was warmer than usual, the same temperature as the air, and when the rain wet the sky, I leapt up and down in the growing waves, unable to feel the difference between air and water, lake and rain. The three of us played together that time; even my father remained near shore rather than striking east to swim past the white buoys. We were joined in this favorite element, splashing, ducking. I waved my arms over my head. My father pretended to be a great whale, heavy in the surf, now and then spouting streams of water from his mouth. He chased me. My mother laughed.

Dad died in 1973 when I was eleven years old, before my mother and I moved to the apartment on the lake. We always thought it such a shame he didn't get to make that move with us. He would so have enjoyed finding Lake Michigan in his backyard.

We buried him in Albany, New York, because that is where he was raised. My mother was born in North Dakota, and I was born between them, in Chicago. There is a good chance we shall not all rest together, our stories playing out in different lands. But I imagine that if a rendezvous is possible—and my mother insists it is—we will find one another in this great lake, this small sea that rocks like a cradle.

We are strong swimmers in our separate ways, my mother like a turtle, my father like a seal. And me? I am a small anonymous fish, unspectacular but content.

NATALIE KUSZ

atalie Kusz, currently a Briggs-Copeland Fellow
in the Creative Writing Department of Harvard
University, finds herself about as far from her
native homeland, Alaska, as one can get.
Despite an often rugged upbringing there,
Kusz remains deeply attached to Alaska,
returning frequently. Her first memoir,
Roadsong, depicts with unstinting candor the
vicious attack by dogs that left her scarred for
life. "Fire in the Valley," sometimes wryly
humorous in tone, is about the importance of
fire to Alaskans, the delicate truce humans
must strike with natural elements they harness.
But "Fire in the Valley" is also about human
vulnerability, the edgy awareness that life in all
its seeming security can be destroyed in a
second, without a second's notice.

F I R E
I N T H E
V A L L E Y

WHAT YOU HAVE ENVISIONED OF ALASKA IS TRUE: THE VAST AND craggy mountains, retaining their snow cover year round; the wild-life—bears, moose, snowshoe hares—even city dwellers encounter on occasion; the long, bright nights of summer followed by the eternal twilit winter. And the cold. Growing up in this place, I read all the works of Jack London, and I remember my amazed recognition of his landscapes—their heavy great silence, their ruthless temperatures, the leaden fog that they made of one's breath. These were not the total of my experience, but they were London's most clearly drawn images, and at nine years old I was astonished by his accuracy, his devastating clarity of perception.

For cold, and the fire we use to combat it, have always been part of regional lore, the education one received through daily practice. You could, in fact, give a thermodynamics quiz to most of the school-children here, and they could tell you the relative heat value of many diverse items on a list. In many of their houses, the kitchen holds two trash cans: one for burnables, one for all else. These kids learn early that paper towels and junk mail, although their heat value is low, will satisfy the furnace for a moment. Eggshells, too, are worthy, and newspapers and old phone books—these last rating high because of their density. My widowed father, when his children were all grown, would phone me to say that aluminum cans had helped stretch the firewood, had indeed burned and provided heat, though they left a funny residue in the ash box. I didn't quite believe this then, but were I ever to get low enough on fuel, I know I would try it myself.

Everything, when the hard cold comes, receives a valuation based upon its heat content. "Don't throw that out," parents say, when their children go to clean the garage. "There's an hour of fire in that. Just put it by the woodpile in pieces." I've heard this exchange with regard to broken furniture, decayed books, even blankets and clothing beyond their prime. Firewood itself, collected all summer and stacked near the house, has its own special set of heat ratings. Birch is very good for kindling, its papery bark so easy to ignite. Poplar, too, is fine, though very young trees are too wet to be useful. Spruce is tricky, because although it burns longer than, say, willow, its resin produces much creosote, coating and inflaming the stovepipes. Still, my parents achieved longer shifts of night sleep by stoking the stove with dry wood and then putting a spruce log on top, knowing its embers would last until they dragged themselves awake in a few hours. Baseboard heat became a thing of fond dreams, the first item on the list if they won a sweepstakes.

And it remained first on the wish list as we children grew up, as our mother died, as one by one we moved away to college, then to various jobs, each of us hoping fervently to Make It first: to earn many thousands and surprise our dad one cold Christmas with radiators, a thermostat, and a huge throbbing boiler to run it all. As the oil boom went bust, we began leaving this depressed economy to find work Outside, as we call it, in the States, planning one day to return, like Columbus, our ships full of plundered foreign exotica. Even now, nearly a decade after moving away, I myself claim not to have *relocated*, per se: Never mind that I spend nine months teaching near Boston and only three months here, tending the land; I still tell people that I "winter" Outside, and that I "live," officially, in this place, in the house my parents built so slowly all the wood-burning winters and wood-gathering summers of my childhood. Situated on the outskirts of a farming town, on the hundred acres still left of my family's original two hundred sixty, the place has passed from my parents to me, and I come here every warm season to occupy the house, the land.

The homecoming procedure remains much the same every year. I arrive with my daughter and unlock the doors, carry in our luggage, and spend two days hauling off dust sheets, hanging our clothes, and putting away the supplies we bought cheaply Outside: ant powder and bug repellent, housepaint sometimes or roofing tar, toilet paper and dry goods and canning jars. I check the water pipes—though a friend has looked in on them all winter—to see that none of them has burst, and I light a great fire in the furnace to blow out the remaining spring damp. After this there are the ritual visits, not to people so much as to places: my mother's grave and, since last year, my father's, five or so miles away at the cemetery; the pond on our property where the moose come to drink, and where you can never predict if this year's snowmelt will be neck-deep or hardly enough to cover the frog eggs; the cabin ten acres from the house, that private retreat which was the last thing my dad built with me before he died; and the tourist information center in town, to see what new mushroom or berry-picking guides have been published, and to ask at the desk the status of the summer fires.

For here is what we all have in common, I and the people who abide here year-round: Fire. Fire in winter is a necessary thing, that small tongue of energy between us and total loss—of possessions, of homes, of life. But after breakup, with the ice gone and the earth turned dry, the spruce needles and underbrush gone brittle—now is when things grow complex, when the beast we have tended so carefully in our furnaces comes alive, here and there, and goes roaring. You will hear, on occasion, that a lightning bolt started it, but most often it was we ourselves—our untended campfires, our controlled garbage burns breaking loose, and once, rumor has it, a farmer going bankrupt lit rags on his tractor, hoping to collect the insurance: that fire accelerated almost into town, and they say a million acres lay scorched. A tourist at the gas pump complained to me that summer how he might as well have stayed in L.A.; his asthma, he said, was even worse here, and this after all he'd read of the clear and untainted Arctic air. I had no real comfort to give the man, except to point toward the mountains, saying that on the other side the smoke wasn't bad, they were having a good year compared to ours.

It is true that there are better years than others, months when you might travel every road and never see the sky going yellow. You could ask and be told that yes, a hundred thousand acres were burning out west, but "out west" could mean six hundred wilderness miles, someplace only a bush pilot might encounter. Other seasons, when the winter snowfall was low or the summer rains brief and paltry, the atmosphere turns the same silty color as the rivers that converge here and suggest Delta's name. The eyes run. The throat sticks together. Families stop at the post office for weather reports. This valley tends toward windiness, and the manner of that wind is a vital sign, telling us which way the flames will veer, and how fast. Out at the barley projects, farmers pay up the insurance on their fields, their cattle, their machinery. Cabin dwellers in endangered strands of forest collect what valuables they have—photo albums, clothing, guns—and lay them up ready in their cars. And the young men and women in town go to the forestry station, hire on as firefighters, and go out to earn their summer's income.

Half a generation ago it was our parents who did this, waited through the spring jobless season and then, when the first of the smoke reports emerged, rejoiced with quiet guilt in their hearts. They signed the white job forms and climbed into school buses, rode to where the forest rangers took them, and went forth with state-issued hatchets, shovels, and water cannisters to contain what they could of the danger. If disaster were his source of income, my own father would say, then at least he would keep that disaster very small.

In this way, our covenant with fire remains constant year-round, a symbiotic pact no visitor will know. In the warm months those younger adults with families or educations to support, as well as those out of other work, will hope the summer fires come early, before the freezer runs empty, or the bill collectors phone, or the roof gets beyond quick repair. At the first call for workers, they rush in to be early, wearing their oldest or most disposable clothing, aware they could be in it for days. They find out now where the work will be, ten miles away or two hundred, and if the site is close, some of them drive their own cars so as to be able to come home between shifts.

The shifts are long, twelve or more hours sometimes, but the people who do this job say it is hardly dangerous, for the ground crews do not work in live flames. Instead, while the small planes drop water or retardant on the burning parts, the people below manage "containment," limiting however they can the fire's spread. Modern workers each carry a *Pulaski*—a short-handled tool with an ax facing one way and a small hoe facing the other—and they chop, dig, and scrape a wide circle around the live fire, removing all possible fuel sources from its reach. From the Fedco water cannisters on their backs, the crews dampen the fire break and the still-safe trees; if the work gets very urgent, a forty-pound Fedco might run empty in five minutes, sending its wearer running for a refill at the huge Porta-Tank on safe ground. When the fire uses up a spot of land and moves on, the men and women move in to reclaim the place: spraying, chopping, patting out embers.

It is this part of the job which gives rise to yearly rumors—that now and again some firefighters, in the interest of job security, fail to quash the last smoking coal, turning away and leaving it to reignite, or to creep out slowly toward new wood, dry by the next day and combustible. And who knows, perhaps this does happen, perhaps even, as some people say, the original fire is sometimes set, deliberately lit by an out-of-work local with kids. Plenty of arguments go on in environmental circles here, about how wildfires are natural and the earth in fact *requires* them, depends on a periodic clean start. Perhaps on occasion, when the unemployment checks stop, someone decides that, so long as no houses are touched, a little lighter fluid a hundred miles away could mean something more than rice on the table and, incidentally, could be a truly helpful little gesture for the land.

My father speculated on these things, but believed mostly that flames reignited because of human stupidity. The system, he said, the forestry system, was lazy. As a crew boss, he made his workers dig up the soil in squares, turning it over so the smoking side suffocated underneath; other crews sprayed a little water and went on as if their job were finished, but in the end, he said, his fires were the ones that stayed out. If he told this story and a newcomer heard him, the invariable reaction was horror. How, the visitor would say, how could other workers stop before seeing that the flames were really dead? And these rumors that they did it deliberately—did anyone know if they were true?

I understand the visitors' incredulity, for when you first encounter this country—the delicious and unkempt forest, the vast and inaccessible mountains—the thought that someone might disfigure it, even that they might leave evidence of their visit, seems obscene. But what the mere passer-through cannot see is this: that in summer even firefighters hold arson in their hearts, for they must welcome each flare-up if they are to support their own lives in this place. Contain it they will, and all of us expect this, but the yellow beast is a necessary if untrustworthy companion, as essential now, perhaps, as in snowtime when we bring it inside.

And the relationship is not comfortable even then, even with every safeguard installed. You might invest in asbestos stovepipe, an airtight furnace, and the cleanest-burning wood or oil fuel, yet still be aware that unless you watch it every minute, the flame with which you warm the rooms can sneak out to the rooftop and smolder. Every householder here has a method to forestall this. Some people swear by Red Devil, a powder you sprinkle in the woodstove, which travels up the chimney, igniting all the soot collected there, burning it off and dropping it down. My family would throw in the powder and go outside, staring up at the roof for wayward sparks, ready to climb up and remove them. Other people clean the stovepipes by hand, attaching an old broom or wire brush to a handle as long as the chimney. They go up to the rooftop, remove the chimney hat, and shove the brush down, scrubbing the piping the way you would a baby's bottle, up and down many strokes. Between times, then, they knock hard on the pipe from inside, and the sound of falling soot is like the tinkling of china, clattering down to the fire and reburning.

This, though, is all a matter of restraint, of holding in check an element we must have beside us in limitation. The bulk of winter work, especially for wood-burning families, involves *nurturing* fire, sustaining it, tending its life as their own. When my father was growing weaker with the lung disease he would finally die of, I bought an oil furnace and had it delivered to him. I was already living, by then, Outside, warmed myself by apartment radiators, and the winter back home had grown particularly fierce, 80 below zero for days. The Alaskan weather had made national news, and people at my job would stop in to say, "How's your dad? I bet he's staying indoors." And he was, but not for the reasons they meant, that the cold outdoors was so brutal; no, on the phone he spoke entirely of tending the woodstove, waking every two hours to feed it, closing off unused rooms so they wouldn't steal the heat. Having been frail already, his body was collapsing tired, and I could hear its slow surrender in his voice. So I discarded my bill statements for that month and the next, telephoned the builder's store in Delta, and had them take Dad an oil furnace.

It was not the radiator heat system of our childhood dreams, not the great surprise we siblings had competed to buy first, but rather an ungainly heat blower in the basement, situated near the staircase in hopes that some warmth would travel upward. Still, it would run by itself and require no stoking, and if we all chipped in for oil bills, it would be a good-for-now gift for our father. Ah, he told us when it was installed, ah, the luxury. He could sleep almost five-hour stretches now, before he grew nervous and went down to the heater, making sure it had kept burning without him.

It is this same furnace I turn on now, luxuriously, every fall, when the last of the tourists is gone and I make my way ready to follow. Dust sheets cover the furniture then, and plastic seals up all the windows. I set the thermostat at fifty degrees Fahrenheit, put the good photos in a flame-proof box; I close the door and go away. An old local friend comes once a week all winter to check on things, to change the furnace filter or to see if the oil tank needs filling. Someday, we both know, in spite of our precautions, in spite of the heating man's yearly maintenance—someday it is possible that the beast will erupt, that when I arrive for the summer I will note how my dad was quite right: you can't look away for an instant, can't leave a fire unwatched. In that year I will find not much left but the freezer, perhaps, and a few nails that failed to ignite. I will dig in the ashes for the fireproof box, and will see that already, as with the summer forest fires, the earth is emerging from beneath it all, pushing up weeds through the rubble, converting the cinders to dirt. It is a future memory I try hard to avoid by sending in my friend every week. This is a large favor to ask, but this man doesn't mind, understanding that, in the way of pet wolves, which some people keep here, a flame will never domesticate; you can tend it with love, but only in a cage, and you must never leave your children to feed it. Tame-looking or not, by nature it is wild; rein it in, give it limits, and know that in spite of all this it may creep out at night and consume you.

ROBERT FINCH

obert Finch, naturalist and essayist, writes often
about his native Cape Cod. The author of
several collections of essays about this place,
Finch's pieces are elegant meditations on the
relation of inner spirit to landscape. Often, they
capture the rare stand of mind, reminiscent of
Thoreau and Henry Ward Beston, of someone
who has achieved real solitude. "A Day of
Roads" finds Finch wandering familiar terrain
with new eyes, and a sense for the almost
sedimentary layers of history and geography
contained in this place, the literal and spiritual
paths that crisscross its terrain.

A Day

of

Roads

When I pulled into Newcomb Hollow in Wellfleet, the beach was curiously empty. There were only three cars in the parking lot, and two of those left almost immediately. The waves were low and quiet, silently tossing massive logs and bright flags of sea lettuce about in the surf. A muffled fog was sitting on the beach like a cool shroud, though I could feel the hot sun, like a weight, beating down upon it.

In August the beaches of Cape Cod are normally paved with human bodies. Here, on the Lower Cape, the flexed forearm of this glacial peninsula, some five million people each year visit the Cape Cod National Seashore, most of them during the summer months. A century and a half ago the Cape's most famous literary visitor, Henry David Thoreau, remarked on this very stretch of beach that "a thousand men could not have seriously interrupted it, but would have been lost in the vastness of the scenery as their footsteps in the sand." Even Thoreau's perceptive vision, however, could not have imagined the extent to which humanity would someday occupy these sands, so that those same footsteps would actually threaten to alter the scenery itself.

As a year-rounder, I usually avoid the ocean beaches in summer, saving my walks there for the off-season. But this morning, all it had taken was a little moisture and sea breeze to blow the crowds away like sea foam and restore the beach to its ancient vastness and majesty, and so I came, with no purpose in mind except to experience the beach in its unaccustomed solitude.

I began walking north, my eyes smarting from a stiff, moist north wind. Above me, on my left, loomed the sand cliffs of the outer beach, part of a nearly continuous twenty-six-mile marine scarp running from Coast Guard Beach in Eastham to High Head in North Truro, interrupted only by a series of dips, or "hollows," in the cliff wall. At Newcomb Hollow the bluffs are about fifty feet high and nearly completely barren of growth, in part from the constant foot traffic of the beach users. Farther on, the cliffs double, then triple in height, and the vegetation begins to reassert itself, climbing up the smooth slopes out of the wrack line. At the base were the stitched lines of compass grass, tracing circles in the sand with their hard-tipped, shiny blades; above them were clumps of fleshy-leaved sea rocket, bristly sea burdock, seaside goldenrod, spiraled stems of beach pea, and tufts of dusty miller with its lobed, silvery-green leaves and long stalks of yellow flower clusters.

A dense fog continued to blow down the beach, shrouding visibility at both ends. In the distance I saw what appeared to be figures on the beach. But when I came closer, they proved to be improvised driftwood structures, decorated with colorful bits of washed-up fabric, netting, and lobster buoys, the kind of whimsical sculpture one often finds here. In places, footprints and vehicle tracks were so numerous that the beach resembled a railroad yard done in sand, yet I neither met nor saw another soul from Newcomb Hollow to Brush Valley in Truro, nearly three miles away. This abundance of mute signs, the strange absence of people, and the desolate feeling of the fog, gave the impression of a mass exodus, a ghost beach.

As the cliffs began to rise, near the Wellfleet-Truro town line, I left the beach, climbing up one of those diagonal foot trails cut into the face of the scarp—something like a mountain path, narrow and flat, and comparatively firm after the recent rain. Reaching the top, I continued on the path that runs along the crest just back from the edge. This path, like the beach itself, is both a permanent and ephemeral road, in this case man-made, but constantly forced to relocate as the cliffs recede from year to year.

I looked out over a vast and undulating plain of stunted vegetation, across one of the most dramatic stretches of the outer beach of Cape

Cod. To the north the bluffs dip and rise precipitously in long, rolling, waves. They rise up out of wooded hollows to the west, cresting in shaggy, grassy overhangs at the cliff edge, so that they appear as massive frozen swells, terrestrial counterparts of the ocean breakers that nibbled away at their foundations below.

With the drifting patches of fog both softening its details and intensifying its colors, the whole plain appeared as a series of distinct and varied north-south bands of green: shimmering hillocks of poverty grass, carpets of bearberry, and waves of beachgrass near the cliff edge, giving way to the deeper hues of beach rose, bayberry, and beach plum, backed in turn by darker bands of shiny scrub oak and dusky pitch pine. I have been to seashores in many parts of the world, and yet it is this distinctive tapestry of vegetation, as much as the topography of the glacial bluffs, that makes this landscape as recognizable and unmistakable as a familiar face.

Here, I thought, is one place where the Cape's extremes are vertical as well as horizontal. The highest point of land on the Outer Cape is along this stretch of cliff, a summit officially designated on the U.S. Geological Survey maps as "Pamet," which climbs a giddy 177 feet above the beach (though this figure likely changes from year to year). Yet everything is on the Cape's characteristically diminutive scale, so that one feels like a giant striding in several minutes from one summit to another along a sandy mountain range, complete with miniature peaks, cirques, bowls, and knife edges. As the crest trail swung out to the edge, I peered over and startled a flock of gulls that were roosting on the slope, sending them out into the fog where they disappeared, reassembling farther north. Each time I caught up with them they flew, as if newly startled, and waited for me farther on— a kind of larger version of the shepherding game one plays with flocks of shorebirds along the beach.

At intervals the crest trail swung inland and joined a wider and more substantial Jeep sand road. Along its soft surface were numerous fresh tracks of deer that had apparently been coming in my direction, had scented or heard my approach, and turned off the road. I could feel their presence nearby, bedded down probably within yards of me somewhere in the low, dark green thicket of scrub oak, but I knew I could wait there all day and never see or hear a sign of them.

I strode, with my folded umbrella set over my shoulders like a yoke, across an open field of bright, rounded tufts of beach heather surrounded by tall, waving beachgrass, among hardy stands of knarled and weathered chokecherry, through thickets of beach plum with their hard green fruits already as large as marbles in this year of excellent berry sets. Their stiff twigs were entwined with numerous vines of wild grapes, all sprouting clusters of lime green fruit as yet no bigger than grape seeds, glowing beneath the broad, arched grape leaves. How lush and thick, how heavy with promise these eroding fragments of beach bluff can be!

Shortly beyond the Pamet summit I descended to the beach road again, staying on it until I reached a break in the cliff face at Brush Valley, a short distance south of Ballston Beach in Truro. As I walked up the hard, narrow path of this ancient glacial valley, the uninterrupted hills of scrub oak rose sharp and huge into the fog. The screams of the invisible gulls loomed over me, dwarfing my presence. And I felt: how we need to be overwhelmed like this, from time to time, by some unpeopled expanse of the land where we live, even to fear it a little. It goes on so long without us.

I came out of Brush Valley onto the paved surface of South Pamet Road near the head of the Pamet River Valley. The Pamet is a tidal river basin, which comes in from Cape Cod Bay a few miles to the west and ends just behind a thin line of ocean-fronting dunes—thus nearly cutting the Cape in two. North and South Pamet Roads run roughly parallel on either side of the river and once formed a loop road that ran directly behind the dunes at the head of the valley.

Less than two decades ago, a small but important environmental decision was made here. During the great winter storm of February 1978, the ocean breached this dune line, spilling over into the headwaters of the Pamet River and temporarily separating the northern half of Truro and all of Provincetown from the rest of Cape Cod. The dune line had been breached before, but in the wake of this storm it became apparent that the paved loop road had been preventing the natural landward migration of the dunes in the face of beach erosion. This, coupled with excessive foot traffic on the dunes themselves in recent years, had seriously weakened the dune system and threatened to make this most recent break a permanent one. As a result, the town of Truro decided to close off the valley loop road at its head—

thus turning North and South Pamet Roads into deadends—and to fence off the dunes to walking. For several years the strategy appeared to work: the dune line migrated completely over the old paved road surface and beachgrass began to weave its network of underground runners, like a hair transplant, beneath the sand surface. Then, during the five-day blow of the Halloween Gale of 1991, the ocean breached again, dumping thousands of gallons of salt water and spreading a five hundred-foot plume of sand into the upper river. Once again, however, the dune appeared to be stabilizing, and at least has the option to continue migrating landward.

I was struck at the time by the town's original decision to close the road, not merely because it showed uncommon environmental sense (allowing, as it were, the dune to continue to march down its road unobstructed), but because it ran directly against the grain of road history in our time. It is unusual enough to hear of any established road being closed or abandoned, but in this case the passage being terminated was one of the oldest in existence in New England. According to several eighteenth-century maps, this section of the Pamet Road was part of the original King's Highway, the first road running the entire length of the Cape, laid out during the reign of Charles II. Yet this historic thoroughfare had been sacrificed, truncated, at no small inconvenience to some of the local residents, for the long-term good of a natural system.

I emptied the beach sand from my shoes and continued along the narrow, winding course of the South Pamet Road toward Truro Center, about a mile and a half to the west. Across the river the soft, rounded, bearberry-draped ridges of the Pamet Hills, known locally as "hogbacks," rose to the north. In the last century most of Cape Cod had a similar appearance: treeless heath, sandplain, or dune. Timothy Dwight, the president of Yale, traveling through Truro in 1815, referred to its landscape as "a vast Sahara," and Thoreau, traveling the same route a few decades later, described the countryside as "for the most part, bare, or with only a little scrubby woods left on the hills." But forests, though still scrubby by mainland standards, have reclaimed all but a few sections of this peninsula. Today they probably more closely resemble the original forests encountered by the *Mayflower* passengers in 1620 than at any time since.

Still, certain areas of the Cape have always been comparatively fertile, and the narrow floodplain of the Pamet River is one of those. This lovely low valley, filled with old farmhouses, orchards, marshside gardens, and the strong smell of a few remaining cowyards, breathes a rural use and settled continuity that is rare to encounter here any more. Many of the old houses today are occupied by summer residents, retirees, artists, and writers, but it is a benign occupation, full of deference for the past. At one spot there is even a small brook running under the road into the marsh that Thoreau took notice of in 1849. He had read somewhere that there were no fresh brooks in Truro, but noted, "I am pretty sure that I afterward saw a small fresh-water brook emptying into the south side of the Pamet River, though I was so heedless as not to taste it." A century and a half later I decided to rectify his uncharacteristic oversight, and so I knelt beside the stream and drank. It is, indeed, Henry, sweet and fresh.

Farther down the road I came upon two frizzy-haired young women standing beside their car and looking at it as though it were a sick cow. They had just come off one of the dirt side roads, they told me, where they had rammed a fender against one of Truro's rare glacial boulders. The left front wheel looked seriously out of alignment and the radiator was dripping.

"The radiator? Oh, is that what that water is?" said one. "Well, Marian, it's not a very big leak, is it? I bet if we stopped and put water into it every half-hour we could make it back to Brookline."

I persuaded them that they should have it looked at first, gave them directions to a garage south of Truro Center, and watched them as the car went roaring, weaving, and squealing off down the road, looking for all the world as if they were riding a wild pig. Ten minutes later, when I reached the town center and came out onto Route 6, I was surprised to see them again, driving by me in the breakdown lane, emergency lights blinking, the left wheel protesting loudly, as they headed, not off-Cape, but north toward Provincetown. They saw me and waved, with hopeful, trusting, desperate looks on their faces. Innocents from Boston, I thought—another venerable Cape tradition.

Perhaps, though, they felt safe from disaster having gotten back to the familiarity of Route 6, which is the main tourist highway running down the spine of Cape Cod from the Bourne Bridge at the canal to the Cape's tip at Provincetown. Pedestrians, however, risk their lives crossing this road in summer. I had planned to wait in Truro Center for the afternoon bus to take me back from Wellfleet, but by the time I finished lunch I felt refreshed, the fog had lifted, and I decided to complete the circuit on foot.

I struck off south on one of the narrow dirt roads east of Route 6, intending to make my way back to Newcomb Hollow along a network of wood roads shown on my 1972 U.S. Geological Survey map. But the road I had chosen soon began to peter out in the puckerbrush, and I realized that it currently existed more on my map and in my mind than in reality. Nonetheless, I forged ahead, the passage growing leafier and needlier, until with each step I had to push the branches ahead of me with both arms, as if doing the breaststroke, so that I seemed to be swimming through a layered green sea of foliage. It occurred to me that I could very well be the last person ever to attempt to walk this particular road, and I was just about to give up and retrace my steps when I suddenly emerged back out onto the paved highway.

This was not Route 6 itself, but one of those old side loops of the original highway that were cut off, like oxbows on an old river, when the road was straightened and widened in the 1950s. There are a dozen or more of these little bits of old Route 6 along the Lower Cape, curving off the main highway here and there for a few hundred feet before rejoining the mainstream of traffic. (It is easy to see where they veer off, for the telephone lines, installed down the Cape before the road was straightened, still follow the old route.) Some are completely barricaded off now, the pavement bulldozed over and replanted with bayberry and other native shrubs. One is a storage area for the state highway department. Most, however, are still accessible by car, and for years I had promised myself I would someday trace their route. But always, while driving, I seemed to be too pressed by the surrounding traffic or my own momentum to pull off and do so.

So I decided to walk them now, following the old, nearly continuous route as it weaved its way back and forth across the busy new highway like the loose end of thread in a needle looped across the taut strand. On one loop were a few old houses from the 1700s and 1800s, set off like roadside exhibits from a previous age; on another, some modest pondshore cottages built in the 1930s, 1940s, and 1950s, before President John F. Kennedy, a summer resident of the

Cape, signed the National Seashore into being in 1961, effectively preventing new building within its boundaries; and on yet another an unpublicized parking area on a small pond.

It occurred to me that the history of most roads seems to be the opposite of that of rivers, in that roads seem to grow younger, straighter, more rapid with age, meandering less and less, cutting their channels deeper and faster through the surrounding terrain, by-passing more and more of the old roads, villages, even—in the case of Interstates—entire towns and cities, some of which in time grow more sluggish, cut off from the main flow, and are left to stagnate and silt in at their own, unremarked pace.

As I traveled these older side loops of Route 6, it seemed that I had been unintentionally exploring a variety of thoroughfares all day—from the sand road of the beach and the cliff path in the morning, down the truncated loop of the Pamet Valley at midday, and now, in the afternoon, along vanishing wood roads and this inter-mingling of old and new highways. I have, in nearly three decades of living here, covered a great deal of this peninsula on foot, retracing many of my favorite routes year after year, carving, no less than the bulldozers, my own personal history here. My first set of USGS maps, printed in the late 1950s and now retired, are heavily annotated with exclamation points, where I noted enthusiastic first discoveries of bank swallow colonies, prime beachplum or bayberry sites, fox dens, wild cranberries, hidden ponds, the remains of shipwrecks, eagle sightings. The notes on my current set of maps, themselves nearly a quarter-century old, are less excited, and tend to record the passing of things: beach cottages claimed by the ocean, shifting sandspits, encroaching woodlands, whole sections of town lost to development, abandoned cranberry bogs, and old wood roads become impassable with time. Sometimes, after walking what I thought was some unexplored stretch of road or section of beach, I have been surprised to find it recorded on one of my earlier maps, unrecognized after many years.

This afternoon, however, for the first time, I began to see that whatever personal map I had traced for myself along the Cape's various thoroughfares existed within a larger, more public history of roads that I had also begun to subsume into my vision of this place. The highway I was on now, Route 6, is one of a series of roughly parallel roads that run down the lower arm of the Cape from Orleans to Provincetown, and in so doing weave deeply through the Cape's history, each strand having a traveled and storied history of its own.

Route 6 (that is, in its original, more loopy configuration) represents the first continuously paved road down the Outer Cape, completed in 1923. Along its length came the first large waves of motor tourists to Provincetown in the years after World War I. Provincetown's art colony flourished in those days, and the tourists were joined by hosts of painters, writers, and theatrical figures—Eugene O'Neill, Karl Knaths, Jack Reed, Mary Heaton Vorse, William Daniel Steele, Edward Hopper, Edna St. Vincent Millay, Edmund Wilson, Conrad Aiken, John Dos Passos, and many others—all traveling this road.

More than a mile to the west, running close to Cape Cod Bay, is the abandoned bed of the Old Colony Railroad, which first reached Wellfleet in 1869, and Provincetown four years later. Its tracks and ties, now long torn up, provided the fastest passage down-Cape before the advent of paved highways. It conveyed such distinguished figures as President Theodore Roosevelt, who laid the cornerstone of the Provincetown Monument in 1907, and such disgraced ones as the Reverend Horatio Alger, who fled his Unitarian pulpit in Brewster a few decades earlier. According to the records of Brewster's First Parish Church, Alger was dismissed by the church elders for "molesting young boys" and was ordered to take the next train out of town—to Boston or Provincetown. He chose Boston, where he later made his literary fortune with a series of rags-to-riches pulp novels about young, enterprising boys.

Lying between the old railroad bed and the present Route 6 is Old County Road, running its irregular course through all the town centers, along the borders of the marshes and through the woods on the Bay side. Thoreau traveled portions of this road on foot in 1849, remarking that it was so sandy "a horse would sink into its fetlocks there." A long, narrow, winding stretch of this old nineteenth-century road runs from Wellfleet Center to Truro Center, mostly within the National Seashore. To some of the older inhabitants it is still known as "Whiskey Road," reflecting its history as a thoroughfare of choice for transporting local bootlegged goods during Prohibition.

Only a few hundred yards east of Route 6's roaring summer traffic one can still find portions of the original Old King's Highway, the colonial road first built over three hundred years ago. It was in November 1778, following the wreck of the British man-of-war *Somerset* on Truro's backside, that 480 survivors of the Royal Navy, in the custody of Captain Enoch Hallett and the home guard, were marched down this road from North Truro to Boston through a chain of cheering and jeering villagers. Sixty years before that shipwreck another captain, Cyprian Southack, was sent to Wellfleet in 1717 by the colonial governor to recover the bullion that had come ashore when "Black Sam" Bellamy's pirate ship *Whydah* wrecked near Cahoon Hollow. Captain Southack also walked the King's Highway, knocking futilely on the doors of some of the two hundred Wellfleetians who had descended on the *Whydah*'s carcass and stripped her clean. Most of the locals denied knowledge, not only of the treasure but also of the wreck itself, leaving the captain to retrace his steps, fuming and empty-handed.

And further east still lies the oldest land road of all, the beach itself, the most changing and unchangeable of our thoroughfares, walked over the centuries by the Pamet, Punonakanit, and Nauset Indians, by the first hapless shipwrecked sailors, by early beachcombers and professional wreckers, by generations of lantern-carrying surfmen of the Life Saving Service, and by countless vacationers and beachgoers today.

I have walked or ridden each of these north-south routes at one time or another, but now, crisscrossing the stream of roaring trucks and buzzing cars on Route 6, I was struck anew at the cumulative history they represent, and at how various, and for what various purposes, have been the routes by which we have all made our way up and down this peninsula. Each way has taken precedence at different times in our collective history and at different seasons in our individual lives, and each is, to a remarkable degree, still here, intact and available for passage, if not by vehicle, then on foot.

But where did we think we were going all this time? Perhaps that is the question I had been wordlessly framing for myself as I started out on the beach earlier in the day—a day, it had turned out, of roads. Perhaps it is useful, on occasion, just to wander like this, along the thoroughfares of one's home ground, with no purpose in mind, just to try to get some sense of where it is they have led us after all these centuries of earnest and frivolous travel.

At the Wellfleet town line, I struck off west on the first dirt road through the woods toward Newcomb Hollow. About a third of a mile in, I came to the longest remaining continuous section of the original 1660 King's Highway. At this point the old colonial road is no more than a narrow dirt cartpath running through shady and quiet woods, indistinguishable from any of the other wood roads that labyrinth their way through this section of Wellfleet. Indeed, I wondered at first if this was in fact the Old King's Highway as designated on the map, for it ran due south over a fairly steep hill that would have been difficult for wagons and coaches to negotiate. One would think that if the early settlers had taken the trouble to lay out a road, they would have chosen an easier route. But I soon passed a brass plaque, set in a granite slab beside the road, which read:

> KINGS HIGHWAY
> HERE WAS BUILT
> THE FIRST
> SCHOOLHOUSE
> IN WELLFLEET
> W.R.

No dates, no hint of who the local historian or grown-up schoolboy "W.R." might have been, and of course no sign of the vanished schoolhouse itself. But farther along there are eighteenth-century Cape farmhouses, the sites of old stagecoach inns, and ancient pear and apple orchards that still grow heavy with fruit in late summer, all giving further evidence that this out-of-the-way cartpath in these semi-isolated woods was once a vital artery running through active settlements.

To the east I began to hear music. The secluded pine woods rippled and hummed with the muted and overlapping sounds of drums, cornets, mandolins, guitars, and stereos. They came from a scattered, extensive community of summer cottages, most of them older ones predating the National Seashore, which were strung out around the ponds at the head of the Herring River and along a bewildering complex of sand roads. The varying and broken strands of music that filtered through the afternoon air had an informal, lackadaisical quality to them, starting and stopping in mid-phrase, like birdsong.

In their haphazard rhythms and snatches of melody, I sensed the strong role that these woods and the houses they hide play for their seasonal inhabitants, a role which they can never play for one who, like myself, lives here year-round and who comes to them, not so much to get away as to revisit and attend not only to the changes and continuities in the landscape but to those in myself as well. That is the great value, and lasting novelty, of staying put in one place, so that we can say with Thoreau of our well-thumbed landscapes that "I was promised the greatest novelty the world has ever seen or shall see, though the utmost possible novelty would be the difference between me and myself a year ago."

But for these summer refugees it must be a place out of their accustomed life, removed from its resigned and inexorable flow, a locale of wide margins where, for a weekend, two weeks, a month, or a season, they can still be who they once dreamed they were, lost in a maze of unregulated soft dirt roads, identified only by some rough wooden sign tacked to a pine trunk at an unnamed intersection in the woods, relaxing and making tentative music for its own sake, music that echoed anonymously back and forth across the waters that separated them.

So musing as I walked, I came at last to where the Old King's Highway crosses the Herring River, not far from its headwaters in Wellfleet's Herring Ponds, and only another twenty minutes to my car. Here the "river" is a shallow stream only a few feet wide, deep-sunk, slow-moving, well shaded, and extremely clear. On the downstream side, it exits from beneath the road out of a concrete culvert. There was a slight commotion in the water here, and I saw that thousands of small herring fry, each about three inches long, were circling and swimming downstream in thick clumps, like swirling patches of long, slender blades of grass. These were the year's crop of alewives—migratory herring which each spring make their way up hundreds of New England rivers and streams to spawn in freshwater ponds, and then shortly return, leaving the young to hatch and make their own precarious way back out to sea in late summer and early fall.

The culvert out of which they swam—or, more accurately, were carried—was dark beneath the road and seemed to issue out of the earth itself, gushing up wave after wave of tiny fish that already seemed ocean-bent in their determined motions. They would cross, before they reached the Bay, the entire series of roads and thorough-fares striating the width of the Cape, in a largely unrecognized and unnoticed journey. Yet here was perhaps the oldest road of all traveled by life on this peninsula, predating all highways, railroads, wagon paths, and Indian trails. It is a road originally laid out, not by men but by tremendous ice sheets, plowing down from Canada's Lauren-tian Shield while Europeans huddled in caves in France and Spain. Its course was dug and graded, not by bulldozers but by the melt-waters of the glaciers' retreat, perpetually maintained and resurfaced by the flow of the ponds above it. For how many thousands of springs have alewives come in from the cold seas, making their way up this watery highway to spawn, leaving these tiny young to yield to late summer currents, to be carried out like autumn seeds to the unfath-omable waters of their maturity?

Once navigable, the river has been shrunken by dikes and filled in by marsh over the centuries, so that it is a way we rarely travel any more. Nor are we likely to be aware of these herring fry as we speed over them on our various human highways. My own way home that afternoon lay in an opposite direction to that of the fish, but watching their little forms darting through the lucid waters with such fresh and undiminished energy, I could not help but feel in some measure brought back to my own beginnings.

D O N A L D   H A L L

onald Hall, while known mostly as a poet and critic, has written some of the finest descriptions of landscape in recent literary history. "Winter," originally published as a part of *Seasons at Eagle Pond*, is a structurally complex mixture of literal portrait and metaphorical one. In it, Hall describes the almost overpowering cold and snow that come over his terrain each winter, sending its inhabitants into the warm safety of their firelit abodes. "Winter" also describes the history of this place through several generations, the sense of permanence, repetition, and rootedness it lends. A poetic love song, it expresses the joy and solace one might find in going absolutely nowhere, and in accepting the definition of self that a place bestows upon its inhabitants.

WINTER *

IN NEW HAMPSHIRE WE KNOW OURSELVES BY WINTER—IN SNOW, in cold, in darkness. For some of us the first true snow begins it; for others winter begins with the first bruising assault of zero weather: there is yet another sort, light-lovers, for whom winter begins with dark's onset in mid-August. If we wake as we ought to at 5:30, we begin waking in darkness; and dawn turns throaty with the ululations of photophiliacs, noctophobics, some of whom are fanatical enough to begin lamentation late in the month of June—when dawn arrives at 4:32 A.M. and yesterday it arrived at 4:31:30. On June 22 my wife exchanges postcards of commiseration with a fellow in Michigan who is another amorist of light. Fortunately this mountain has an upside as well as a downside. When in January daylight lasts half a minute longer every day, Jane's faint green leaves take on color, she leans south toward Kearsarge and the low, brief but lengthening pale winter sun; an observer can spy the faint buds that will burst into snowdrops in April, daffodils in April, tulips in May . . .

Some of us, on the other hand, are darkness-lovers. We do not *dislike* the early and late daylight of June, whippoorwill's graytime, but we cherish the gradually increasing dark of November, which we wrap around ourselves in the prosperous warmth of woodstove, oil,

* From Hood Museum of Art Exhibition Catalogue. A version of this essay also appeared in *Harper's Magazine*.

electric blanket, storm window, and insulation. We are partly tuber, partly bear. Inside our warmth we fold ourselves in the dark and the cold—around us, outside us, safely away from us: we tuck ourselves up in the long sleep and comfort of cold's opposite, warming ourselves by thought of the cold, lighting ourselves by darkness's idea. Or we are Persephone gone underground again, cozy in the amenities of Hell. Sheltered between stove and electric light, we hollow islands of safety within the cold and dark. As light grows less each day, our fur grows thicker. By December 22 we are cozy as a cat hunkered under a Glenwood.

Often October has shown one snow flurry, sometimes even September. For that matter, it once snowed in New Hampshire every month of the year. In 1816, it snowed and froze in June, in July, in August—the Poverty Year, season of continuous winter when farmers planted over and over again, over and over again ripped out frozen shoots of corn and pumpkin. A volcanic eruption in the South Seas two years earlier did it, though at the time our preachers thought the source more local and divine wrath explicit.

Winter starts in November, whatever the calendar says, with gray of granite, with russet and brown of used leaves. In November stillness our stonewalls wait, attentive, and gaunt revenant trunks of maple and oak settle down for winter's stasis, which annually mimics and presages death for each of us and for the planet. November's palette, Braque's analytic cubism, static and squared with fieldstones, interrupts itself briefly with the bright-flapped caps of deer hunters and their orange jackets. Always it is modified by the black-green fir, enduring, hinting at permanence. Serious snow begins one November afternoon. Gradually Mount Kearsarge, south of us, disappears into white gauzy cloud, vanishing mountain, weather-sign for all of us to its north. For one hundred and eighty years the people of this house have looked south at dawn's light and again at sunset to tell the coming weather, reliable in 1802 when the first builder put in the south windows, reliable still. When Kearsarge disappears, the storm comes closer. Birds gather at the feeder, squabbling, gobbling their weight. When they are full they look for shelter, and we do the same, or at least we bring wood from the shed to stack beside the old Glenwoods and the new Jøtul.

Every year the first snow sets us dreaming. By March it will only bring the grumps, but November snow is revenance, a dreamy restitution of childhood or even infancy. Tighten the door and settle a cloth snake against the breeze from the door's bottom; make sure the storms are firmly shut; add logs to the stove and widen the draft. Sit in a chair looking south into blue twilight that arrives earlier every day—as the sky flakes and densens, as the first clear flakes float past the porch's wood to light on dirt of the driveway and on brown frozen grass or dry stalks of the flower border. They seem tentative and awkward at first, then in a hastening host a whole brief army falls, white militia paratrooping out of the close sky over various textures making them one. Snow is white and gray, part and whole, infinitely various yet infinitely repetitious, soft and hard, frozen and melting, a creaking underfoot and a soundlessness . . . But first of all it is the reversion of many into one. It is substance, almost the idea of substance, that turns grass, driveway, hayfield, old garden, log pile, Saab, watering trough, collapsed barn, and stonewall *into the one white.*

We finish early in November the task of preparing the house for snow—tacking poly over the low clapboards, raking leaves against the foundations as high as we can rake them. When the first real snow arrives, no dusting half inch but a solid foot, we complete the insulation, for it is snow that keeps us warm. After a neighbor's four-wheel-drive pickup, plow bolted in front, swoops clean our U-shaped driveway, and after we dig out the mailbox for Bert's rural delivery, it is time to heap the snow over leaves and against poly, around the house, on all sides of the house, against the granite foundation stones. Arctic winds halt before this white guard. When bright noon melts inches of snow away from the house, reflecting heat from the snowy clapboard, it leaves cracks of cold air for us to fill when new snow falls all winter long.

But November, although it begins winter, is only winter's approach, with little snow and with cold that announces itself only to increase. The calendar's winter begins at the solstice, Advent's event: the child's birth who rises from winter to die and rise again in spring. November is autumn's burial and the smoke of victims sacrificed is thanks for harvest and magic as we go into ourselves like maples for winter's bear-sleep. We make transition by way of least and anticipatory snow, toward the long, white, hard hundred days of the true winter of our annual death. We wait for December to feel the *cold.* I mean COLD, like thirty-five degrees below zero Fahrenheit. Seldom does it stay *cold*, or COLD, for longer than a week, but we are ready now for snow.

The first *big* snow accumulates one night. Kearsarge may disappear at noon, and darkness start early. In teatime twilight, big flakes slowly, as if hesitant, reel past the empty trees like small white leaves, star-shaped and infrequent. By bedtime, driveway and lawn turn shaggy with the first cover. It is good to go to bed early in winter, and tonight as we sleep our dreams take punctuation from the thudding of snowplows as they roll and bluster all night up and down Route 4, shaking the house yet comforting our sleep: Someone takes care, the solitary captains in their great snowships breasting through vast whiteness, fountaining it sideways into gutter drifts. If we stir as they thump past, we watch revolving yellow lights flash through our windows and reflect on the ceiling. We roll over and fall back into protected sleep. In a house full of cats we sleep not alone, for the snowplows that reassure us frighten our animals like thunder or riflefire; they crawl between our warm bodies under warmer electric blankets.

When we become aware, by the plows' repeated patrols, that the first deep snow accumulates; when the first intense and almost unbreakable sleep finishes and we enter the frangible second half of the night's house, I pull myself out of bed at two or three in the morning to inspect the true oncoming of winter's work. I walk through the dark house from one vantage to another—parlor window that looks west toward pond, kitchen from which I look toward Kearsarge, dining room that gives on the north, and if I twist, back to the slope of Ragged Mountain rising east above us. The night's flaking air breaks black sky into white flecks, silent and pervasive, shuttering the day's vista. This snow fills the air and the eyes, the way on spring nights peepers fill the ears. Everywhere I look, limited by snow-limits, cold dewy whiteness takes everything into itself. Beside the covered woodshed, side by side, I see the shapes of two small cars rounded and smooth like enormous loaves of dead-white bread. Where the woodpile waits for final stacking in the shed, a round mound rises with irregular sticks jagging out of it. Up on the hill the great cowbarn labors under a two-foot layer of snow, its unpainted vertical boards a dark upright shadow in all the whiteness, like the hemlocks above it on Ragged's hill. Although snowplows keep Route 4 passable, they do not yet scrape to the macadam: In the darkness the highway is as white as the hayfields on either side. Down the road white cottage disappears against white field, green shutters a patch of vacancy in the whiteness. In the stillness of 2:00 A.M., in a silent unlit moment with no plows thudding, I regard a landscape reverted to other years by the same snow—and I might be my great-grandfather gazing from the same windows in 1885. Or it might be his mother's eyes I gaze from, born on a Wilmot hill in 1789. Or maybe I look, centuries earlier, from the eyes of a Penacook wintering over the pond. If I squint a little I cannot see that this depression is a road.

But now the snowplow's thunder signals itself, and I watch the revolving yellow light reflect upward into white prodigious air, and hear the great bruising barge roar and rumble past the house, 1985 and grateful, as a steel prow swooshes high waves of whiteness up and over the gutter almost to the front of the house, and buries the mailbox.

One year the first great snow came Christmas Eve after the family had struggled to bed. When we lit the tree in the morning, the day was thick and dark past the windows, and as we opened our presents the snow deepened in yard and hayfield outside, and on Christmas Day, all day, the great plows of state and town kept Route 4 clear. Snow stopped at three in the afternoon, and when Forrest rolled in to plow the driveway in the early blue twilight, Jane heaped slices of turkey between homemade bread to comfort him in his cab as he drove over the countryside digging people out.

The next morning was cold, thirty below, cold enough to notice. January is the coldest month, in fact, although many would argue for February. Usually our cold is dry, and it does not penetrate so much as damp cold. December of 1975, our first full winter here, I tried starting the Plymouth one morning with normal confidence in the old six and without cold-weather precautions; I flooded it. When I looked at the thermometer I was astonished to find it minus seventeen degrees, for my face and forehead had not warned me that it was *cold*. I had lived in Michigan where the winters were damp, and Ann Arbor's occasional zero felt harsher than New Hampshire's common twenty below. Later that winter we did not complain of the mildness. In January of 1976, morning after morning was thirty below; one morning on the porch the thermometer read thirty-eight degrees under—a temperature we did not equal again until 1984. My grandmother had just died at ninety-seven, and she had spent most of her late winters going south to Connecticut. The house had grown unaccustomed to winter, the old heavy wooden storm windows broken, no central heat, and no insulation. Jane and I had never lived without central heat. Now we had a parlor Glenwood stove for heating, two kerosene burners in the kitchen, and on occasion an electric oven with the door left open. This twelve-room house, in January of 1976, dwindled to a one-room house, with a kitchen sometimes habitable. Working at the dining room table, twenty feet from the living room's Glenwood, I felt chilly. At the time, we were too excited or triumphant to complain. We were camping out; we were earning our stripes. The next summer we added aluminum combination storms and screens together with some insulation; we added two more small woodstoves, one for each study so that we could each work despite the winter. My grandparents survived with only two woodstoves because they bustled around all day; in our work we sat on our duffs and required extra stoves. When February came we learned we had passed our initiation, for it had been the coldest January since New Hampshire started keeping records more than a hundred years earlier. In all my grandmother's ninety-seven Januarys she had not known so cold a month.

My grandfather worked all day without any heat except for the bodies of his cows. When he sat at morning and evening between two great steaming black-and-white Holstein hulks, pulling the pale thin tonnage of blue milk from their cud-chewing bodies, he was warm. I can remember him, on my winter visits to the farm as a boy, scurrying into the house for a warm-up between his other daily chores, rubbing his hands together, opening the drafts of one of the woodstoves and looming over it for a moment. Early and late, he moved among cold sheds and unheated barns. In the cowbarn, he fed the cattle hay, grain, and ensilage, and provided his horse Riley with oats and hay and water. He let the Holsteins loose to wander still-legged to the old cement watering trough next to the milk room, from which he first removed a layer of ice. Their pink muzzles dipped one by one into the near-freezing water. And he fed the sheep in sheepbarn and sheepyard. From the sheep's trough he dipped out water for the hens, who lived next door to the sheep, and carried feed for his hens from the grainshed beside the cowbarn.

He would start these chores early, most days of deep winter, rising at four-thirty, perhaps three hours before the sun, to do half the daily chores of feeding and watering, of milking and readying milk for the trucker, because the special daily chores of winter were the year's hardest. The pains of minus twenty were exacerbated by pains of hard labor. To chop wood for next year's stove the farmer stalked with his ax into his woodlot after chores and breakfast, and often marched far enough so that he carried with him his bread and butter, meat and pie, and thermos of coffee for dinner. Setting out with a great ax, usually working alone, the farmer chopped the tree down, trimmed branches, cut the trunk into four-foot sections, and stacked it. Later he would hitch oxen to the sledge and fetch the cordwood downhill for cutting in the barnyard to stove-length pieces, and for splitting. Maybe ten cord of a winter for the house—more for the sugaring in March.

In January he harvested another winter crop—the crop that people forget when they think of the needs of an old farm—which was the harvest of ice, cut in great oblongs two or three feet thick from Eagle Pond, ox-sledded up to the icehouse in back of the cowbarn's watering trough, packed against warm weather six months hence. Each winter the farmer waited for a cold stretch, augering through the pond ice to check its thickness. Then he cut checkerboard squares with his ice saws. He kept himself heavily mittened not only against cold and wind rattling over the open desert lake, but also against the inevitable clasp of near-frozen water. A crew of them—neighbors cooperated to fetch ice—sawed and grappled, lifted and hauled, hard work and cold work. In the icehouse they stacked layers of ice, thickly insulated with sawdust, to last from the earliest warmth of April through hot spells of June and the long summer hay days of July and August through autumn with its Indian summer until the ice froze again. In the hot months my grandfather brought one chunk a day downhill from the icehouse, great square balanced with ice-tongs on his shoulder, to the toolshed behind the kitchen where my grandmother kept her icebox, drip drip. Most ice went to cool the milk, hot from the udders of Holsteins, so that it would not spoil overnight in the hot summer. July and August, I was amazed every time we dug down through the wet sawdust in the cool shade of the icehouse to find cold winter again—packed silvery slab of Eagle Pond preserved against summer, just as we hayed to preserve for the winter-cattle summer's hay. On the hottest days when we returned sweaty from haying, my grandfather cracked off a little triangle of ice for me to suck on. Every January when he dug down in the icehouse to bury his crop of new ice, he found old ice underneath it. After all, you never wanted to find yourself all out; some years, there might be hot days even in November when you would require a touch of ice. One long hot autumn, he found at the bottom of the ice shed, further than he ever remembered digging, a small coffin-shaped remnant from times past, ice that might have been five years old, he told me; maybe older . . .

And my grandfather told me how, in the state of Maine especially, in the old days, clipper ships loaded up ice and sawdust, at the end of winter, and sailed this cargo—transient mineral, annual and reproducible reverse-coal tonnage—down the East Coast to unload its cool for the South that never otherwise saw a piece of ice: ice by the ton for coastal cities like Charleston, South Carolina. Sometimes they sailed all the way to the West Indies with their perishable silvery cargo: Maine ice for the juleps of Charleston, northern January cooling Jamaica's rum.

By tradition the hard snow and heavy cold of January take a vacation for the eldritch out-of-time phenomenon of January thaw. Sometimes the January thaw comes in February, sometimes it never arrives at all, and on the rarest occasions it starts early and lasts all winter . . . Mostly the January thaw lives up to its name. Some strange day, after a week when we dress in the black of twenty below, we notice that we do not back up to the fire as we change our clothing. Extraordinary. Or at midday we pick up the mail in our shirtsleeves, balmy at forty-two degrees. (It is commonplace to observe that a temperature which felt Arctic late in August feels tropical in mid-January.) Icicles drip, snow slides off the south roof in midday sun, and mud season takes over the driveway. Snow melts deeply away from clapboard and poly. Or the January thaw comes with warm rain. ("If this was snow we'd have twelve feet . . .") And if warm rain pours for three January days, as I have known it to do, Ragged's melt floods our driveway, snow vanishes from all hayfields, and water drowns the black ice of Eagle Pond. Our small universe confuses itself with false spring. Bears wake perplexed and wander looking for deer corpses or compost heaps, thinking that it's time to get on with it. I remember fetching the newspaper one morning at six o'clock (I pick up the *Globe* outside a store nearby that does not open for customers, slugabeds, until eight o'clock) on the third day of a warm rain. Chugging through deep mud in my outboard Nissan, I pulled up at the wet porch to see a huge white cat rooting about in perennials beside the walk, a white pussycat with black spots . . . Oh, no . . . Therefore I remained in the front seat, quietly reading the paper, careful not to make a startling sound or otherwise appear rude—until the skunk wandered away.

Until we replaced rotten sills three years ago, a family of skunks lived in our rootcellar every winter. We never *saw* them, but we found their scat; we found the holes by which they entered and exited; we confirmed their presence by another sense. In the spring they sometimes quarreled, possibly over the correct time and place for love, and we could hear them snapping at each other, and, alas, we discovered that skunks used on each other their special skunk-equipment: Once a year in February or March we threw our windows wide open. On one occasion, Ann Arbor friends visited in March, dear friends notable for the immaculateness of their house in a culture of unspotted houses. When we brought them home with their skis from the airport, and opened the door, we discovered that our rootcellar family had suffered a domestic disagreement; therefore we opened all downstairs windows, although it was of course fifteen below. As we prepared to take our friends upstairs to their bedroom, where the air would be purer, we opened the doorway upstairs to discover a dead rat on the carpet, courtesy of a guardian cat. Welcome to the country.

January thaw is dazzling, but it is a moment's respite. If this were January in England we would soon expect snowdrops; here we know enough to expect replacement battalions of snow's troopers following on coldness that freezes the melt, covering it with foot upon foot of furry whiteness and moon-coldness. We return to the satisfactions of winter, maybe even to the deliverance and delirium of a full moon.

In New Hampshire the full moon is remarkable all year long, because we suffer relatively little from garbage-air and even less from background light. The great cloudless night of the full moon is werewolf time, glory of silver-pale hauntedness whenever it happens—but in winter it is most beautiful. I set the internal alarm, maybe three or four nights in a row, and wander, self-made ghost, through pale rooms in the pewter light while the moon magnifies itself in bright hayfields and reflects upward, a sun from middle earth, onto shadowy low ceilings. High sailing above, higher than it has a right to, bigger, the February full moon, huge disc of cold, rides and slides among tatters of cloud. My breathing speeds, my pulse quickens; for half an hour I wander, pulled like a tide through the still house in the salty half-light, more asleep than awake, asleep not in house or nightshirt in 1985 but in moon, moon, moon . . . What old animal awakens and stretches inside the marrow of the bones? What howls? What circles, sniffing for prey?

It's no winter without an ice storm. When Robert Frost gazed at bent-over birch trees and tried to think that boys had bent them playing, he knew better: "Ice storms do that." They do that, and a lot more, trimming disease and weakness out of the tree—the old tree's friend, as pneumonia used to be the old man's. Some of us provide life-support systems for our precious shrubs, boarding them over against the ice; for the ice storm takes the young or unlucky branch or birch as well as the rotten or feeble. One February morning we look out our windows over yards and fields littered with kindling, small twigs and great branches. We look out at a world turned into one diamond, ten thousand karats in the line of sight, twice as many facets. What a dazzle of spinning refracted light, spider webs of cold brilliance attacking our eyeballs! All winter we wear sunglasses to drive, more than we do in summer, and never so much as after an ice storm with its painful glaze reflecting from maple and birch, granite boulder and stonewall, turning electric wires into bright silver filaments. The snow itself takes on a crust of ice, like the finish of a clay pot, that carries our weight and sends us swooping and sliding. It is worth your life to go for the mail. Until sand and salt redeem the highway, Route 4 is quiet; we cancel the appointment with the dentist, stay home, and marvel at the altered universe, knowing that midday sun will strip ice from tree and roof and restore our ordinary white winter world.

Another inescapable attribute of winter, increasing in the years of postwar affluence, is the ski people, cold counterpart of the summer folks who have filled New Hampshire's Julys and Augusts ever since the railroad came in the 1840s. Now the roads north from Boston are as dense on a February Friday as they are on a July; and late Sunday afternoon Interstate 93 backs up from the tollbooth. On twenty thousand Toyotas pairs of skis ride north and south every weekend. At Christmas vacation and school holidays every hotel room fills all week with families of flatlanders. They wait in line at the tows, resplendent in the costumes of money, booted and coifed in bright petrochemical armor. They ride, they swoop, they fall, they drink whiskey . . . and the bonesetter takes no holiday on a New Hampshire February weekend, and the renter of crutches earns time and a half. Now that cross-country rivals downhill, the ski people grow older and more various; tourism, which rivals the yard sale as major north country industry, brings Massachusetts and New York money for the thin purses of the cold land. And by the fashionable areas—much of Vermont, and the Waterville Valley in New Hampshire's White Mountains—restaurants and boutiques, cute-shops and quiche-cafés buzz like winter's blackflies.

The snowmachine breaks trails for cross-country, and it is also the countryman's ski outfit. Few natives ski, though some have always done, and in our attic there are wide heavy wooden skis from the time of the Great War on which my mother and her sisters traipsed all winter, largely doing cross-country but perfectly willing to slide down a hill. Old-timers remember the horse as ski-tow, pulling adventurers uphill.

The motorcycle roar of snowmachines, from a distance indistinguishable from chainsaws, interrupts the down-quiet of midweek evenings, as kids roar along disused railroad tracks and over the surface of frozen lakes. Mostly kids. The older folks, men mostly, park their bobhouses on thick ice of winter lakes, saw holes in the ice, light a fire, warm themselves with a pint of whiskey, and fish for the wormless perch of winter. Like deer-hunting in November, of course, this fishing is not mere sport; it fills the freezers of ten thousand shacks, trailers, and extended farmhouses. On Eagle Pond just west of us we count six or a dozen bobhouses each winter, laboriously translated by pickup and pushed or slipped across the ice to a lucky spot. Most springs it seems one fisherman waits too late. How many little houses, some with tin stoves flaking away, raise a freshwater Davy Jones's condominium on the bottom of Eagle Pond?

After the labor of cordwood and ice in the old days, in March, as the winter ended, followed the great chore of maple sugaring. It still arrives, though without so much labor. Usually it comes in March, one stretch, but on occasion the conditions for sap turn right for two weeks in February, go wrong for twenty days, then right again—a split season of sugaring. Right conditions are warm days when the snow melts followed by cold nights when it freezes. Nowadays people suction sap from the sugarbush with miles of plastic tubing. In the old time, you pounded the spigot into the tree—several of them in a good-sized three-hundred-year-old maple—and hung a bucket from each for the sap to drip into. My grandfather trudged from tree to tree every day, wearing a wooden yoke across his shoulders; long pails hung from the ends of it, narrow on top and wide on bottom, for collecting sap from each bucket. He emptied these yoke-pails into a great receptacle sledged by an ox—oxen were especially useful in the winter, slow but unbothered by snow—and when he filled this great sledge-kettle, his ox pulled it to a funnel and pipe whence the sap flowed downhill to a storage tank behind the saphouse.

Gathering sap was a third of the work, or maybe a quarter. There was cordwood to cut and burn under the trays boiling the sap down. Someone had to tend the fire day and night, and to watch and test the sap on its delicate journey to syrup. In 1913 my grandfather corked five hundred gallons at a dollar a gallon, big money in 1913, with the help of his father-in-law Ben Keneston, cousin Freeman, and Ansel the hired man. When we remember that it takes about forty gallons of sap, boiled down, to make one gallon of syrup, we begin to assess the labor required.

But the sweetness of the task was not only the cash crop. With honey from the beehive next to the barn and the hollyhocks, my grandfather and grandmother grew and produced their own sweetening. With the cash from the syrup—sometimes from wool and baby lambs—they bought land and paid taxes. Often their tax was little or nothing, for in the old days many farmers paid their taxes by doing road work—scraping and rolling the dirt roads, filling in with hardpan, and in winter rolling down the snow on the road to make it fit for the runners of sleighs, taking on a mile of Wilmot's Grafton Turnpike.

March was always the month for blizzards. Still is. It is the time when we all tell ourselves: *We've had enough of winter.* Old folks come back from Florida and Hilton Head: younger ones, fed up, head off for a week where the weather performs like May or June in New Hampshire. Every morning the *Globe* measures a word from Florida: *baseball* . . . In New Hampshire, tantalizing melt is overwhelmed with four feet of snow, drifts to twelve feet . . . We comfort each other, when we use the form of complaint for our boasting, that even if we lost the old outhouse yesterday, or the '53 Buick that the chickens use for summer roosting, what comes quick in March goes quick in March, and three or four days from now it'll melt to reveal the lost Atlantis of the family barnyard. Of course three or four days later, we find another four feet.

Blizzards happen in March, like the great one of '88, which the old people still bragged about in the 1940s. My Connecticut grandfather and my New Hampshire one, who shared little, shared the blizzard of '88: a great watershed for bragging, or for telling lies about. And in the 1980s I still ask old people what they remember that *their* old people told them about '88, much as the '88ers themselves asked their old-timers about the Poverty Year of 1816. Great weather makes great stories. Paul Fenton told me a story he heard as a boy, not about '88 but just about "the big snows we used to have, back in the old days." It seems that a bunch went out after a heavy snow, dragging the roads with the help of oxen so that people could use their sleighs and sledges, when one of the oxen slipped and got stuck, couldn't move at all: got a hoof caught in something . . . Well, they dug down, dug around, trying to free the ox's hoof, and what do you know . . . That ox had stuck its foot into a chimney!

Now, the blue snow of 1933 is *not* a lie. I am sure of it, because of the way Ansel Powers tells me about it, because his wife Edna confirms it, because Les Ford from Potter Place, who has never been known to collaborate on a story, remembers it just as well and tells the same stories. It may be hard to believe: *but it was blue.* You stuck a shovel in it, and it was *blue*, blue as that sky, blue as a bachelor's button. It fell in April, a late snow, and it fell fast. Les remembers that he'd been to a dance at Danbury, and when he went to bed at midnight the sky was clear and full of stars; when he woke up in the morning, there was three feet of blue snow. The snowplows were disassembled for summer; the road agent had to start up the old dozer and go up and down the road with it, to clear a way for the Model T's—and a few shiny Model A's. Nobody *saw* it snow except Sam Duby, the same blacksmith who made the first snowplows in Andover. He woke up at two or three in the morning and had to do something, you know; well, the outhouse was across the road in the barn, and he came out on the porch and it was snowing to beat the band and he just dropped a load right there . . . He's the only one who saw it snow; the rest of us went to bed under stars, woke up to the sun shining in three feet of *blue snow*.

In *The Voyage of the Beagle* Charles Darwin wrote about finding red snow, *Protococcus nivalis*, on the Peuquenes Ridge in Chile in 1835. "A little rubbed on paper gives it a faint rose tinge mingled with a little brick-red." When he examined it later, Darwin found "microscopical plants." As far as I know, no one took our blue snow into a laboratory.

Of course it snows in April, every year, most often white, but you cannot call it winter anymore. Snow sticks around, in the north shade, most years until early in May, but it is ragged and dirty stuff, and we overlook it as we gaze in hopeful amazement at this year's crop of daffodils. Every year the earlier daffodils fill with snow, bright yellow spilling out white crystals, outraged optimism overcome by fact. And the worst storm I have driven through, after ten New Hampshire winters, occurred a few years back on the ninth day of May.

But annual aberration aside, March is the end of winter, and the transition to spring is April's melt. One year not long ago we had an open winter, with very little snow, *no* snow we all said; we exaggerated a little for we had an inch here and an inch there. The winter was not only dry but mild, which was a good thing, for an open winter with cold weather destroys flowers and bushes and even trees, since snow is our great insulator. As it was, in our open winter we suffered one cold patch—twenty below for a week—and in the spring that followed, and in the summer, we discovered winterkill: A few rose bushes and old lilacs, plants and bulbs that had survived for decades, didn't make it that year. When spring came without a melt, when mild days softened with buttery air and the protected daffodils rose blowing yellow trumpets, we felt uneasy; all of us knew: Lacking the pains of winter, we did not deserve the rapture and the respite of spring.

Our annual melt is the wild, messy, glorious loosening of everything tight. It is gravity's ecstasy as water seeks its own level on every level, and the noise of water running fills day and night. Down Ragged Mountain the streams rush, cutting through ice and snow, peeling away winter's cold layers. Rush, trickle, rush. Busy water moves all day and all night, never tired, cutting away the corrupt detritus of winter. Fingers of bare earth extend down hillsides. South sides of trees extend bare patches farther every day. Root-patterned rivulets melting gather downhill to form brief streams. Dirt roads slog, driveways turn swamps, cars smithereen transmissions. Rural delivery, which survives ten thousand blizzards, sticks in the mud of April.

Then it dries. Last snow melts. Trees bud green. Soft air turns. Who can believe in winter now?

All of us. We know that winter has only retreated, waiting. When the bear comes out of its winter sleep, winter itself goes into hibernation, sleeping off the balmy months of peeper-sing until the red leaf wakes it again and the white season returns with the New Hampshire by which we know ourselves.

JOY WILLIAMS

ne of the more polemical essays in *The Place Within*, "Florida" reveals an author straddling an uncomfortable fence. In her fiction, Joy Williams has often "used" her native Florida as a setting. She has also "used" it in *The Florida Keys: A History and Guide*, which, she recounts with no small irony, "has sold better than any of my fiction." As an environmentalist, however, Williams is aware that writing about places, while assuaging our guilt, does little to save these places from destruction. It is with this ironic, often angry awareness that "Florida" is written. The essay is a bold warning about the contradiction inherent about environmental work on the one hand, and the "literature of landscape" on the other.

FLORIDA

At any of Florida's state parks you can get a car tag that says: *"Florida State Parks—The Real Florida,"* with the silhouette of a panther on it. It's like saying the Real Iceland, with a picture of the auk, which was exterminated by some guy, some genetic predecessor of the Wise Use movement undoubtedly, who killed the last nesting pair and smashed their single egg in 1844. If the "real" Florida, the natural Florida hasn't utterly disappeared, it has certainly been pushed to its last redoubt. And still it never ends: the destruction and diminishment. The desecration and degradation. Of Florida.

Poor Florida. Once so pretty and now so battered and worn, she still presents a sunny countenance. Sunny, self-destructive, over-crowded Florida. Where realtors scramble and claw their way to the highest offices in the Audubon Society.

In Europe, Florida is known as Orlando. For many decades, she's been touted as "Vacationland." But the last winter here was cold and wet and many vacationers vowed they would not return, never return, for Florida had become too "unreliable" as a destination. If the sky's not blue and the sun don't shine, what's the point of coming down after all?

And there are those unpleasant incidents—attacks in highway rest areas, murders at tiki bars, bodies being discovered by the maid under the box springs in perfectly nice hotels, jet skis attacking the boats of "wilderness" guides. But Florida hardly needs the vacationer any more. There is no "season": Florida has maxed out with her permanent occupiers. Banks sponsor gala celebrations with fireworks and parades when a city, Jacksonville, hits the one million population mark. Tampa has become Sarasota. Fort Meyers, Naples. Miami sprawls everywhere. But Florida is still a very large state, and as Jax struts and hollers its way into the future as Queen of the Mildew Belt, one thousand miles to the south is the one-of-a-kind, quietly suffocating Everglades.

When I first came to Florida, I was ignorant enough to think that the Everglades National Park *was* the Everglades, when in fact the entire bottom half of the state is; or was, until fifty years ago, when it was diked, drained, channeled and farmed and 'burbed out. The Everglades is a delicate and beautiful ecosystem unequaled on this planet, but it was considered nothing more than a plumbing problem, and treated accordingly. Everyone had pretty much written it off except for some screaming and fussing environmentalists, and it seemed destined to die under the observant eyes and tinkering hands of state bureaucrats, sugar and development interests, and water management boards.

But in February 1996 the Clinton administration did what it had long promised to do and made the shrunken River of Grass the nation's top environmental priority, pledging hundreds of millions of dollars to restore it. Farmland will be bought and turned back to marsh, which sounds wonderful, of course, except to those farmers whose T-shirt of choise says EVERGLADES FARMER—AN ENDANGERED SPECIES. The difficulty is that no one has exactly figured out how farmland is metamorphosized back into viable marsh. When the state recently acquired some long-sought-after farmland that it considered key to its plans for "freshening"—*resuscitating* is more accurate—Florida Bay, the Everglades's immense saltwater nursery, it leased the land back to farmers to farm while it figured out how this restoration idea would proceed. Florida is not a state of mind, but of irony.

Not long ago, on a panel about "place" at a literary seminar in Key West, I remarked that Florida was "toast." This enraged certain members of the audience, who had paid good money to hear how lovely and unique the place was, and to be assured that they had not made a mistake by moving down here. They were sick of people like me, always bad-mouthing everything. Florida wasn't a vanished world, she was still here, wasn't she? There was a lot to still like about Florida, a lot. The weather was still okay. And it's recognizable, the aura. People recognize it as providing the backdrop for lots of nifty crime novels. Writers become "Florida writers" by writing in this genre. They use her as bright and sleazy background. She's reduced to a lurid sunset, a contrivance. She serves, in all her sunny rottenness, as fictive amusement.

Even for the non-genre writer, of course, place matters. Florida has impelled and infused my own writing for twenty-five years. I began on the St. Marks River in northern Florida, then lived for many years on Siesta Key off Sarasota on the west coast. Now I'm as far down as you can go in this exquisitely and peculiarly shaped state: Key West. Florida has served me as backdrop, framework, ambience. I've *used* her. Water and weirdities. Bright irreality. Palmy irresponsibility. Her residents a bit batty. A swell place. Odd but accessible, very accessible. Oh, it was fun. And everything was willing to be shown. The palm would surrender its intense heart for a salad alone. The shark would rise to the bloody bait. Florida was stage and tone. She was my familiar. Surreal and ironic, ironic because her stupendous beauty was so dismissed and debased.

Here in Key West, we have a few salt ponds. A few remnant salt ponds hemmed in by the airport and crisscrossed by filled-in marly trails. People like to come out here, finish off large bottles of vodka, and change the oil in their vehicles of choice. No state-regulated waste disposal fees for them. They're anti-bureaucrat. They prefer to leave the oil where they wish, in this case, in plastic milk jugs at the water's edge. All manner of grotesque debris can be found here, arriving daily. Toilets, gas grilles, construction debris. An existential touch (Oh, the environment is a hostile place and man must oppose it by exercising his free will . . .) is the discarded box that once contained *Barbie's Housekeeping Set*—a gift to some lucky little girl—placed on top of a junked sofa, an engine block, some fast-food containers, the entire arrangement nestled in the mangroves. You can see almost anything out at the salt ponds. The place is practically . . . hypnotizing. But it would be rare indeed if you saw any birds. Where *are* the birds? In the Keys there seem to be more birds in the Wildlife Rescue and Rehabilitation Center in Key West and in Islamorada than in the air, and these birds in general are missing something—

an eye, a foot, a wing. They're not *entire* birds. Where are the birds? Where's the reef? Where's the view?

For the writer who lives in Florida and was ever nurtured by its natural strangeness and beauty—the beauty and strangeness of the ray and egret, the mangrove and palm—landscape, with its connotations of source and strength, has been replaced by lifeless scenery, something even less than scenery. Florida has been assaulted by mankind for over a hundred years now. She has not withstood that assault. Habitat has been leveled into just another place to live. It all looks pretty much the same now, urban and suburban. Key West is the most "interesting" city in Florida, which of course doesn't mean that it's beautiful, though it has many charms, one of which is that it is not at all representative of the rest of the state. The marvelous poet Elizabeth Bishop, who lived here in the 1940s, wrote: "When somebody says 'beautiful' about Key West you should really take it with a grain of salt until you've seen it for yourself. In general it is really awful and the 'beauty' is just the light or something equally perverse."

The light. Maybe we'll all, in the end, just settle for the light.

Nature writing is enjoying a renaissance. This seems to be in lieu of nature itself, which is not. The humanities in America's colleges have become "green." Environmental Studies is the new hot academic major, with literature professors becoming ecocritics discovering anew how language constitutes reality, and making remarks like: "Environmentalism is ultimately a question of design—of ethical design," and, "We're seeing a return to realism, to exact and aesthetically pleasing descriptions of nature." All of which is fascinating, given that nature is becoming less aesthetically pleasing all the time, falling as it is to the unethical plow, the bulldozer, the saw, and the ghost net.

Nature is receding in many different ways at once and may in fact, in our time, be utterly subsumed by language, by the writers'—some writers'—increasingly frantic attempts to capture it and preserve its image, somewhat like a pressed fern, between the pages.

Where is literature in all this? Maybe it's too late for literature in this "world of wounds," as Aldo Leopold calls it. Maybe there is just a world of warring words. They are there when I read that businessmen in Crystal River, Florida, although realizing that the manatee is a resource they can capitalize on, nevertheless think that its protection has gone too far when tourists can't swim with it. Or when I read that Miami developers can now get rid of their wetland mitigation obligations (wetland *protection* was an eighties thing) by paying into a wetland bank somewhere else, away from their golf courses and zero-lot line developments. Or when I read the many complaints from people who weren't able to "use" the wilderness areas of the Everglades and Fort Jefferson National Park in the Dry Tortugas during the government shutdown, including the lament of a *Miami Herald* columnist that the fish were lonely, lacking as they did the fishermen. When I read such things, does it drive me to literature? These are assaults on nature at the most careless, unthinking, or cynical level, and it takes more than literature to deal with them.

I think you have only one chance at *place* in this life, your life. A place where your spirit finds a home, a place you cherish and want to protect. All this can take a lifetime. And you can miss your place. Or not recognize it. You can be faithful steward to the wrong place. And when do you leave, abandon it to others? When you see the two-lane bridge to the beach become four? When the four-lane road becomes eight? When you hear motel owners complain bitterly that turtles don't pay taxes, that property owners and tourists do, and that turtle nests just mess up the beach and prohibit proper human use? When a hundred-year-old live oak is slain for a Hooters? When you see an egret trying to fish in the soiled, rain-filled pit of a construction site once too often? When do you leave; what will it take?

Sometimes I despair, which I've heard philosophically speaking is an immature response to reality; joy, in fact, always joy, is the proper, integrated reaction. But sometimes, I must admit—frequently, actually—I despair. Florida has perhaps lost her distinction of place, her vital mystery, and those who love her might be laboring in the wrong vineyard. Knocking at the wrong door. Praying at the wrong church.

But for those who love her this cannot, of course, must not be so.

JEFFREY A. HOFFMAN

lthough an astronaut by trade, Jeffrey A. Hoffman has the spirit of a poet. In "A Place Above America," Hoffman writes movingly, with beautiful clarity, about what it is like to view America from a unique perspective. "Seen from space at night," he writes, "America is a place of glorious lights. At first glance, these lights form a beautiful chaos, but a space traveler soon learns to recognize patterns of light and associate them with a mental geographical map, navigating from city to city much as a stargazer uses one constellation to find another." Hoffman has been a NASA astronaut since 1979, making his first space flight as a Mission Specialist in 1985. Since then, he has logged over one thousand hours in space, working on the Hubble Space Telescope and other missions. Hoffman has a promising literary career ahead of him, should he ever tire of traveling in space.

A P L A C E
A B O V E
A M E R I C A

AMERICA IS MADE UP OF MANY INDIVIDUAL PLACES, BUT FLYING IN
a spacecraft over the entire North American continent in ten minutes
creates a sense of all America as one place. Only from space have I
experienced America as an island continent, different from the much
larger African-Eurasian landmass.

I fly over America several times during each twenty-four hours.
Each time, I first experience America as a welcome change from the
endless Pacific Ocean, over which our west-to-east orbit inevitably
carries us before we reach the country's West Coast. Circled every
ninety minutes, the entire Earth seems small, but when thirty of these
minutes are spent looking at an unbroken expanse of water, I realize
how big the Pacific Ocean truly is. While flying over the ocean, I
often look toward the horizon, straining to get an early glimpse of
the oncoming land, much like a sailor looking out from atop a ship's
mast. The difference is that, even on a clear day, the sailor's horizon
is only tens of miles away, while my horizon stretches over a thousand
miles.

There is an even more fundamental difference between an astronaut's horizon and a sailor's. Instead of a huge blue sky coming down
to meet the ground, I see above the horizon the deep blackness of
space, the blackest black I have ever seen. Separating it from the Earth
is a thin but intense blue line. It is hard to believe that the "big,
blue sky," which looks so immense from below, is actually so small.

As a space traveler, I keenly feel the hostility of space to life. Outside our spaceship, or on any other planetary surface in our solar system, I would not survive unprotected for even fifteen seconds. The Earth is unique. From space, I see our atmosphere as the protective cocoon that shields us from the hostile universe and permits life to exist. This thin blue line is so small and vulnerable, though, that the life-nurturing power of the Earth seems particularly precious.

Spaceflight tends to engender this kind of "planetary conscious-ness," and long periods of flight over the Pacific Ocean are a good time for such contemplation, but planetary thoughts give way to thoughts of America as dry land finally appears over the horizon. From far away, the first things I notice are the contrast between the different regions of the continent. I can see the Pacific Coast merging into the basin and range country of the Rocky Mountain states, the Sonoran Desert thrusting northward from Mexico, and the abrupt delineation of the Rocky Mountains and Great Plains stretching north and south for over a thousand miles. The broad swath of the Gulf Coast is a special place for astronauts, since we live in Houston. I remember the first time I flew over Houston as a space rookie. I could easily make out with my naked eye the pattern of freeways that crisscross the city. Then I took a look through high-powered binoculars and was amazed that I could see all the buildings of the Johnson Space Center, where I work. I quickly swept my gaze a few miles to the east and was actually able to see my own house! I got so excited I felt like waving out the window at my family, until I remembered that they were staying in Florida for the duration of the flight. Of course, moving at five miles every second, it wasn't long before we were flying over them. Florida's Cape Canaveral is another place astronauts always look out for, since it is where we leave the Earth and where we usually return. Looking down, it is easy to see our launch pad as well as the long runway especially built for Shuttles to land on. As we approach the end of a space flight, we take a close personal interest in watching the weather patterns approaching Florida and trying to predict if we will be able to land there or will have to divert to the California desert.

I have always been struck by the contrast between having such a vast view from orbit, spanning thousands of miles from horizon to horizon, and yet still being able to pick out individual buildings and roads right below me. People are often surprised that objects can be seen so sharply from a distance of hundreds of miles. When something is directly below us, however, we only have to look through the equivalent of a few miles of atmosphere, which is why on a clear day it is so easy to make out city streets, individual buildings, and even moving vehicles when we fly right over them. As our gaze goes further out to the horizon, light has to travel through a lot more atmosphere before it reaches our eyes. The scattering of light reduces the sharpness, contrast, and color differences of terrestrial features, so we can only see large-scale changes of color and texture that mark the boundaries between different geographical regions. The detail necessary to pick out cities is lost, and instead we notice geographical features like lakes, rivers, and mountains. The closer we look toward the horizon, the more America looks like the place it probably was before Europeans ever arrived.

All this is true by day. At night, the sense of place changes completely. We fly over some parts of the globe where the only lights at night are lightning storms and an occasional fire. Pre-Revolutionary America must have looked like this, but industrialization has changed America's nights. Our society produces millions of tiny points of electric light, which shine like stars below us as we pass overhead. The contrast between a point of light and a dark background is so great that bright lights can be seen all the way out to the horizon. Seen from space at night, America is a place of glorious lights. At first glance, these lights form a beautiful chaos, but a space traveler soon learns to recognize patterns of light and associate them with a mental geographical map, navigating from city to city much as a stargazer uses one constellation to find another. The thrill of recognition as each new landmark is identified can be experienced by cross-country airplane travelers flying over familiar territory, but the scale of the vista seen from space is vastly greater, spanning the whole continent.

Flying over America at night, the sense of place is very strong because, knowing the geography in great detail, I can make sense of the patterns of light. This is in great contrast to, for instance, East Asia. The lights on the west coast of the Pacific Rim are as impressive as in America, but I am not so familiar with Asian geography and hence do not derive the same excitement at being able to navigate my way around the city lights. I have flown with several crew members who were military pilots with experience in Asia, who knew the geography much better than I. They got much more excited than I did when we flew over that area, because they recognized it. Every time I fly over America, especially at night, I get the pleasure of recognizing a place I know.

The tiny dots of Hawaiian lights break up our nighttime orbit over the dark Pacific Ocean and signal me to look for the glow of California on the horizon. The thin blue line I could see on the horizon during the day is no longer visible. Instead, the Earth is now surrounded by an even thinner ethereal orange-brown halo, caused by molecular activity high in the atmosphere. It is easy to mistake this line for the actual horizon, except that setting stars continue to shine through the halo and remain visible below it until they actually set behind the Earth. On a moonless night, the entire ocean below me is invisible. All I can see is this ghostly halo stretching around the horizon and the glorious stars, which seen from space do not twinkle. This is when I feel most removed from everything on the Earth. With the overwhelming presence of the Sun hidden from me and with no visible terrestrial landmarks, I could be anywhere in the galaxy.

This reverie is interrupted as the first lights of California appear over the horizon. I am no longer floating somewhere in the galaxy, I am back over America, trying to pick out familiar places. The ring of lights surrounding a black hole is San Francisco and the Bay Area. Starting the process of mental navigation, I realize that the two lights just to the east must be Sacramento and Reno. Then I look south and see the huge expanse of light coming from the Los Angeles basin. San Diego is shining brightly just to the south, but most amazing is the intensely bright light to the east. It is not large compared to the enormous expanse of Los Angeles, but its intensity far surpasses anything else in the world. It is Las Vegas, outrageously bright, shining like a nova outburst in the black space of the surrounding desert. Even with my naked eye I can clearly see the Strip from orbit.

I continue my visual navigation as I fly east. "That's Denver, so those two lights to the south must be Colorado Springs and Pueblo . . . That huge light with the dark area over it must be Chicago and Lake Michigan, so directly north is Milwaukee and the double light further west must be Minneapolis–St. Paul . . . The big blob of light on the Gulf Coast is Houston, so the other two points of the triangle must be Austin and San Antonio, and the Dallas–Fort Worth area is just to the north."

Flying over Houston, I am in the middle of the continent, and looking out opposite windows of the spacecraft, I can see all the way back to the West Coast on one side and out to the East Coast on the other. By this time, I am thoroughly used to translating the lights below into a mental map of American cities, and from this central point I take in the entire country, "from sea to shining sea." Soon, moving inexorably eastward at eighteen thousand miles an hour, I lose sight of the Pacific Coast and concentrate my gaze on the eastern half of the country. Without the vast desert and mountain expanses of the West, the East is almost completely covered with lights. The cities of the eastern seaboard are strung out like a shining necklace. Miami is at the core of a huge blob of light in southern Florida, which sports a tail (the Keys). Atlanta is the next major point of light to the north. There is a strange darkness, however, stretching to the northeast from Atlanta, in marked contrast to the overall brightness of the eastern half of North America. Suddenly, feeling once again the thrill of recognition, I realize that I am seeing the economically less developed Appalachians. It is an easy task now to work my way up the coast past Charleston, Richmond, Washington, Baltimore, and Philadelphia. I lived for many years in New York and Boston, so it is especially exciting to be able to pick them out at the end of the luminous chain of East Coast cities. The view is brief, though. Only ten minutes after I first picked up the lights of California, I now watch the lights of the eastern seaboard gradually disappear over the western horizon, leaving behind America.

ABOUT

THE

CONTRIBUTORS

DIANE ACKERMAN is the author of twelve books, including *A Natural History of the Senses*; *A Natural History of Love*; the essay collection *The Moon by Whalelight: Other Adventures Among Bats, Penguins, Crocodilians and Whales*; several volumes of poetry; and, most recently, *The Rarest of the Rare: Vanishing Animals, Timeless Worlds*. She lives with her husband, writer Paul West, in upstate New York.

SUZANNE BERNE's essays and short stories have been published in numerous periodicals, including *The Quarterly, Agni, The Threepenny Review*, and *The New York Times Magazine*. She is also a frequent contributor to the *New York Times Book Review* and *Travel* sections. Berne's first novel, *A Crime in the Neighborhood*, will be published by Algonquin Books in 1997.

HARRY CREWS is the author of nineteen books, including two novels, *Body, Scar Lover* and *The Mulching of America*, and a memoir, *Childhood: The Biography of a Place*, as well as numerous articles and columns. Crews lives in Gainesville, where he teaches at the University of Florida.

JODI DAYNARD, editor of *The Place Within*, is an essayist and fiction writer. Her essays have been published in numerous periodicals, including *The New York Times Book Review, Harvard Magazine, The*

Harvard Review, The Paris Review, and in several anthologies. Her current project is a memoir, *The Consolation of Things: Memoirs of a Suburban Childhood*. Daynard has taught at Harvard University and at MIT.

GERALD EARLY is the Merle Kling Professor of Modern Letters and director of the African and Afro-American Studies Program at Washington University in St. Louis. He is the author of a memoir, *Daughters: On Family and Fatherhood*, and a collection of essays, *The Culture of Bruising*, which won the 1994 National Book Critics Circle Award for criticism. He is currently working on a book about Fisk University.

GRETEL EHRLICH was born and raised in California, and has returned there to live after many years in Wyoming. She is the author of *The Solace of Open Spaces* and *Islands, The Universe, Home*, as well as the novel *Heart Mountain*. Ehrlich's story of being struck by lightning, *A Match to the Heart*, is her latest book.

ROBERT FINCH, a resident of Cape Cod since 1971, is the author of four essay collections, *Common Ground, The Primal Place, Outlands*, and *The Cape Itself*. He is editor of *The Norton Book of Nature Writing* and *Place Apart: A Cape Cod Reader*. Finch's current projects include the forthcoming *Smithsonian Guide to Southern New England* and a book about Newfoundland.

DONALD HALL is the author of numerous prize-winning volumes of poetry—including *The One Day*, winner of the National Book Critics Circle Award for Poetry—as well as essays, children's books, and criticism. His most recent books are *Their Ancient Glittering Eyes* and *The Museum of Clear Ideas*. Hall lives on his family farm in New Hampshire with his wife, the poet Jane Kenyon.

JEFFREY A. HOFFMAN has been a NASA astronaut since 1979. He received his Ph.D. in astrophysics from Harvard University. Dr. Hoffman has logged over 1,000 hours in space as a NASA Mission Specialist, working on the Hubble Space Telescope and other projects, including EVA, the development of a high-pressure spacesuit for use on the Space Station.

WILLIAM KITTREDGE is the author of two essay collections, *Who Owns the West* and *Owning It All*; the memoir, *Hole in the Sky*; and two short story collections, *The Van Gogh Field and Other Stories* and *We Are Not In This Together*. Kittredge also co-edited *The Last Best Place: A Montana Anthology*. He is the recipient of numerous awards, including the National Endowment for the Humanities' Charles Frankel Prize for service to the humanities. Kittredge is Professor of English and Creative Writing at the University of Montana.

NATALIE KUSZ is the author of the memoir *Roadsong*, and a recent recipient of a National Endowment for the Arts grant in Creative Non-Fiction for her second memoir. She is a Briggs-Copeland Fellow at Harvard University.

ALAN LIGHTMAN is the author of ten books, including the novels *Einstein's Dreams* and *Good Benito*, and three essay collections, *A Modern Day Yankee in a Connecticut Court*; *Time Travel and Papa Joe's Pipe*; and, most recently, *Dance for Two*. Lightman is professor of science and writing at the Massachusetts Institute of Technology.

PHILLIP LOPATE's books include *Bachelorhood, Against Joi de Vivre, The Rug Merchant, Being with Children*, and *The Art of the Personal Essay*. He holds the Adams chair at Hofstra University, and has written extensively on urban issues.

ELLEN MELOY's portrait of a remote canyon in southern Utah, *Raven's Exile: A Season on the Green River*, won the Spur Award for contemporary nonfiction. Her natural history essays are widely anthologized, and she is a regular commentator for National Public Radio in Utah. A forthcoming book, *The Last Cheater's Waltz*, will be published by Holt in 1997. She lives in Utah and Montana.

BRADFORD MORROW is the author of the novels *Come Sunday, The Almanac Branch, Trinity Fields*, and *Giovanni's Box*, and the editor of the literary journal *Conjunctions*. A Bard Center Fellow at Bard

College, he divides his time between New York City and upstate New York.

KATHLEEN NORRIS's nonfiction books include *Dakota: A Spiritual Journey* and *The Cloister Walk*. Her most recent book of poetry is *Little Girls in Church*. She is a recipient of grants from the Bush, Echoing Green, and Guggenheim foundations, and a contributing editor of *The American Benedictine Review* and *Hungry Mind Review*.

SUSAN POWER's first novel, *The Grass Dancer*, won the PEN/Hemingway Award for Fiction in 1995. She is a graduate of Harvard University and Harvard Law School. *War Bundles*, her second novel, will be published by Putnam in 1997.

RICHARD RODRIGUEZ is the author of two collections of essays, *Hunger of Memory: The Education of Richard Rodriguez* and *Days of Obligation*. Born to Mexican-American parents, Rodriguez writes frequently about issues relating to heritage and assimilation.

SCOTT RUSSELL SANDERS is the author, most recently, of *Writing from the Center*, *Secrets of the Universe*, and *Staying Put*. His collection of essays, *The Paradise of Bombs*, won the Associated Writing Programs Award for Creative Nonfiction. In 1995, Sanders won the Lannan Literary Award for Nonfiction. He teaches at Indiana University in Bloomington, where he lives with his wife, and where their two grown children also live.

JOY WILLIAMS is a novelist and short story writer whose works include *Taking Care*, *Breaking and Entering*, *State of Grace*, and *Escapes: Stories*. She is also the author of *The Florida Keys: A History and Guide*. In 1993, she received the Strauss Living Award from the American Academy of Arts and Letters. She lives in Key West with her husband, Rust Hills.

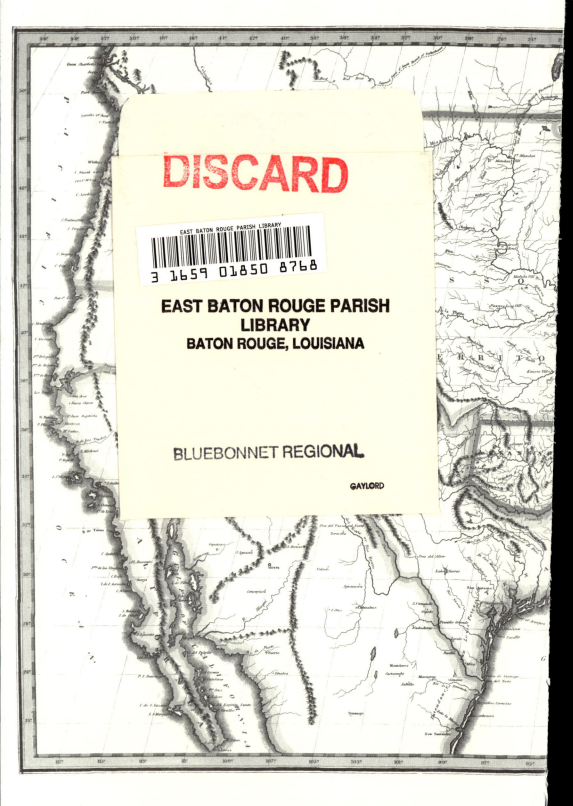